Higher Education in India

Higher Education in India:
Interdisciplinarity and Inclusion

Dr Vikas Mane

GenNext Publication

ISBN: 978-93-5663-008-6

"An Imprint of Kalpaz Publication"

First Published, 2022

Published by

GenNext Publication
5, Ansari Road
Daryaganj, New Delhi-110002
Phone: 011-47034999, 9811692060
E-mail: gennextpublication@hotmail.com

Printed at: Gyan Press, Delhi.

Contents

Preface

The Indian higher education system is rigidly compartmentalised along disciplines. This has hampered holistic knowledge building, equitable employment opportunities and a dynamics of the mental and manual labour for optimum outputs. The access to higher education is regulated by the performance at the memory based secondary and higher secondary level examinations. Due to historical social traditions of pre-ordained duties and divided expertise into mental and manual professions, the traits still lingering, the scheduled castes and tribes have generally been unable to effectively handle the present competition-based education system. So the scheduled castes and tribes are disproportionately represented in the social sciences with least employment and entrepreneurial opportunities. So this unilinearity could only be rectified by interdisciplinarity in higher education i.e. interweaving the natural sciences with the social sciences rooted into the larger socio-economic matrix, along with suitable application and procedurally achieving social inclusion in higher education. This is attempted with an indicative interdisciplinary higher education curriculum.

And finally and most importantly I expressed my sincere gratitude towards my institute, the Indian Institute of Education – its faculty and staff, who whole-heartedly supported me in pursuit of the completion of this book to satisfaction. I also am grateful to my family, especially my late mother who kept my morale high and took care of the family.

Thanks to the Indian Council of Social Science Research, New Delhi for financing the project of significance on higher education that has been published in the form of a book.

This book shall be useful to the policy makers, academicians and intellectuals along with college and university student's and teacher's to understand the various parameters of higher education and it's interweaving nature with Interdisciplinarity and inclusion for an intellectually and skillfully enriched students.

June 2022

Dr Vikas Mane

Pune

Abbreviations

1. B.A. - Bachelor of Arts
2. B.B.A. - Bachelor of Business Administration
3. B.C.A. - Bachelor of Computer Applications
4. B.E. - Bachelor of Engineering
5. B.Ed. - Bachelor of Education
6. B.Sc. - Bachelor of Science
7. B. Tech. - Bachelor of Technology
8. GOI - Government of India
9. Govt. - Government
10. HE - Higher Education
11. HEIs - Higher Education Institutions
12. ID - Interdisciplinarity
13. IGNOU - Indira Gandhi National Open University
14. IIM - Indian Institute of Management
15. IIT - Indian Institute of Technology
16. INI - Institute of National Importance
17. L.L.B. - Bachelor of Law or Laws
18. M.A. - Master of Arts
19. M.B.A. - Master of Business Administration
20. M.Com. - Master of Commerce
21. MHRD - Ministry of Human Resource Development
22. M.Sc. - Master of Science
23. NCRHE - National Council for Rural Higher Education
24. NIH - National Institute of Health

Chapter - 1

Indian Higher Education- A Retrospective

Introduction

Education is the paradigm of life which creates humanity from living beings. It is the most vital input for the growth and prosperity of a nation. It provides core matrix, strength, sensitivity and resilience to enable people to respond to the changing needs of the society. Education is the key to unlock the main gate to civilisation and modernisation. It is the most important mean to develop individuals and nations and to bring about the desired social reforms in this fast changing world of ours. Education is the solution for world peace because it is one of the universal ingredients in the development of mankind and it is indispensable for economic growth and prosperity. Although the world is changing more rapidly than its education systems, yet education continues to protect society, to promote knowledge and to preserve stability by passing on the culture from one generation to another; at the same time it plays a pioneering role in innovation.[1]

Education is the backbone of social mobility to translate into national endeavours of progress. It has the power to transform human beings into human resource. We cannot build a sustainable and prosperous nation without human resource development, which mainly depends on the health and vitality of higher education. Apart from primary and secondary education, higher education is the main instrument for development and transformation even while providing trained personnel for teaching at the initial levels of education. The higher education institutions are recognised as the most important agency of social change involved in the human resource development of any country. Higher education has special value in the contemporary knowledge society, which contributes both directly and indirectly to the wealth of a nation.

In India, education, especially higher education, is extremely disciplined and compartmentalised. This compartmentalisation into the social sciences, pure sciences and professional streams has led to the exclusion of variety. Firstly, at the intellectual level all the proceedings of these faculties have been denied of the perspective and experiences of the others, leading to unidirectional knowledge and tool outputs. Secondly, rigid compartmentalisation has led to a massive army of unemployable graduates, especially from Scheduled Castes and Scheduled Tribes, who cannot enter pure sciences and professional streams in numbers as they languish in the merit list, due to obvious socio-economic and educational handicaps. Lastly, the marks based admission process to all these faculties (especially the professional) has led to huge drop-outs from higher education. So the Gross Enrollment Ratio (GER) today is languishing at a lowly 24 percent.

Our higher education has evolved from Macaulay's minutes. 'Lord Macaulay, a profound scholar came to India in 1834 as Law Member of the Governor's Executive Council. In 1935, he suggested the government a detailed plan of British education in India, popularly known as "Macaulay's Minute". Through this plan, he urged the government to undertake a formal western type of higher education imparting knowledge of European literature and science through the medium of English. Macaulay's minute became major guideline for the British Government to develop higher education in India during the remaining period of British rule. The Plan was widely accepted not only by the government circle but also by the enlightened Indians and therefore it became a foundation stone for modern Indian education.'[2]

'Lord Macaulay was a supporter of the "Downward filtration theory". He remarked that, it is impossible for us with our limited means to attempt to educate the body of the people. We must at present do our best to form a class who may be interpreters between us and the millions whom we govern; a class of persons, Indian in blood and colour, but English in taste, in opinions in moral and in intellect'.[3] It means in British period education was not open to all and we also have a cultural history of limiting access to education. These factors have ensured that our higher education system stood elitist and inaccessible to the masses, especially the socio-economically backward castes of our society. After independence our constitution guaranteed equal rights to all irrespective of caste, creed, sex or any such differences. But it seems as if the policies and legislations are just documented in the papers without any practical implications in real life. Every corner (including education) of Indian society is a case of discrimination and we find people suffering in the midst of it.[4] That's the reason India has to wait for more than 50 years to make education as a fundamental right. Even though right to education has been sanctioned but still we can notice discrimination and exclusion in education.

The worst fallout of our compartmentalised higher education system has been the in-accessibility to fields of higher education to aspirants due to a pitiable admission system based on marks in exams further based on rote learning rather than understanding and application. An evaluation system that gives much less significance to manual work vis-à-vis mental work leads to a uni-sided understanding of a process. Once inside the compartmentalised system of higher education, the students willy-nilly has to limit his/her field of interest to his/her discipline. Inclusiveness on systemic and individual levels are a biggest casualty in this hierarchical and compartmentalised higher education system.

Due to compartmentalisation, every discipline works in a limited area of knowledge. That is why it does not suffice to meet the requirements of the problem with a single or compartmentalised system of knowledge. In order to give justice to the issues undertaken an interdisciplinary approach is always feasible and appropriate.

At the individual level more and more people will be inducted or accommodated in the interdisciplinary approach. The overall benefits of interdisciplinary approach of knowledge will break the barriers of established knowledge. And hence the overall system of knowledge will have a comprehensive and elevated scope.

In the name of specialisation, less and less inclusiveness is achieved whereas in case of interdisciplinarity it moves in reverse order, from narrow to greater and a higher state. Hence more and more people shall be accommodated in the stream of knowledge, leading to inclusiveness of the individual and the system.

This book tries to study the higher education system in India, at a macro level, leading to the studies of streams from the social sciences to the professional. It shall ultimately come up with a curricular fabric integrating the social sciences and pure sciences including technology, to come up with a curricula that creates holistic human resources with a balance between the mental and the manual and thus leading to inclusiveness of the individual and social variety.

Indian Higher Education – From Ancient to Modern

Higher education is not a recent phenomenon for India it has had long historical roots through which a modern system of education has been evolved. The higher education in India has evolved through different periods, viz., ancient, mediaeval, colonial, post-independence and contemporary. The Vedic period in which two types of educational system were present, viz., the Brahminical and the Buddhist systems of education. The Brahminical system of education was regulated by religious values, while the Buddhist form of education, even when religious, was also secular and utilitarian in nature. But the major change in Indian higher education took place through the initiatives of British rulers that made an impact both in positive and negative ways. Here on is presented a short review of the characteristics of Indian higher education through the different periods of history.

(a) Higher Education in Ancient India

Education in ancient India was predominantly religious in character but with evidence of princes receiving training in warfare and statecraft. Craftsmen received and imparted vocational education through their caste guilds. But formal education was focused mainly on the imparting of the knowledge of various concepts of religious discourse to the upper three castes and primarily to Brahmans through the guru-shishya tradition. Two broad trends of educational systems are found, the Brahminical and the Buddhist education systems.

According to University Education Commission (1948-49), during Vedic-Upanishadic period, India made significant contribution to knowledge through institutions of higher learning. The main objective of higher learning during the ancient times was "pure knowledge for its own sake" without any concern about its "utility for life". The philosophical and religious systems dominated the foundations of education with "idealism" occupying a prominent position and without any place for materialism and physical aspects of life. Social service was the greatest ideal for which the entire educational system strove. A scholar drew the best satisfaction in social service which gave him the joy of achievement and excellence. Subjects like Philosophy, religion, logic, mathematics, medicine, astronomy, astrology, pedagogy, politics, fine arts, military science and horticulture were studied with great enthusiasm.[5]

(b) Brahminical Education

The early Vedic period was marked by stratified, though essentially, non-class society. Without any monopolisation of education by any particular social group, the Rigvedic education concerned itself only with an attempt to preserve contemporary religious text through oral transmission. On receiving the sacred texts, the pupils after memorising, contemplated on them and participated in learned assemblies which were institutions of higher learning. Woman also enjoyed equal status with men in the sphere of education in the Rigvedic period.

In the later Vedic period, education was still an oral tradition but took a decisive turn in favour of the ritualistic and sacrificial religion. Higher education became subservient to the requirements of the priesthood and the ritualistic religion and to be monopolised by the upper castes, especially the Brahmans, from the later Vedic period which saw the crystallisation of the caste system.

The post-Vedic period (600-300 BC) saw the elaboration of rituals relating to education and the life of the student was regulated on the principle that he must do what is pleasing and serviceable to his teacher. A list of instructions to be observed by the student is found in the Brahminical literature of the post-Vedic period.

Information of formal secular and military education is also seen from Kautilyas' Arthasastra (400-300 BC) providing details of the studentship of a prince. He had to acquire the knowledge of religion, philosophy, agriculture as well as trade and statecraft.[6] The Sanskrit texts also speak of vocational education which was imparted through the caste guilds or through apprenticeship under certain craftsmen. The Sushruta Samhita provides elaborate information regarding medical education.

(c) Buddhist Education

For the first time in India and perhaps in the world a type of educational institution comparable with modern universities was seen under the Buddhist influence. Education through monasteries superseded Brahminical education of mainly functioning from the home of the individual teacher. The nature of administration in the Buddhist educational centers was secular and republican and was not enmeshed in ritualism.[7]

Buddhist education, religious as well as secular, centered around monasteries and was delivered by the monks. The most important aspect of Buddhist education was that it remained open to all persons irrespective of castes except slaves, army-deserters, the disabled and the sick. It grew out of the teachings of the Buddha and classified as Vinaya (monolithic discipline), Sutta (group discourse) and Abhidhamma (works of doctrine).[8]

The courses of study in Buddhist education included subjects such as the Lokayata System, astrology and witchcraft. A Buddhist text of the Christian era also mentions courses taught as the four Vedas and Vedangas, astronomy, interpretation of omens, philosophical systems of Sankhya, Yoga, Nyaya, Vaisheshika, music, medicine, magic, art of war, poetry, a number of arts as well as crafts and committed to writing for quite some time.[9] The students' choice of subjects was not restricted by their caste. For instance, a Brahmin could study archery and a Kshatriya could study the Vedas. Panini, the renowned Sanskrit Grammarian, and Kautilya, the author of the Arthasastra, were reputed to have studied in Taxila which flourished as a great educational center until the middle of the 3rd century A.D.[10]

The universities of Nalanda, Vikramshila and Vallabhi were perhaps the most important universities of ancient India. Nalanda University was an institution of higher studies situated in Bihar and was known for Buddhist studies, attracting students from China, Nepal, Tibet, and Korea, who went there to study valuable Buddhist manuscripts. The University curriculum included a wide range of subjects from Brahminical and Buddhist, Sacred and Secular to Philosophical and Practical. It is worth mentioning that the University was run on democratic principles. The center at Vallabhi, situated in Gujarat, was a rival to Nalanda. It specialised in Hinayana Buddhism, whereas Nalanda specialised in Mahayana Buddhism. It promoted all branches of higher learning from all types of religious systems. Vikramshila was situated in the present day Bhagalpur district of Bihar. Teaching at Vikramshila was controlled by a board of eminent teachers and this board also administered the affairs of Nalanda. Other centers of learning included Odantapure and Jagaddala (both Buddhist), Kanchi and Ujjain. The latter, capital of Avanti, was noted for secular learning and specialised in astronomy and mathematics. Kanchi (Kanchipuram) was the greatest center of Sanskrit learning in South India. Vatsyyayana, the logician who lived in the 4th century A.D., was a Pandit (Scholar) of Kanchi. The great scholar and teacher, Dinnage, is also said to have received his training in Kanchi. In South India, Ghattikas were famous schools of learning.[11]

The Viharas functioned as residential schools where various groups of students and teachers stayed together. Although the Buddhist canonical texts do not talk about fees, the Jatakas refer to the practice of paying fees exemplified by the University of Takshashila charging 1000 pieces of money. Poor student were, however, allowed to pay in the form of services to their teachers. Sometimes the community also helped the needy student to pay their fees. The fee paid by student was not the individual earning of any teacher but went to the Vihara.[12]

The position of women in the Buddhist system of education was better than the Brahminical system and produced numerous learned women. Buddhism came in the forefront as a challenge to Brahmanism, possibly because it offered a simple way to reach salvation.

(d) Higher Education in Medieval India

During the medieval period, a long time of over 300 years from 1210 A. D. to 1525 A.D. is described as a period of conquest, destruction and loot. Most of the institutions of ancient period lost their importance. Sultan Mohammed Ghori was the first Muslim ruler who started religious schools (Madarsa) at Ajmer. Some Mughal emperors encouraged higher education by grants of land or money. Schools and colleges were opened at several places such as Lohore, Delhi, Rampur, Lukhnow, Allahabad, Jaunpur, Ajmer, Bidar, Fatepur Sikri and Agra.[13]

The mediaeval era in the history of India signified a major phase of social and cultural synthesis. In fact, the history of education in mediaeval India reflects a part of the wider study of the history of society, social history broadly interpreted with politics, economics and religion. The mediaeval state in combination with various other agencies such as Sufism and Bhakti ideology played a crucial role in the protracted process of integration and co-existence. Despite their diverse religions and cultures, these agencies brought the people together through their common experience in public as well as in private.[14]

The early Indian education system and many of its centers continued, if not with their erstwhile grandeur, in the middle ages. There were important Southern Indian Centers in the Chola, Pandya, Hoysala kingdom of its successors, in Northern India Banaras, Prayag, Hardwar, Nadia, Ujjain and Mithila were noted for their pathshala and tolls of early Indian pattern where Brahmin teachers and scholars devoted their entire lives to the study of the Vedas, Shastras and the Puranas. This period also saw the rise of the Madrasa developed by the Muslim settlers from central and west Asia. The medieval Indian Madrasa responded to the existing social norms as much as it responded to them. The early Indian tradition of learning, thus, co-existed with the newly instituted Madrasa, marking continuity and changes both as important features of the history of higher education during the period.[15]

Madrasa were primarily theological institutions, providing instruction in language and other secular subjects as a subsidiary activity, and were supported or aided by the government of the day. The Madrasa were generally attached to mosques in the same way as the Maktabs. The courses of instruction in the Madrasa included grammar, logic, rhetoric, theology, metaphysics, literature, jurisprudence and science. Some of the Madrasa enjoyed the status of universities. The medium of instruction was Persian but Arabic was obligatory for all Muslims. In the twelfth century A.D., Lahore became a center of Muslim learning.[16] Other subjects were also taught such as Agriculture, Accountancy, Astrology and Astronomy, History, Geography, Mathematics, Islamic Law and Jurisprudence and Statecraft or the art of administration.[17]

The education of girls and women was not neglected in the Mughal period. The fact that Gulbadan Begum, sister of Humayun, wrote the Humayun Nama shows that there were learned women during this period. Hence, a major achievement of mediaeval intellectuals was that the mediaeval people learned to live together. People were educated to ensure a measure of balance between the aspirations and actions of different social groups.

(e) Higher Education in Colonial India

In pre-independent India, the Britishers can be credited for bringing a revolution in the Indian higher education system. Modern universities came into being during the British period towards the later half of the 19th century on the recommendations of Wood's Dispatch (1854) to that effect. The first three universities at Calcutta, Bombay and Madras were established in 1857 exclusively as examining bodies for conduction of examination for the students of existing 25 colleges which were still affiliated to the university of London. These three universities were modeled on the University of London. Later on, two more universities were set up – Punjab University at Lahore (1882) and University of Allahabad (1887), thus raising the number of universities to 5 with about 190 affiliated colleges and less than 18000 students towards the end of the Century.[18]

Indian higher education was influenced by their colonisers, the British and began with the first Europeanised institution of higher learning, the Hindu College, Calcutta in 1857. The language of instruction was English and aim was the cultivation of European literature and European science. The first and later universities were modeled on the London University, but the British models could not be successfully replicated in India because conditions and circumstances in India were different. As a result, Indian higher education developed certain peculiar features of its own.

The Indian urban elite wanted English education not only because it gave avenue to jobs, but felt Western secular education had a special role to play in the social and political regeneration of India that would create the capacity for self-rule. The elites were the beneficiaries of this system and hence had a vested interest in its continuance.

The East Indian Company, actually having no interest in imposing a Western English education system on its Indian subjects did so for practical consideration. They started the Calcutta, Madras and the Banaras Sanskrit College to fulfill the need of making officers well versed in Sanskrit, Persian and Arabic to assist them in governing the country, as well as to cultivate the goodwill of the traditional Hindu and Muslim elites.

But the policy of encouraging oriental education was soon challenged by the Evangelicals, the liberals and the utilitarian's, who believed that Indian society had to be radically transformed. They believed that the ignorance of Hindus could only be rectified by the propagation of Christianity, Western Science and making the Indians consumers of Western goods.

The earliest efforts to introduce to any form of education beyond the indigenous emanated from the missionaries such as Schwartz in South India along with rich Indian citizen of Calcutta and Bombay. Ram Manohan Roy, along with British officials founded the Hindu College (Later Presidency College) in 1817, leading to an intellectual ferment and Bengal renaissance. A number of colleges were found in the following years in Bengal.

English was not meant for the masses. It was argued that the improvement in Education, which in Lord Auckland's Minute of 1839, would most effectively contribute to elevate the moral and intellectual condition of the people, especially the education of the higher classes, of the persons possessing leisure and natural influence over the minds of their countrymen.

British rule thus gradually supplanted the pre-colonial indigenous system of education and imposed a new language and curricula. In the traditional Indian institutions, education had mainly a religious and cultural aim while the new English high schools and colleges were degree granting institutions which enabled student's access to power in the colonial, political and economic system.

The London University served as a model for establishing Indian Universities because its administrative structure would enable an Indian University to unite in one system the colleges scattered in different parts of a presidency. Such a university was also not likely to cost much and would be self-supporting, it would by-pass the problems of religious education by having non-residential universities. All first three Indian Universities Bombay, Calcutta and Madras, founded in 1857, were to be affiliating and examining bodies without any teaching or research functions.

Indian Universities were instruments for strengthening British cultural, intellectual and political domination and European learning was the staple of the curriculum.

Despite the alien character, there was an eager response to the new university education, especially in metropolitan cities of Calcutta, Bombay and Madras where the opportunities for Indians to find jobs in the government or in the professions was greatest. Indian education had a predominantly literary bias, in that the number of Arts colleges far outnumbered the professional colleges.

Initially law colleges were the most popular and engineering education in India, till the first world war, was mainly geared to providing recruits to the Public Works Department. The Indians also started the Victoria Jubilee Technical Institute in Bombay in 1857 and the Ranchodlal Chhotalal Technical Institute at Ahmadabad in 1910. The Indian Institute of Science was established at Bangalore in 1915.

Little attention was paid to Agriculture education during the colonial period. Medical Colleges were founded in Calcutta and Madras in 1835 to impart, through a scientific system, the benefit of medical instruction to the natives of Western India.

The first university to elevate from the affiliating model was Benaras Hindu University, set up in 1916. The Osmania University was established in Hyderabad in 1918, experimenting with teaching in Urdu. The Sadler commission (1917) recommended need for unitary, teaching and residential universities on the Oxbridge model. The Aligarh (1920), Lukhnow (1921), Dacca (1921), Delhi (1922), Nagpur (1923), Andhra (1923), Agra (1927) and Annamalai (1929), came up within the next decade of the commission's recommendation, with only Nagpur, Andhra and Agra being affiliating universities. Later only Travancore, Utkal (1943), Sagar (1946) and Rajasthan (1947) universities were established.

Universities in India, then, were under strict government control and examinations dominated the higher education system. Teachers just delivered lectures without emphasis on discussion or seminars. The curriculum was too biased towards the west and ignored Indian history, culture, philosophy and India's contemporary problems. The system also tended to de-emphasize scientific, technical and vocational education.

Dissatisfied by the western higher education system a series of national universities were founded by Gandhiji during the first non-co-operation movement in 1920-22, including Gujarat Vidyapeeth, Kashi Vidyapeeth, Bihar Vidyapeeth, Tilak Maharashtra Vidyapeeth and Jamia Millia Islamiya. In these universities the emphasis was on character formation and the staff and students were concerned more with building the national movement and fighting the Raj, than in cultivating the intellect. Hindi or the vernacular was the medium of instruction.

This pre and post-independence approach towards higher education, with emphasis on nation building and character seem to be the roots of imbalanced approach and expansion of the social science in the later periods. This ultimately seems to have been the ultimate obstacle to an interdisciplinary knowledge building at higher education levels.

Rabindranath Tagore started the Vishwa Bharati in an attempt to synthesize the Asian and western cultures. He worried about the alienation that the English language created among the intelligentsia towards the common people.

Annie Besant started the Central Hindu College and the Banaras Hindu University to uphold Indian Values and ancient traditions.

Educational Institutions were also started by the Christian missionaries, the Arya Samajists and the Singh Sabha movement. Patriotism was the flavour of these indigenous institutions but were not able to provide a viable alternative for Indian Education system.

A women's university, the first of its kind, was started by D. K. Karve in 1918 in Poona, later developed into the SNDT Women's University.

The British and Indian higher education institutions were concentrated to Calcutta, Bombay and Madras and thus were spread unevenly. The Indian upper castes responded to this education while the deprived were left out, creating an iniquitous and regionally unbalanced higher education system.

(f) Higher Education after Independence to-date

After independence, India inherited a system of higher education, which was an integral part of the colonial set-up impregnated with colonial needs and wedded to the achievement of colonial objectives. It was not only quantitatively small and microscopic but was also qualitatively anemic and dysfunctional in relation to the tasks of building a self-reliant and growth oriented economy, an integrated nation and a forward looking society. The country was faced with the challenge of bringing about a basic transformation in the inherited structure so as to provide the necessary support system for a self-reliant, integrated and progressive India. In the light of the complexities of the situation, the development trajectory of higher education, which was considered to be the modernisation of tradition, could not and did not take a linear path but proceeded through contradictory pulls, within a tangle of forces with its three apices located in quantity, quality and equity. A literate workforce was considered to be as essential in this context as the education and training of an adequate pool of highly skilled manpower. Considerable emphasis was placed not only on rapid expansion of elementary education but also simultaneously strengthening higher education, which performs the mother function for the educational system as a whole and particularly to scientific and technological components therein, so as to meet the requirements of high level capabilities in the realm of knowledge as well as skills.

While the University Grants Commission (UGC) was set up as the apex national organisation, concerned with the setting up of and maintenance of standards in higher education throughout the country, the parliament as well as the Union and State governments, have been devoting considerable attention to the task of providing the general directions of public policy in this vital sphere of national life. The UGC acts as the vital link between the policy making bodies of the government and institutions of higher education. Broad guidelines and mid-course correction committees were set up for the purpose. Lately the present government is intending to setup the 'Higher Education Funding Agency' (HEFA) for funding of universities and higher education institutions relegating the UGC to an academic regulatory body.

Higher Education Policy Evolution

Origin of the higher education System in India

The modern higher education started with the Wood's Despatch (1854) described as 'The Magna Charta of English Education in India'. This despatch described the government to take up the responsibility of 'creating a properly articulated system of education from the primary school to the university' and of establishing university at the Presidency towns, on the model of London University. This university should be conferring degrees to such persons as would come from any of the affiliated institutions after passing some required examinations. Accordingly, university of Calcutta, Bombay and Madras were founded in 1857.

Points below highlight the evolution of the Indian higher education system:

(i) Wood's Despatch of 1954 on Education: Wood's Despatch came to be known after the name of Sir Charles Wood who was the President of the Board of Control. It directed Governments to pay attention to Primary and University Education. It advocated Grant - in - Aid System, based on Secular Education. The diffusion of European Knowledge was the primary object of Wood's Despatch. This Despatch marked the beginning of Mass Education which was a departure from the Filtration Theory.

The salient features of the Wood's Despatch were:

- The constitution of Separate Department for the Administration of Education.
- Establishment of Universities in the Presidency Towns.
- Maintenance of existing colleges, high schools and increasing their Numbers.
- Expansion of mass education through vernaculars.
- Medium of Instruction - English for higher branches and Vernacular for lower level.
- Stressed the importance of training of teachers for all classes.
- Insisted on Female Education.
- Established New Middle Schools.
- Advocated Grant - in - Aid System based on perfect religious neutrality.
- Anglo - Vernacular Colleges for a careful cultivation of the vernacular languages.
- Encouraged the students with stipends, scholarship and reward of merit.
- Liberal Rewards for best elementary treatise in specified languages.
- Pointed out the indispensability of Examination.
- Demanded periodical report of Government Inspectors.

- A comprehensive System of Scholarship was introduced so as to connect lower schools with higher schools and higher schools with college.

(ii) The Education Commission of 1882: In 1882, the Government of India appointed a Commission, known as the Hunter Commission, "to enquire into the manner in which, effect had been given to the principles of the Despatch of 1854 and to suggest such measures as it may think desirable in order to further carrying out of the policy therein laid down". The commission, inter alia, recommended the gradual withdrawal of the State from the direct support and management of institutions of higher education.[19] With regard to vocational and technical education, the commission recommended that in the particular class of high schools there should be two avenues, one leading to the entrance examination of the university and the other of a more practical character intended to fit the youth for commercial, vocational and non-literary pursuits.

The main recommendations of the commission are as follows[20]:

1. The legal powers of the older universities should be enlarged so that all the universities may be recognised as teaching bodies.
2. The local limits of each university should be more accurately defined and the affiliated colleges in the central provinces, united provinces etc., should be removed from the Calcutta University.
3. The senate, the syndicate and the faculties should be enlarged and made more representative than before.
4. The affiliation rules should be so framed that no institution once admitted to affiliation be allowed to fall below the standard of efficiency required for affiliation.
5. There should be properly constituted governing body for each college.
6. The courses and methods of examination should be reorganised.
7. Attention should be paid to the residence and discipline of students.

(iii) The Universities Commission of 1902: Lord Curzon appointed the commission in 1902, "to inquire in to the conditions and prospects of the Universities established in British India, to consider and report upon any proposals which have been or may be made for improving their constitution and working, and to recommend to the Governor General-in-Council such measures as may tend to elevate the standards of university teaching and to promote the advancement of learning."[21]

Recommendations of the commission[22]:

(i) The reorganisation of the administration of universities and the territorial jurisdiction of each university to be defined.

(ii) A much more strict and systematic supervision of the affiliated colleges by the university, and the imposition of more exacting conditions of affiliation.

(iii) A much closer attention to the conditions under which students live and work; provision of adequate library facilities etc.

(iv) Substantial changes in curricula, and in the methods of examination.

(v) The assumption of teaching functions by the university within defined limits.

In spite of the specific recommendations of the commission for fitting the youth for- commercial, vocational or non-literary pursuits, neither the public nor the government seem to have appreciated the value of suggestions with the result that the recommendations were practically ignored. More strict and systematic supervision of the colleges by the university; and the imposition of more exacting conditions of affiliation; a much closer attention to the conditions under which students live and work; the assumption of teaching functions by the university within defined limits; substantial changes in curricula and in the methods of examination. As a result of the recommendations of this commission secondary schools came to be more under the domination of the universities; under the Indian Universities Act of 1904, schools had to be recognised by the universities, and rules and regulations were framed for this purpose.

(iv) Educational policy (1913): The Education policy of 1913 proposed the establishment of new teaching and residential universities within each of the provinces. The Banaras Hindu University and Aligarh Muslim University these two universities were set up by Acts of Central Legislatures. Universities were also established at Mysore, Hyderabad, Patna and other places by this time.[23]

There was a growing popular demand in the country for mass education. A Government Resolution on education policy was issued in 1913.

Major suggestions regarding the higher education in the resolution are as follows[24]:

(i) The Resolution provided for the expansion in University education. The existence of 5 Universities and 185 colleges was considered to be insufficient in view of the vast needs and demands of the country.

(ii) The Resolution suggested that Universities and high schools should be assigned distinct spheres of activities.

(iii) The Universities should be relieved of the responsibility of granting recognition to high schools and they should be kept under Provincial Governments.

(iv) The establishment of teaching universities was suggested by emphasizing the separation of the two functions of the Universities teaching and examining.

(v) Recommendations were made concerning the inclusion of subjects of industrial importance in the curriculum and provision of facilities to the students desirous of prosecuting research work.

Though the Resolution was immediately carried into effect, the outbreak of the World War-I delayed the developments planned in the Resolution. However, some new universities were established.

(v) The Calcutta University Commission of 1917: The next important stage was the appointment of the Calcutta University Commission in 1917 under the chairmanship of the late Sir Michael Sadler. This commission went into the question of secondary education and held the view that the improvement of secondary education was essential for the improvement of university education.

The commission made the following important recommendations[25]:

(i) Intermediate classes should be separated from universities and a curriculum spreading over three years should be prescribed for the degree of B.A. The stage of admission to the university was to be intermediate and not matriculation examination.

(ii) Intermediate college should be established for the sake of completing the first stage. These colleges should conduct teaching in Arts, Science, Medicine, Engineering, Education, Agriculture and Commerce.

(iii) A separate higher school and intermediate board should be formed in every province, consisting of representatives of the government, universities, high schools and intermediate colleges, for the sake of managing secondary education.

(iv) The commission recommended the use of the mother tongue as medium of instruction in intermediate colleges.

The reports of the commission contain the most comprehensive and authoritative study of the Indian education system from the secondary stage to the university. It is, therefore, quite natural that they have greatly influenced the subsequent course of secondary and higher education in the country.

(vi) The Hartog Committee Report (1929): In 1929, an auxiliary committee of the Indian statutory commission, known as the Hartog Committee, after its chairman Sir Philip Hartog, was appointed to review the position of education in the country. The observation of the committee on higher education is as follows:

> 'Many of the universities and colleges show marked improvement in their methods of teaching and in the amount of original work which they have produced and in some of them there is undoubtedly a better training for corporate life than formerly. But the theory that a university exists mainly, if not solely, to pass students through examinations still finds too large an acceptance in India; and we wish that there were more signs that the universities regarded the training of broad-minded, tolerant and self-reliant citizens as one of their being over-crowded with students who are not fittest by capacity for university education and of whom many would be far more likely to succeed in other careers'.[26]
>
> In the opinion of this committee, the matriculation of the university still dominated the whole of the secondary course. In order to obviate this defect, the committee recommended that a large number of pupils intending to follow certain avocation should stop at the middle school stage and there should be "more diversified curricula in the schools". The committee also recommended diversion of more boys to industrial and commercial careers at the end of the middle stage, preparatory to special instruction in technical and industrial schools. The committee also reviewed the problems relating to the training of teachers and the service conditions of the secondary teachers.

(vii) The Sapru Committee (1934): The Sapru committee appointed in 1934 by the U.P. government to enquire into the causes of unemployment in U.P. came to the conclusion that the system of education commonly prevalent prepared pupils only for examinations and degrees and not for any avocation in life. The committee suggested that:

(i) Diversified courses at the secondary stage should be introduced, one of these leading to the university degree;

(ii) The intermediate stage be abolished and the secondary stage be extended by one year;

(iii) The vocational training and education should begin after the lower secondary stage; and

(iv) The degree course at the university should extend over a period of three years.

(viii) The Abbot-Wood Report (1936-37): On its revival in 1935, the Central-Advisory Board of Education recommended the appointment of a committee to make recommendations for the reorganisation of education in view of the fact that a large number of graduates going out of the universities were unable to secure employment of the kind for which the education qualified them. Two expert advisers, Messrs Abbot and Wood were accordingly invited in 1936 to advise the government "on certain problems of educational reorganisation and particularly on problems of vocational education". The Abbot-Wood Report, submitted in 1937, suggested a complete hierarchy of vocational institutions parallel with the hierarchy of institutions imparting general education.

As a result of their recommendations "a new type of technical institution called the Polytechnic has come into existence". The provinces also started technical, commercial, or agricultural high -schools conducting non-literary courses.

(ix) The Sargent Report (1944): In 1944, the Central Advisory Board of Education submitted a comprehensive report on post-war educational development, known as the Sargent Report, visualising a system of universal, compulsory and free education for all boys and girls between the ages of 6 and 14, the senior basic or the middle school to be the final stage in the school career of majority of the pupils. The Report also recommended that at the middle school stage, provision should be made for a variety of courses, extending over a period of five years after the age of 11. These courses while preserving an essentially cultural character should be designed to prepare the pupils for entry into industrial and commercial occupations as well as into the universities. It was recommended that the high school course should cover 6 years, the normal age of admission being 11 years and that the high schools should be of two main types (a) academic, and (b) technical. The objective of both should be to provide a good all-round education combined with some preparation in the later stages for the careers which pupils will pursue on leaving schools.

The report made some recommendations on university education as follows[27]:

(i) Indian universities, as they exist to-day, despite many admirable features do not fully satisfy the requirements of a national system of education.

(ii) In order to raise standards all round, the conditions for admission must be revised with the object of ensuring that all students are capable of taking full advantage of a university course. The proposed reorganisation of the high school system will facilitate this. Adequate financial assistance must be provided for poor students.

(iii) The present intermediate course should be abolished. Ultimately the whole of this course should be covered in the high school, but as an intermediate step the first year of the course should be transferred to high schools and the second to universities.

(iv) The minimum length of a university degree course should be three years.

(v) The tutorial system should be widely extended and closer personal contacts established between teachers and students.

(vi) The importance of establishing a high standard in postgraduate studies and particularly in pure and applied research should be emphasized.

(vii) Steps should be taken to improve the conditions of service, including remuneration of university and college teachers where those now in operation are not attracting men and women of the requisite caliber.

(viii) An Indian University Grant Committee should be constituted for the purposes and with the terms of reference set out in this chapter.

(ix) To provide for the increased number of able and well prepared students which a national system of high schools may be expected to produce, approximately 2,40,000 places, or double the existing number, should be available in universities.

(x) The University Education Commission of 1948-49: The era of educational reconstruction inevitably followed in the wake of social and economic reconstruction initiated by the national government after 1947, education being the chief instrument for reconstruction and transformation of society. The first steps taken in the direction of educational reconstruction were the appointment of a series of commissions to survey, study, review and recommend improvements in the different sectors of education.

To look into the problems of University education, the University Education Commission was appointed by the Government of India in 1948, under the chairmanship of Dr. S. Radhakrishnan in pursuance of the recommendations of the Central Advisory Board of Education and also of the inter-university board. The Radhakrishnan commission recommended that in the inevitable expansion of higher education in India, a fair proportion of the additional facilities be directed to meeting the needs and developing the opportunities of rural areas.[28]

The commission made important suggestions for improving the standard of university education in the country. Introduction of a three-year degree course for the first university degree, greater use of tutorial system of instruction, formulation of new aims, emphasis on developing knowledge and critical thinking rather than mechanical passing of examinations, establishment of rural universities and introduction of moral education were some of its salient recommendations. The commission, however, thought it unfortunate that neither the public nor the government had realised the importance of intermediate colleges in the Indian educational systems. To coordinate university education in the country, the establishment of the University Grants Commission was also recommended. The commission came into being immediately there after.

Major recommendations of the University Education Commission are as follows[29]:

(i) Teaching Staff:- There be four types of teachers- Professor, Readers, Lecturers and Instructors. Promotions from one category to another be on grounds of merit.

(ii) Standard of teaching:- Admission to the university courses after completion of 12 years study at a school and an intermediate college.

(iii) To avoid overcrowding maximum number of admission at university to be fixed at 3000 and in an affiliated college at 1500.

(iv) Number of working days shall be 180 in the year, exclusive of examination days.

(v) Courses of Study:- Principles and practice of general education shall be introduced at the degree level.

(a) Ph.D. student should grasp his subject by breadth and depth.

(vi) University teacher should give the community punctuality, efficiency and devotion to duty in relation to their teaching work.

(vii) Medium of Instruction:- The federal language be developed through the assimilation of words from various sources and the retention of words which have already entered into Indian languages from different sources.

(a) International technical and scientific terminology be adopted; the borrowed words be properly assimilated.

(b) For the medium of instruction for higher education English be replaced as early as practicable by an Indian language which cannot be Sanskrit on account of vital difficulties.

(c) Pupil at the higher secondary and university stages be made conversant with three languages- the regional languages, the Federal language and English.

(viii) Examinations:- A university degree should not be required for government administrative service. Special state examinations for recruitment to the various services should be organised.

(a) No credit is given, at present, for class work in courses except sometimes in the case of practical work. Such credit should be given.

(b) Three years will be involved for the first degree.

(c) The standards for success at the examination should as far as possible, be uniform in the various universities and should be raised. We suggested that a candidate should get 70% or more marks to secure a first class, 55% to 69% for a second and at least 40% for a third.

(ix) Students, their activities and welfare:

(a) Two years of physical education be required for all students, men and women, except those who are physically unfit or who are in the National Cadet Corps.

(b) Hostels be constructed in blocks of not more than fifty students per block, with common rooms and dining halls for four or five blocks.

(c) University union should be as free as possible from political activities.

(d) An Advisory Board of Student Welfare be organised in universities which do not have such a body.

(x) Women's Education:-

(a) Women students in general should be helped to see their normal places in a normal society, both as citizens and as women, and to prepare for it college programmes should be so designed that it will be possible for them to do so.

(b) Standards of courtesy and social responsibility should be emphasized on the part of men in mixed colleges.

(xi) Constitution and Control:-

(a) University education be placed on the Concurrent List.

(b) The concern of the Central Government with the universities be with regard to finance, co-ordination of facilities in special subjects, adoption of national policies, ensuring minimum standards of efficient administration and liaison between universities and national research laboratories and scientific surveys etc.

(xii) Finance:- The University Grants Commission be set up for allocating grants.

(xiii) Rural universities:- Special attention be paid to the development of higher education in rural areas.

(xi) Report of the Three-Year Degree Course Estimates Committee (1956): The Education Ministers Conference held on the 2nd – 3rd September, 1956, recommended the appointment of a Committee to work out the estimates of expenditure connected with the introduction of Three-Year Degree Course in Universities and affiliated colleges so that it might be possible for all ties to change over to the new pattern. In accordance with the above recommendation a Three-Year Degree Course Estimates Committee was set up on 1st October, 1956.

Major Recommendations -

1. Three-Year Degree Course should be introduced in as many universities as possible during the Second Five- Year Plan period.
2. The unit of reorganisation should be a university and not a college, so that no university will give two types of degrees for the same courses.
3. During the transitional period, student passing the Intermediate examination should be admitted to the second year of the Three Year Degree Course.
4. The total amount which would be required to introduce the reform including recurring expenditure for four years will be about Rs 25 crores.
5. The expenditure involved in introducing the reform should be shared between the Central and State Government in equal proportion.

6. During the Second Five-Year Plan period, the Central Government should give Rs 7.5 crores, including Rs 2.5 crores to be made available by the University Grants Commission. A similar amount should be found by the State Government including contributions from Private Management. This total amount available will thus be Rs 15 crores which will be sufficient for upgrading 180 Intermediate Colleges and reorganising 300 Degree Colleges which should be taken as the targets for the Second Five-Year Plan.
7. There should be a public examination at the end of the Pre-University class.
8. Professional colleges should ether conduct their own admission tests or select candidates for pre-professional courses on the basis of Higher Secondary/ Pre-University examination.
9. The number of students should be restricted to 800-1,000 per college.
10. While the Three-Year Degree Course is introduced, steps should be taken to improve quality of collegiate education in general. For this purpose from the grants available, it is necessary to revise syllabuses, introduce General Education Courses, reduce over-crowding in colleges, improve the teacher-pupil ratio, strengthen laboratories, replenish libraries and wherever possible institute tutorial system.
11. The State of U.P. will present a special problem because of the entirely different system operating in that state.[30]

(xii) Report of the Committee of Member of Parliament on Higher Education (1963): On the recommendation of the Informal Consultative Committee of Members of Parliament on Education that university education should be a Union subject, the Ministry of Education set up a Committee of certain Members of Parliament in 1963 under the Chairmanship of Shri P. N. Sapru for the purpose of examining the constitutional provisions on higher education.

Major Recommendations -

1. University and higher education should be transferred from the State List to the Concurrent List, retaining intact Entry 66 in the Union List Under this arrangement the State Governments will continue, as at present, to be responsible for the maintenance of Universities.

2. The University Grants Commission should have 15 members, of whom at least five should be full time members, men of the highest standing in the educational world. They should be persons of the status of Vice Chancellors. Serving Vice-Chancellor should not be appointed as members of the Commission.
3. Both State Government and Universities find it difficult to provide matching funds. Depending on the merits of the case, the condition of grant should be liberalised.
4. Step should be taken to see that more and more colleges adopt the pay scales prescribed by the Commission for affiliated colleges.
5. Professional education cannot be completely divorced from general education. Professional education including medical (Basic), Agriculture, Engineering and Law should also come within the purview of the university.
6. A real improvement in university education is not possible without a corresponding increase in the efficiency of our secondary education. Vigorous steps should be taken to improve the quality of secondary education.
7. The number of scholarship for university education and research should be considerably increased in institution of higher education.
8. The number of scholarship for higher education for women students should be considerably increased.
9. The University Grants Commission Act should be so amended as to make it obligatory on the part of a State Government to consult the Commission before setting up a new university. This change cannot be effected if education is not made a Concurrent subject.
10. The Inter-University Board should be made more effective and it should be more and more regarded as the spokesman of University option.
11. The universities should be pursue a common policy in regard to admissions.
12. Morning, evening colleges and correspondence courses should be established for the benefit of those who are unable to pursue regular courses.[31]

(xiii) Report on Standards of University Education: One of the important functions of the University Grants Commission is to take, in consultation with the universities or the other bodies concerned, all such steps, as it may think fit for the promotion and co-ordination of university education and for the determination and maintenance of standards of teaching, examination and research in universities.

In order to undertake a systematic and objective investigation of problems relating to the standards of higher education in Indian Universities, the University Grants Commission appointed a Committee in August, 1961.

Major Recommendations -

1. **Aim of University Education in India:** The pursuit of liberal values should be a perennial activity. The universities have to preserve and communicate the existing knowledge and to advance the frontiers of knowledge. They should try to develop in them a modern Indian outlook, which requires a reinterpretation and adoption of our traditional values in the context of the contemporary situation. A national outlook and purpose has also to be cultivated by a deliberate pursuit of national ends in preference to local interests.

2. **Evaluation of Standards:** For a variety of reasons, a categorical answer cannot be given to the question whether standards have deteriorated during the last 10 or 15 years. Standards are said to have declined from the point of view of examination results as also with reference to the expectations entertained by the employing agencies and general public.

   The general opinion, however, seems to be that while the quality of the best students is as good, as ever, the average of an Indian university does not compare favourably with his counterpart in some of the well-known universities in the world.

3. **Admission Policy:** There are several ways in which a more careful selection of student could be made such as approving only such student as have secured a fairly high percentage of marks at the school examinations or special weightage being given to marks in important subjects like languages and mathematics.

   The school system should contain a number of terminal points from which students could be diverted to technical and vocational courses.

   Another solution consists in a large scale expansion of facilities for correspondence course, part-time courses, etc.

4. **Course of Study:** The problem of formulation of suitable courses of study in Indian universities has to be judged in the light of the

rapid advances being made in the field of knowledge, particularly in science and technology.

5. **Undergraduate Education:** In recent years there is a general agreement on the total duration of school and university education being 15 years.

   The pattern of having 10 years of school education followed by two years in an intermediate or junior college and three years in a degree college deserves serious consideration. The junior college could provide an opportunity to large number of students who require a university degree without having to proceed further, besides being a point for dispersal to vocational and technical courses.

6. **Postgraduate Studies and Research:** The chief aim of postgraduate education should be the acquisition of specialised knowledge. The course should produce competent scholars and scientist for employment mainly in the learned profession.

   The proper method of developing postgraduate education in the colleges is to organise it in place where at least 3 to 4 good colleges may pool their resource in equipment and teaching personnel.

7. **Science Education:** Standards of science teaching should be improved at the school level in order to provide adequate foundation for upgrading standards at the university level.

   The programme undertaken by the University Grants Commission of organising summer institutes for improving the teaching of science in school needs considerable expansion.

   Student with scientific potentialities should be identified sufficiently early and given special attention and care.

8. **Improvement of Teaching:** The dictation of notes in university classes should be discouraged. It will however be useful if the teacher prepares a synopsis of his lectures containing carefully selected bibliography and makes it available to the student for their guidance.

   Encouragement should be given to students to go to the library, select books and read for themselves. One method of doing this would be to insist upon more written assignments and tutorials during the course of the year.

9. **Medium of Instruction:** Change over to the regional as the medium of instruction at the university stage requires careful preparation. Unless an Indian language has grown up to its full

academic stature, it would be unwise to introduce it as the medium of instruction at the university stage.

Before any change-over is brought about, universities must satisfy themselves about the competence of teachers to teach in the language concerned and about the availability of sufficient number of good books.

10. **Examination Reforms:** There should be a combination of different methods of evaluation as well as the objectives and written types of examination.

    Universities should arrange convenient spacing of examination. The system of holding a final comprehensive examination has become outdated in view of the rapidly growing content of knowledge which has considerably heightened the burden of the student.

11. **Colleges:** There should be a reasonably uniform system of granting affiliation to colleges all over the country. The norms and conditions formulated by the college committee of the UGC in regard to staff requirements and physical and other facilities should be strictly adhered to.

    The system of government meeting 90 percent of the deficit of the constituent colleges of Delhi University should be extended to other colleges also.

12. **Organisation of the University:** University should have a high degree of autonomy. They should have the freedom to choose their students, to appoint their staff, to organise their courses of study etc.

    Participation of lay-men in the legislative and administrative organs of the university may be desirable, but in no case, should they be allowed to become a hampering factor in the performance of academic activities.

13. **Maintenance and coordination of standards:** (i) The academic activities of the University Grants Commission such as the holding of seminars and conferences, appointment of review committee, setting up of centers of advance study, etc., need to be strengthened further.

    (i) Unless the present outlay on higher education as also the cost per student is sufficiently increased, many of our institutions will not be able to rise above sub-standards.[32]

(xiv) Report of the Committee on Colleges: The unprecedented rise in the number of colleges and their enrolment does not merely pose a challenge to the physical and financial resources of the country, nor is it merely a question of providing more space, more equipment, more money, and more teachers. Here, one has to reckon with the problem of providing a worth-while and meaningful education to mass of young persons who have vast individual and group differences in ability and achievement, aptitude and ambition. In September 1962, a small committee was constituted to advise the University Grants Commission on the general policy to be followed in developing colleges, to make suggestion regarding the proper and effective utilisation of the limited resources available for this purpose and to recommend collegiate education. In April, 1964 this committee was reconstituted.

Major Recommendations -

(1) Reorganisation of under graduation: (i) The school and pre-university course should extend for at least 12 years. This would ensure a minimum entrance age of 18 to the first degree course, assuring they will be admitted to schools at six. (ii) It would be desirable to have two public examinations first, at the Matriculation stage and, the second, at the old, intermediate level which may now be called the pre-degree of pre-university course. (iii) For student who do not intend or cannot pursue further education after graduation, a 2- year first degree course of balanced education after 12 years of schooling should be deemed sufficient. (iv) There may be honors courses of 3 years apart from the Pass course for the better students after a 12-years period of schooling. Those undergraduate students who have demonstrated an aptitude for scholarly work in the 2-years Pass course could be given 3rd year of honors course. (v) Admission to post-graduate course of 2 years duration may be open only to honours students.

(2) The tutorial system: A system of tutorials should be provided to the student, personal contact with the teacher both in and outside the classroom for discussion of individual and personal problems, for planning and executing a good programme of studies and for stimulating the student to a pursuit of meaningful goals and intellectual attainment.

(3) New colleges: New colleges should be started only after exploring the capacity of the existing ones for further growth and development.

(4) **Condition of affiliation:** No college should, however, be affiliated without the express approval of the university. It is desirable that the University Grants Commission lays down some minimum standard condition of affiliation.

(5) **Grant in- aid code/rules:** (i) One way of dealing with the problem of liberalising grant-in-aid-code/ rules would be to assign the function of reviewing these codes/rules together with the salary scales of college teachers to what may be called the Collegiate Grant Committee to be set up by the State Government whose advice should be accepted in regard to such matters. (ii) The pattern of grant-in-aid given by the University Grants Commission to colleges in Delhi would seem to be the best way of meeting the requirement of the affiliated colleges.

(6) **Postgraduate education:** No single college should start post-graduate courses without co-operative assistance from the university and unless it has a minimum staff of three qualified teachers for each subject.

(7) **Autonomous college:** One of the practical methods of improving the standards of higher education in India would be to select a few colleges on the basis of their past work, influential traditions, maturity and academic standards and give them an autonomous status with freedom to develop their personalities, experiments with new ideas, frame their own syllabi in consultation with the university, devise and conduct their examination and initiate new measures. This does not mean that the autonomous college will have a university (degree giving) status.

(8) **Other conditions of excellence:** (i) Colleges may be encouraged to admit students from other states and, if necessary, subsidized for the purpose. (ii) All teachers, teaching at university level, should be classified into three main categories- Professors, Readers and Lecturers. The present disparities in respect for pay between teachers in colleges and those in the universities should be reduced to minimum, if not completely eliminated.

(9) **U.G.C.s assistance to affiliated college:** (i) the present scheme of University Grants Commission aid to affiliated colleges may continue during the Fourth Plan period. (ii) The scheme of Summer Institutes may be extended to cover all subjects including humanities and the Social Sciences. (iii) The students unions in the colleges may be encouraged and welcomed and sometimes

even assisted instead of being merely tolerated as at present. Healthy unions are those which satisfy the following three conditions:

(i) The constitution of the union should have an article that its member may not practice, preach, encourage or even tolerate direct action. (ii) The accounts of the union should be submitted at regular intervals for independent audit, and (iii) office-bearers of the union should give to the head of the institution prior information of the union's programmes and activities.[33]

(xv) Kothari Commission (1964-66): Kothari Education Commission was appointed under the chairmanship of Dr D.S. Kothari to deal with all aspects and sectors of education and to advise Government on the evolution of a National System of Education for the country. Based on this commission's report, the educational policy 1968 was formulated.

The report made very important recommendations covering all aspects for the future development of national education. The Report emphasized the need for a built-in flexibility in the system of education, and for the necessity of education to be science-based and coherent with Indian culture and values.[34]

The Kothari Commission revealed that Indian education needs a drastic reconstruction, almost a revolution. We need to introduce work experience as an integral element of general education to improve quality of teachers at all levels to strengthen centers of advanced studies and strive to attain in some of our universities, at least, higher international standards; to lay special emphasis on the combination of teaching and research; and to pay particular attention to education and research in agriculture and allied sciences.

The report stressed that there had to be:[35]

- a radical improvement in the quality and standard of higher education and research,
- expansion of higher education to meet manpower requirements of the Nation and the rising social ambitions and expectations of the people, and
- improvement of university organisation and administration.

The commission recommended special measures for major universities to ensure quality of research development of other universities and affiliated colleges, improvement in teaching and evaluation by re-organisation of courses and examinations, opportunities for part-time education, and special attention to women's education. As far as the implementation of the Kothari Commission is concerned, the recommendations were discussed in both the houses of parliament and there emerged the first national policy in independent India in the form of a resolution in July 1968. Perhaps not surprisingly, the recommendations of the Kothari Commission were progressively diluted at every stage of the discussions, yet the policy that was born out of them remained the basic framework for all governmental action despite an attempt by the Janata Government to revise it in 1979.

(xvi) National Policy of Education, 1968: On the basis of findings of the Education Commission, 1964-66, the Government of India brought out a National Policy on Education (NPE) 1968. The provisions related to higher education are:

(i) Admissions of students to college and university need to be determined according to the infrastructure and facilities available.

(ii) New Universities would be established only after an adequate provision of funds was made;

(iii) Due care should be taken for maintenance of proper standards;

(iv) Special attention should be paid to the organisation of PG courses and improvement of research and training; and

(v) Part-time education and correspondence courses should be developed on large scale at the University state.

(a) Rural Institutes of Higher Education and NCRHE: As per university education commissions' suggestion the central government decided to establish at least one Rural Institute of Higher Education as an experiment in 1956. The Rural Institutes sought to meet the requirements of higher education relating to rural areas. Due to its spectacular success the number of such institute has gone up and these Institutes provided higher education to the rural youth in a rural environment and tried to inculcate in them sympathy and careers in the rural development programmes of the Central and State Government.

(b) Institution deemed to be Universities: Having established the Deemed to be universities the ministry shares the task of maintenance and support of these deemed to be Universities with the UGC. The popularly growing deemed to be universities are not universities in true sense of the term, but function like universities.

(c) Central Universities: At the time of independence the central government took over only 3 institutions called central universities viz. Aligrah Muslim University (AMU), Banaras Hindu University (BHU) and Delhi University. The purpose of these central universities is not merely to act as pace setters in the field of higher education but are major universities meant for qualitative improvement of higher education and meeting the special as well as strategic needs of the country.

(d) Specialised Research Institutions: India has developed a few specialised Research Institutions which do not impart regular instruction or award degree. But they conduct and provide facilities to others for conducting research studies in higher education. Some important of them are- Indian Council of Social Science Research (ICSSR), Indian Council of Philosophical Research (ICPR), Indian Council of Historical Research (ICHR), Indian Institute of Advanced Studies (IDAS) and so on.

As per the NPE, 1986 and modified NPE, 1992 initial attempts were made to delink degrees from jobs and to set up institutions like National Evaluation Organisation (NEO) for conducting tests and developing norms for various jobs.

(e) Institutions of Higher Learning: There are institutions of higher learning of national importance that have been developed in the country. Most of them are voluntary and financed by the Ministry. These are outside the university system and are engaged in the programmes of innovative character. The outstanding institutions are Aurobindo's International Center for Education, Pondicherry, Shri Aurobindo Institute of Educational Research, Auroville, Lok Bharati, Sanorra and Mitra Niketan, Vellanand, Kerala.

(f) Association of Indian Universities (AIU): AIU is an open voluntary educational organisation of Universities with the major objective of promoting and coordinating the activities of higher educational institution which are taken as its members. The major activities of AIU are:

(i) Dissemination of information;
(ii) Carrying out research studies;
(iii) Publication and promotion of literature;
(iv) Co-operation among the institutions in the areas of cultural, sport and allied areas;
(v) Conduct of conferences of vice-chancellors; and
(vi) Organisation of training programme for university administrators.

Besides, various research projects are undertaken to measure efficiency of universities, use of performance indicators, impact of question bank, etc.

(xvii) National Policy of Education (NPE) 1986 and 1992: A nationwide deliberation took place since 1985 on the basis of the government of India's historical document 'Challenge of Education'. A policy perspective for a comprehensive review of the Indian system of Education. In 1986, the NPE finally emerged and was adopted in Parliament. Highlighting the importance and objectiveness of higher education, it stated, higher education provides people with an opportunity to reflect on the critical social, economic, cultural, moral and spiritual issues facing humanity. It contributes to national development through dissemination of specialised knowledge and skills. It is, therefore, a crucial factor of survival. Being at the apex of the education pyramid, it has also a key role in producing teachers for the education system.

The NPE, 1986 rightly observed, that in context of the unprecedented explosion of knowledge, higher education has to become dynamic as never before, constantly entering uncharted areas. In view of the massive growth of higher education it emphasised that urgent steps need to be taken to protect the system from degradation. Courses and programmes would be redesigned to meet demands of specialisation along with special emphasis on linguistic competence and increasing flexibility in the combination of courses.

The National Policy (1986) also suggested for state level planning and coordination of higher education through councils of higher education. It added that the UGC and these councils would develop coordinative methods to keep a watch on standards, provision would be made for minimum facilities and admission would be made regulated according to the capacity. Stress was laid on transformation of the teaching methods, use of Audio-visual aids and electronic media, development of science and technology, curricula and material research and teacher orientation.

Besides preparation of teachers in the beginning of their service, attention has to be paid to their continuing education. The NPE aptly said that teachers performance would be systematically assessed and all posts be filled on the basis of merit. Research in the universities has to be encouraged and its high quality be ensured. The UGC should develop suitable mechanisms for coordinating these activities and set up national research facilities within the university system.

The policy also enjoined, in the interest of greater coordination and consistency in policy, sharing of facilities and developing inter-disciplinary research, a national body covering higher education in general, agriculture, medical, teaching, legal and other professional fields will be setup.

The NPE also stated The Open University system has to be initiated in order to augment opportunity for higher education and as an important instrument of democratizing education.

National Testing service would be established for determining the suitability of candidate for specified jobs and for paving the way for emergency of norms of comparable competence. The Rural University would be consolidated and developed on the lines of Mahatma Gandhi's ideas of education for the transformation of rural areas. The NPE 1992 (Revised) reiterated the above points and stressed both the qualitative and quantitative importance of higher education.

- **Programme of Action (POA) 1989 and 1992:** Formed for realising objectives of the NPE 1988 the POA and revised POA (1992) realised the main features of the programmes and strategies to impart the necessary dynamism to the higher education system, would consist of the following:
  - (i) Consolidation and expansion of institutions
  - (ii) Development of autonomous colleges and departments
  - (iii) Redesigning course
  - (iv) Training of Teachers
  - (v) Strengthening Research
  - (vi) Improvement of efficiency
  - (vii) Creation of structures for coordination at the state and national levels.
  - (viii) Mobility
- **Review of the NPE:** The review committee, under the chairmanship of Acharya Ramamurthy, released a perspective paper entitled 'Towards an Enlightened and Humane Society.' The review committee inter alia reported that quality of higher education is to be improved, to cater to the needs of competitive industry, indigenisation of technology, research and development etc. College and Universities should have curricular and educational process linked to regional development and the improvement of school education. There is need for promoting orderly growth of

higher education, research in social sciences also for study of and research on our classics for their literary eminence and underlying values and traditions.

(a) Development of Autonomous Colleges: The NPE provided that in view of the mixed experiences with the system of affiliation, autonomous colleges would be helped to develop in large number until the affiliating system is replaced by a freer and more creative association of universities with colleges. Fully financed by the central government, a college declared autonomous by its affiliating university is fully accountable for the content and quality of education. Such a college is also responsible for setting its own examination paper and for the conduct of examinations.

(b) International Cooperation: At present there has been growing interaction and interest among the academics of foreign countries and India for development of higher education. A number of schemes are being implemented by UGC for promoting such international cooperation in the area of higher education. Some projects are sponsored by countries like USA, UK, Australia, Canada, etc. for improving mutual relations. The institute set up for ensuring cooperation and understanding through the bilateral agreements are the Shastri Indo-Canadian Institute, U.S. Educational Foundation, American Institute of Indian Studies and so on.

With a steady increase in Universities over the years reaching up to 217 universities and 74 deemed universities up to 2003-04 and 14163 colleges including the general and professional, the higher education institution in India is growing rapidly, especially in the era of globalisation and liberalisation. The enrollment in higher education totalled 10009.1 thousand in 2003-04 including both the general and professional colleges.

(c) Financial Assistance to State Universities and Colleges: As per the UGC act, 100 state Universities excluding Agriculture universities were eligible to receive grants in 1993-94. Developmental grants are provided for infrastructural improvement. Grants for specific schemes are also made available on the recommendation of experts.

Only Colleges recognised by the UGC in terms of section 2 (f) and 12 (b) of the UGCs act are eligible to receive development grants from the commission. The quantum of grants is worked out on the basis of various parameters, such as the level of teaching, students and faculty strength, etc. With a view to removing disparities and regional imbalances, the Commission has related norms for giving development grants to colleges located in educationally backward rural or border areas and to colleges catering to SC/ ST student and women. Grants are generally provided for buildings, hostels, libraries, laboratories and faculty improvement programmes for teachers.

(d) Maintenance and coordination of standards: A number of schemes / programmes have been implemented for maintenance and coordination of standards in teaching, examination, research and other aspects such as:

Academic staff college-Significant innovations in improving the quality of higher education, having come into existence for promoting the professional growth of teachers of colleges and universities. The orientation courses, of 4 weeks duration, are general and mostly multi-disciplinary and refresher courses are usually in-depth and intensive as well as subject-oriented.

The country wide classroom programme (CCP) is broadcast on Doordarshan and on various subjects in English.

(xviii) IGNOU and other Distance Education Agencies: The Indira Gandhi International Open University (1985), established by an Act of parliament for promotion of Open University and Distance Education in the field of higher education, using education technology for providing opportunities to larger segments of the population, particularly the disadvantaged groups. The IGNOU provides an innovative system of higher education, flexible and open in regard to methods and pace of learning, courses of studies, eligibility for enrollment, age of entry, methods of evaluation etc. IGNOU is the open body charged with the responsibility for the coordination and determination of standards in distance education in India.

The Government of India in its document "Challenge of Education: A policy perspective" made a review of the entire educational set-up. In the context of higher education it is reported that there were conflicting views amongst the educationist about the relative importance of school versus higher education. Despite the key role assigned to higher education, the developments in this field have been extremely uneven. The following matters of concern were observed.

(i) **Disparities in Expansions:** Though there is large enrollment in higher education, only 4.8% were from the relevant age group. Rural areas were worse off and proportion of women and deprived sections adverse. And the enrollment pattern was far too much in general education than professional education.

(ii) **Sub-standard colleges:** Qualitatively below par colleges and universities create a big question about the suitable usability of scarce resource, creating a confrontation between the UGC and state governments sponsoring the colleges.

(iii) **Colleges and universities being notorious places:** For rampant regionalism, casteism and inbreeding and politicking

(iv) **Colossal waste of resources:** Effective working days in colleges are too low and hurt the internal efficiency and quality of colleges.

(v) **Low Standards:** A large number of students passes in the IIIrd division or pass class and inflate the unemployment registers.

(vi) **No upto-date curricula:** At college levels no institutional arrangement is available for updation of curricula leading to unilinear syllabi in humanities and faculty and supportive arrangements are not made for science and technology education.

(vii) **Inadequate co-curricular activities:** Like cultural activities, sports, corporate life are inadequate or non-existent.

(viii) **Undue Interferences:** By external agencies intruding into the autonomous and accountable character of higher education institution.

(ix) **Dwindling Status of VCs:** Functioning on the basis of a fast dwindling prestige, since he/she is constantly at the doorstep of government officials for money to keep the university going and on the other hand, he/she has to compromise at every step to get his/her way in university bodies whose member are not accountable for the impact of their decisions on the working of the university.

(x) **Inadequate Resource:** With immense needs for expansion as well as qualitative improvement inadequate funds is the bane of higher education in India.

With dwindling government funds for education the rising of resource through increased fee, accelerated global activity of internationalisation of higher education, sought to be institutionalised through the General Agreement in Trade and Services (GATS). The governments, especially of the developing countries, are facing a resources crunch for education and are under subtle pressure of the agencies of the Bretton woods system. These government are facing the basic question of prioritisation in education and there higher education agencies are facing the challenge of modernisation, relevance and competition in an era of globalisation and commodification of higher education. The government and their agencies have to take the final call on education being a public good or otherwise on the basis of their respective constitution and objectives of social justice.

SALIENT FEATURES OF New Education Policy 2020

NEP 2020 is the first education policy of the 21st century and replaces the thirty-four year old National Policy on Education (NPE), 1986. Built on the foundational pillars of Access, Equity, Quality, Affordability and Accountability, this policy is aligned to the 2030 Agenda for Sustainable Development and aims to transform India into a vibrant knowledge society and global knowledge superpower by making both school and college education more holistic, flexible, multidisciplinary, suited to 21st century needs and aimed at bringing out the unique capabilities of each student.

The policy has been formulated after a very detailed consultative process, unprecedented in depth and scale. Consultation involved over 2 lakh suggestions from 2.5 lakhs Gram Panchayats, 6600 Blocks, 6000 ULBs, 676 Districts. The MHRD had initiated a collaborative, inclusive, and highly participatory consultation process from January 2015. In May 2016, '*Committee for Evolution of the New Education Policy*' under the Chairmanship of Late Shri T.S.R. Subramanian, Former Cabinet Secretary, submitted its report. Based on this, the Ministry prepared '*Some Inputs for the Draft National Education Policy, 2016*'. In June 2017, a *'Committee for the Draft National Education Policy'* was constituted under the Chairmanship of eminent scientist **Padma Vibhushan, Dr K. Kasturirangan**, which submitted the Draft National Education Policy, 2019 to the Hon'ble Human Resource Development Minister on 31st May, 2019. The Draft National Education Policy 2019 was uploaded on MHRD's website and at 'MyGov Innovate' portal eliciting views/suggestions/ comments of stakeholders, including public.

The salient features of the policy are as follows :

SCHOOL EDUCATION

Ensure Universal Access at All Levels of schooling from pre-primary school to Grade 12

NEP 2020 aims to achieve 100% Gross Enrollment Ratio in school education by 2030. The initiatives that will be undertaken for this include provision of effective and sufficient infrastructure, alternative and innovative education centres to ensure that children who are dropping out of school are brought back into mainstream education, universal participation in school by carefully tracking students, as well as their learning levels.

Counsellors or well-trained social workers connected to schools/school complexes and teachers will continuously work with students and their parents to ensure that all school-age children are attending and learning in school.

Early Childhood Care Education

NEP 2020 emphasises on the criticality of the early years to ensure quality early childhood care and education for all children between 3-6 years by 2025. The children in the ages of 3-5 will be catered to by the current system of anganwadis and pre-schools, and age 5-6 will be included with the schooling system in a seamless integrated manner, with a play-way based curriculum to be prepared by the NCERT. A National Curricular and Pedagogical Framework for Early Childhood Care and Education (NCPFECCE) for children up to the age of 8 will be developed by NCERT. The planning and implementation of early childhood education will be carried out jointly by the Ministries of HRD, Women and Child Development (WCD), Health and Family Welfare (HFW), and Tribal Affairs.

New Curricular and Pedagogical Structure

With emphasis on Early Childhood Care and Education, the 10+2 structure of school curricula is to be replaced by a 5+3+3+4 curricular structure corresponding to ages 3-8, 8-11, 11-14, and 14-18 years respectively. This will bring the hitherto uncovered age group of 3-6 years under school curriculum, which has been recognised globally as the crucial stage for development of mental faculties of a child. The new system will have 12 years of schooling with three years of Anganwadi/ pre schooling.The new system will cover four stages: **Foundational Stage** (in two parts, that is, 3 years of Anganwadi/pre-school + 2 years in primary school in Grades 1-2; both together covering ages 3-8), **Preparatory Stage** (Grades 3-5, covering ages 8-11), **Middle Stage** (Grades 6- 8, covering ages 11-14), and **Secondary Stage** (Grades 9-12 in two phases, i.e., 9 and 10 in the first and 11 and 12 in the second, covering ages 14-18).

The curricula will aim for **holistic development of learners,** equipping them with the key 21st century skills, reduction in curricular content to enhance essential learning and critical thinking and greater focus on **experiential learning**. Students will have increased flexibility and choice of subjects so that they choose their own paths according to their talents and interests. There will be **no rigid separations between arts and sciences, between curricular and extra-curricular activities, between vocational and academic streams**. The objective is to give equal emphasis on all subjects-science, social sciences, art, languages, sports, mathematics-with integration of vocational and academic streams in school.

A new and comprehensive **National Curricular Framework for School Education**, NCFSE 2020-21, will be developed by the NCERT.

High-quality textbook materials will be developed by NCERT and SCERTs. States will prepare their own curricula and prepare textbooks incorporating state flavour and material. The availability of textbooks in all regional languages will be a top priority. Reducing the weight of school bags and textbooks will also be ensured by suitable changes in curriculum load.

Attaining Foundational Literacy and Numeracy

A National Mission on Foundational Literacy and Numeracy will be set-up on priority to focus on early language and mathematical skills from Grades 1 to 3 by 2025. Strategies include: developing school readiness through interim 3- month play-based school preparation module for all Grade 1 students; increased focus on reading, writing, speaking, counting, arithmetic, and mathematical thinking; continuous assessment and adaptive testing; national repository of high-quality resources on foundational literacy and numeracy; filling teacher vacancies; peer-tutoring and volunteer activities; setting up school libraries in every village; A National Book Promotion Policy will be formulated, and initiatives to ensure the availability, accessibility, quality, and readership of books across geographies, languages, levels, and genres will be undertaken.

Multilingualism and the power of language

NEP 2020 lays great emphasis on promoting multilingualism so that children know and learn about the rich and vast array of languages of their country. The medium of instruction until at least Grade 5, but preferably till Grade 8 and beyond, will be the home language/ mother tongue /local language/regional language. Every student in the country will participate in a fun project/activity on 'The Languages of India', sometime in Grades 6-8, such as, under the *'Ek Bharat Shrestha Bharat'* initiative. Sanskrit will be offered at all levels of school and higher education as an important, enriching option for students, including as an option in the three-language formula. Other classical languages and literatures of India, including Tamil, Telugu, Kannada, Malayalam, Odia, Pali, Persian, and Prakrit, will also be widely available in schools as options for students. Foreign languages, such as Korean, Japanese, Thai, French, German, Spanish, Portuguese, and

Russian, will also be offered at the secondary level. Indian Sign Language (ISL) will be standardized across the country, and National and State curriculum materials developed, for use by students with hearing impairment.

Assessment Reforms

There will be a shift from summative assessment to regular and formative assessment, which is more competency-based, promotes learning and development, and tests higher-order skills, such as analysis, critical thinking, and conceptual clarity. Board exams for Grades 10 and 12 will be continued, but be reformed to eliminate the need for taking coaching classes. Board exams will be redesigned to encourage holistic development; and will also be made 'easier', by testing core capacities/competencies. All students will be allowed to take Board Exams on up to two occasions during any given school year, one main examination and one for improvement, if desired. All students will take school examinations in Grades 3, 5, and 8 which will be conducted by the appropriate authority.

A new **National Assessment Centre, PARAKH (Performance Assessment, Review, and Analysis of Knowledge for Holistic Development)**, will be set up as a standard-setting body for setting norms, standards, and guidelines for student assessment and evaluation for all recognised school boards of India, guiding the State Achievement Survey (SAS) and undertaking the National Achievement Survey (NAS), monitoring achievement of learning outcomes and encouraging and helping school boards to shift their assessment patterns towards meeting the skill requirements of the 21st century.

Equitable and inclusive education

NEP 2020 aims to ensure that no child loses any opportunity to learn and excel because of the circumstances of birth or background. Special emphasis will be given on Socially and Economically Disadvantaged Groups (SEDGs) which include: gender identities (particularly female and transgender individuals), socio-cultural identities (such as Scheduled Castes, Scheduled Tribes, OBCs, and minorities), geographical identities (such as students from villages, small towns, and aspirational districts), disabilities (including learning disabilities), and socio-economic conditions (such as migrant communities, low income households, children in vulnerable situations, victims of or children of victims of trafficking, orphans including child beggars in urban areas, and the urban poor).

A **separate Gender Inclusion fund** will be created as also **Special Education Zones** for disadvantaged regions and groups.

Children with disabilities will be enabled to fully participate in the regular schooling process from the foundational stage to higher education. Recruitment of special educators with cross-disability training, and establishment of resource centres, wherever needed, especially for children with severe or multiple disabilities will be supported. Schools and school complexes will be supported for providing all children with disabilities accommodations and support mechanisms tailored to suit their needs and to ensure their full participation in the classroom. Assistive devices and appropriate technology-based tools, will be made available to help children with disabilities integrate more easily into classrooms and engage with teachers and their peers.

Every State/District will be encouraged to establish **"Bal Bhavans"** as a special daytime boarding school, to participate in art-related, career-related, and play- related activities. The unutilised capacity of school infrastructure will be used to promote social, intellectual, and volunteer activities for the community and to promote social cohesion during non-teaching / schooling hours and may be used as a "**Samajik Chetna Kendra**".

Teacher recruitment and career path

Teachers will be recruited through robust, transparent processes. Promotions will be merit-based, and a mechanism for multi-source periodic performance appraisals will be put in place. Progression paths to become educational administrators or teacher educators will be available for the teachers. A common **National Professional Standards for Teachers (NPST)** will be developed by 2022, by the National Council for Teacher Education, in consultation with NCERT, SCERTs, teachers from across levels and regions, expert bodies in vocational education, and higher education institutions etc. The standards would cover expected roles of the teacher at different levels of expertise/stage, and the competencies required for that stage. This could be adopted by states to determine all aspects of teacher career management, including tenure, professional development efforts, salary increases, promotions, and other recognitions. The professional standards will be reviewed and revised in 2030, and thereafter every ten years.

School Governance: Schools can be organised into school complexes or clusters which will be the basic unit of governance and administration that will ensure availability of all resources including infrastructure, like academic libraries and human resources e.g. art and music teachers along with a strong professional teacher community.

Standard-setting and Accreditation for School Education

Regulation and operations of schools will be carried out by separate bodies to eliminate conflicts of interest. It is envisaged to have clear, separate systems for policy making, regulation, operations and academic matters.To ensure that all schools follow certain minimal professional and quality standards, States/UTs will set up independent, State-wide body, **State School Standards Authority (SSSA)**. Transparent public self-disclosure of all the basic regulatory information, as laid down by the SSSA, will be used extensively for public oversight and accountability. The SCERT will develop a **School Quality Assessment and Accreditation Framework (SQAAF)** through consultations with all stakeholders.

Public and private schools will be assessed and accredited on the same criteria, benchmarks, and processes, emphasizing online and offline public disclosure and transparency, so as to ensure that public-spirited private schools are encouraged.

Vocational Education: By 2025, at least 50% of learners through the school and higher education system shall have exposure to vocational education. Beginning with vocational exposure at early ages in middle and secondary school, quality vocational education will be integrated smoothly into higher education. Vocational education will be integrated in the educational offerings of all secondary schools in a phased manner over the next decade. Towards this, secondary schools will also collaborate with ITIs, polytechnics, local industry, etc. Every child to learn at least one vocation and exposed to several more. A 10-day bagless period sometime during Grades 6-8 to intern with local vocational experts such as carpenters, gardeners, potters, artists, etc. Similar internship opportunities to learn vocational subjects to students throughout Grades 6-12, including holiday periods. Vocational courses through online mode will also be made available.

HIGHER EDUCATION

Increase GER in higher education to reach at least 50% by 2035.

The aim will be to increase the Gross Enrolment Ratio in higher education including vocational education from 26.3% (2018) to 50% by 2035.

Holistic Multidisciplinary Education

The policy envisages a broad-based multi-disciplinary holistic education at the undergraduate level for integrated, rigorous exposure to science, arts, humanities, mathematics and professional fields having imaginative and flexible curricular structures, creative combinations of study, integration of vocational education and multiple entry/exit points. A holistic and multidisciplinary education will help develop well-rounded individuals who possess critical 21st century capacities in fields across the arts, humanities, languages, sciences, social sciences, and professional, technical, and vocational fields; an ethic of social engagement; soft skills, such as communication, discussion and debate; and rigorous specialisation in a chosen field or fields. Such a holistic education shall be, in the long term, the approach of all undergraduate programmes, including those in professional, technical, and vocational disciplines.

The **undergraduate degree will be of either 3 or 4-year duration**, with multiple exit options within this period, with appropriate certifications- a certificate after completing 1 year in a discipline or field including vocational and professional areas, or a diploma after 2 years of study, or a Bachelor's degree after a 3-year programme. The 4-year multidisciplinary Bachelor's programme shall be the preferred option since it allows the opportunity to experience the full range of holistic and multidisciplinary education in addition to a focus on the chosen major and minors as per the choices of the student. An **Academic Bank of Credit** (ABC) shall be established which would digitally store the academic credits earned from various recognised HEIs so that the degrees from an HEI can be awarded taking into account credits earned.

Model public universities for holistic and multidisciplinary education, **Multidisciplinary Education and Research Universities (MERUs)** will be set up and will aim to attain the highest standards for multidisciplinary education across India.

A number of initiatives will be taken to ensure **optimal learning environments** are created that are engaging and supportive, and enable all students to succeed. All institutions and faculty will have the autonomy to innovate on matters of curriculum, pedagogy, and assessment within a broad framework of higher education qualifications that ensures consistency across institutions and programmes and across the ODL, online, and the traditional 'in-class' modes. HEIs shall move to a criterion-based grading system that assesses student achievement based on the learning goals for each programme, and also move away from high-stakes examinations towards more continuous and comprehensive evaluation.

Universities and colleges will set up **high-quality support centres** and will be given adequate funds and academic resources to encourage and support students from socio-economically disadvantaged backgrounds. **Professional academic and career counselling** will be available to all students, as well as counsellors to ensure physical, psychological and emotional well-being.

Rationalised Institutional Architecture

A new vision and architecture for higher education has been envisaged with large, well-resourced, vibrant multidisciplinary institutions. Higher Education Institutions will be transformed into large multidisciplinary universities, colleges, and HEI clusters/Knowledge Hubs, each of which will aim to have 3,000 or more students. A university will mean a multidisciplinary institution of higher learning that offers undergraduate and graduate programmes, with high quality teaching, research, and community engagement. The definition of university will allow a spectrum of institutions that range from Research- intensive Universities, Teaching-intensive Universities and Autonomous degree- granting Colleges (ACs).

The system of affiliation will be phased out over 15 years and a stage-wise mechanism for granting graded autonomy to colleges, through a transparent system of graded accreditation, will be established. Over a period of time, it is envisaged that every college would develop into either an Autonomous degree- granting College, or a constituent college of a university.

National Research Foundation (NRF)

A new entity will be set up to catalyze and expand research and innovation across the country. The overarching goal of the NRF will be to enable a culture of research to permeate through our universities, helping to develop a culture of research in the country through suitable incentives for and recognition of outstanding research, and by undertaking major initiatives to seed and grow research at State Universities and other public institutions where research capability is currently limited. The NRF will competitively fund research in all disciplines. Successful research will be recognised, and where relevant, implemented through close linkages with governmental agencies as well as with industry and private/philanthropic organisations.

Financial support for students: Efforts will be made to incentivise the merit of students belonging to SC, ST, OBC, and other SEDGs. The National Scholarship Portal will be expanded to support, foster, and track the progress of students receiving scholarships. Private HEIs will be encouraged to offer larger numbers of freeships and scholarships to their students.

Open and distance learning will be expanded, thereby playing a significant role in increasing the Gross Enrolment Ratio to 50%. Measures such as online courses and digital repositories, funding for research, improved student services, credit-based recognition of MOOCs, etc., will be taken to ensure it is at par with the highest quality in-class programmes.

Internationalisation of education will be facilitated through both institutional collaborations, and student and faculty mobility and allowing entry of top world ranked Universities to open campuses in our country.

Motivated, Energised, and Capable Faculty

NEP 2020 recognises that the success of higher education institutions is the quality and engagement of its faculty. HEIs will have clearly defined, independent, and transparent processes and criteria for faculty recruitment. Faculty will be given the freedom to design their own curricular and pedagogical approaches within the approved framework. Excellence will be further incentivized through appropriate rewards, promotions, recognitions, and movement into institutional leadership. Faculty not delivering on basic norms will be held accountable.

Effective Governance and Leadership in HEIs

Through a suitable system of graded accreditation and graded autonomy, and in a phased manner over a period of 15 years, all HEIs in India will aim to become independent self-governing institutions pursuing innovation and excellence. Measures will be taken at all HEIs to ensure leadership of the highest quality and promote an institutional culture of excellence. Institutional governance based on autonomy - academic, administrative and financial -is envisioned with each higher education institution having an Board of Governors. All leadership positions and Head of institutions will be offered to persons with high academic qualifications and demonstrated administrative and leadership capabilities along with abilities to manage complex situations.

Regulation

There will be a single overarching umbrella body for promotion of higher education- the Higher Education Commission of India (HECI)- with independent bodies for standard setting- the General Education Council; funding-Higher Education Grants Council (HEGC); accreditation- National Accreditation Council (NAC); and regulation- National Higher Education Regulatory Council (NHERC). Regulation will be 'light but tight' to ensure financial probity and public-spiritedness to eliminate conflicts of interest with transparent self-disclosure as the norm not an inspectorial regime. The regulatory body will function through a faceless intervention through technology for regulation & will have powers to penalise HEIs not conforming to norms and standards. Public and private higher education institutions will be governed by the same set of norms for regulation, accreditation and academic standards.

Teacher Education: The 4-year integrated stage-specific, subject-specific Bachelor of Education offered at multidisciplinary institutions would be the way forward. A new and comprehensive National Curriculum Framework for Teacher Education, NCFTE 2021, will be formulated by the NCTE in consultation with NCERT. By 2030, the minimum degree qualification for teaching will be a 4-year integrated B.Ed. degree that teaches a range of knowledge content and pedagogy and includes strong practicum training in the form of student-teaching at local schools.Stringent action will be taken against substandard stand-alone Teacher Education Institutions (TEIs).

A **National Mission for Mentoring** shall be established, with a large pool of outstanding senior/retired faculty – including those with the ability to teach in Indian languages – who would be willing to provide short and long-term mentoring/professional support to university/college teachers.

Professional Education

All professional education will be an integral part of the higher education system.Stand-alone technical universities, health science universities, legal and agricultural universities, or institutions in these or other fields, will aim to become multi-disciplinary institutions.

Technology in Education

An autonomous body, the **National Educational Technology Forum** (NETF), will be created to provide a platform for the free exchange of ideas on the use of technology to enhance learning, assessment, planning, administration. Appropriate integration of technology into all levels of education will be done to improve classroom processes, support teacher professional development, enhance educational access for disadvantaged groups and streamline educational planning, administration and management. Technology-based education platforms, such as DIKSHA/ SWAYAM, will be better integrated across school and higher education. HEIs will play an active role in conducting research on disruptive technologies and in creating instructional materials and courses including online courses in cutting-edge domains.

Online Education and Digital Education: A comprehensive set of recommendations for promoting online education consequent in the recent rise in epidemics and pandemics in order to ensure preparedness with alternative modes of quality education whenever and wherever traditional and in-person modes of education are not possible, has been covered. A dedicated unit for the purpose of orchestrating the building of digital infrastructure, digital content and capacity building will be created in the MHRD to look after the e-education needs of both school and higher education.

Adult Education

The policy aims to achieve 100% youth and adult literacy by 2030.

Promotion of Indian Languages

To ensure the preservation, growth, and vibrancy of all Indian languages, several initiatives are envisaged. More HEIs, and more programmes in higher education, will use the mother tongue/local language as a medium of instruction, and/or offer programmes bilingually, in order to increase access and GER and also to promote the strength, usage, and vibrancy of all Indian languages. An Indian Institute of Translation and Interpretation (IITI) will be established. Sanskrit and all Indian language institutes and departments across the country will be significantly strengthened. National Institute (or Institutes) for Pali, Persian and Prakrit will be set up. Efforts to preserve and promote all Indian languages including classical, tribal and endangered languages will be undertaken.

Financing Education

Education is a public service and must not be a commercial activity or a source of profit. Multiple mechanisms with checks and balances will combat and stop the commercialisation of higher education. All education institutions will be held to similar standards of audit and disclosure as a 'not for profit' entity. The Centre and the States will work together to increase the public investment in Education sector to reach 6% of GDP at the earliest.

The **Central Advisory Board of Education will be strengthened** to ensure coordination to bring overall focus on quality education. The remodeled and rejuvenated CABE shall also be responsible for developing, articulating, evaluating, and revising the vision of education in the country on a continuous basis, in close collaboration with MHRD and the corresponding apex bodies of States. It shall also create and continuously review the institutional frameworks that shall help attain this vision.

Ministry of Education: In order to bring the focus back on education and learning, it may be desirable to re-designate MHRD as the Ministry of Education (MoE).

Philosophy of Education

Philosophy is a search for a general understanding of values and reality by chiefly speculative rather than observational means. It signifies a natural and necessary urge in human beings to know themselves and the world in which they live and move and have their being. Western philosophy remained more or less true to the etymological meaning of philosophy in being essentially an intellectual quest for truth. Hindu philosophy is intensely spiritual and has always emphasized the need for practical realisation of truth. Philosophy is a comprehensive system of ideas about human nature and the nature of the reality we live in. It is a guide for living, because the issues it addresses are basic and pervasive, determining the course we take in life and how we treat other people. Hence we can say that all the aspects of human life are influenced and governed by the philosophical consideration. As a field of study, philosophy is one of the oldest disciplines. It is considered as a mother of all the sciences. In fact it is at the root of all knowledge. Education has also drawn its material from different philosophical bases.

The free dictionary defines philosophy as follows:

1. The study of the nature, causes, or principles of reality, knowledge, or values, based on logical reasoning.
2. A system of thought based on or involving such study.
3. The study of the theoretical underpinnings of a particular field or discipline.
4. An underlying theory or set of ideas relating to a particular field of activity or to life as a whole.

Education, like philosophy is also closely related to human life. Therefore, being an important life activity education is also greatly influenced by philosophy. Various fields of philosophy like the political philosophy, social philosophy and economic philosophy have great influence on the various aspects of education like educational procedures, processes, policies, planning and its implementation, from both the theoretical and practical aspects.

- **Meaning of Education:** Etymologically, the word education is derived from educare (Latin) "bring up", which is related to educere "bring out", "bring forth what is within", "bring out potential" and ducere, "to lead". Education in the largest sense is any act or experience that has a formative effect on the mind, character or physical ability of an individual. In its technical sense, education is the process by which society deliberately transmits its accumulated knowledge, skills and values from one generation to another.

Is Education as transmission of knowledge versus education as the fostering of inquiry and reasoning skills that are conducive to the development of autonomy (which, roughly, is the tension between education as conservative and education as progressive, and also is closely related to differing views about human—perfectibility—issues that historically have been raised in the debate over the aims of education); the question of what this knowledge, and what these skills, ought to be—part of the domain of philosophy of the curriculum; the questions of how learning is possible, and what is it to have learned something—two sets of issues that relate to the question of the capacities and potentialities that are present at birth, and also to the process (and stages) of human development and to what degree this process is flexible and hence can be influenced or manipulated; the tension between liberal education and vocational education, and the overlapping issue of which should be given priority—education for personal development or education for citizenship (and the issue of whether or not this is a false dichotomy); the differences (if any) between education and enculturation; the distinction between educating versus teaching versus training versus indoctrination; the relation between education and maintenance of the class structure of society, and the issue of whether different classes or cultural groups can— justifiably—be given educational programmes that differ in content or in aims; the issue of whether the rights of children, parents, and socio-cultural or ethnic groups, conflict—and if they do, the question of whose rights should be dominant; the question as to whether or not all children have a right to state-provided education, and if so, should this education respect the beliefs and customs of all groups and how on earth would this be accomplished; and a set of complex issues about the relation between education and social reform, centering upon whether education is essentially conservative, or whether it can be an (or, the) agent of social change.

It is here that that philosophy of education plays an important role in providing direction to education on the following issues as well as providing a theory of knowledge for education to work upon.

Philosophy of education is essentially a method of approaching educational experience rather than a body of conclusions. It is the specific method which makes it philosophical. Philosophical method is critical, comprehensive and synthetic.

Therefore,

1. Philosophy of education is the criticism of the general theory of education.
2. It consists of critical evaluation and systematic reflection upon general theories.
3. It is a synthesis of educational facts with educational values.

In brief, it is a philosophical process of solving educational problems through philosophical method, from a philosophical attitude to arrive at philosophical conclusions and results. Thus, it aims at achieving general as well as comprehensive results.

(A) Philosophy of Education in Western Perspective: Plato along with John Dewey believes that philosophy of education occupied a central place in philosophical thought. Dewey, in fact, once suggested that *"philosophy may even be defined as the general theory of education."*

Idealistic View:-

The idealists believe that the soul is immortal, the world of ideas is the real world and this world of ideas is not the world of senses. Mind possesses the important power of thought. Butler maintains the Descartes' dictum *"I think, therefore I am"*, is the first step toward all knowledge. Idealist defines man in terms of mental activity, who must recognise a mode of knowing other than experiences.

The Idealist does not object to the schools' attempting to develop physical fitness, social efficiency and vocational competence of the individual but for the idealists the intellectual studies are primary because they are concerned with changeless essences, universals and concepts.

Plato's scheme of education is best described in his *"Republic"*. According to Plato, the aim of education should be for the *"safety of the unity of the state, development of the qualities of citizenship, development of faith in truth, goodness and beauty, development of personality, preservation of social classes and development of human qualities.*" Plato insisted that true knowledge must be elicited from within and sought for ideas and not in particulars of senses. Production of the right type citizen (who is socially, economically, intellectually and politically useful and fit) is the aim of education.

Plato's actual educational practices were derived from his theory of ideas. Ideas constitute the important content of education. Man's superior faculties are attributed to the soul (mind and reason) and inferior attributes to the body (evil, change, corruption and the like). The things of the mind are the concern of education; other activities belong to man's lower nature and should not be dignified by the term education. Rather they should be called training, in the sense that one speaks of training an animal.

Idealism believes that man realizes the spiritual nature of Divine Being, therefore, the educational aim is *'man making'* in its highest capacity.

Even though his specific plan was never put into practice, Plato's view of society as an ordered division of classes has been the ideal of educational conservatives throughout the ages. Like Plato, the medieval educator believed that only the intellectuals should receive advanced education. The modern conservatives also accept the divisions, especially at the higher levels, and call for very rigorous selection of candidates for advanced study according to their intellectual capacities. Plato emphasizes on individual differences which means no human nature is common to all men. But all men possess the same fundamental powers of the soul. But the differences are the harsh realities with which the rulers and educators must work. Again Plato asserts that man's will is free. Recognition of the freedom of the will shows man's responsibility for his actions and the attendant reward or punishment for good and bad behaviour.

Need of curriculum is another great factor for Horne. He suggested that the criteria for selection of curricular content should be the abilities and needs of the learner and secondly, the requirements of society and thirdly, the nature of the universe in which we live. Meeting the students' needs calls for work in the science (knowing), arts (feeling) and the practical arts (doing or willing). Physics, chemistry, biology, sociology, and similar courses give the student the knowledge of the external world. Appreciation of music, drama, literature and the like assist man to make proper emotional adjustment to the world around him. Finally, vocational education provides him with the skills necessary to maintain his own life as well as to become a productive member of the society. Curriculum provided by Idealists is traditional in character. But they liberally granted vocational education also. However, Horne disagreed with Dewey and other liberals who ranked practical and intellectual studies equally.

Horne was one of the first systematic reactions against the liberal philosophy of Dewey. Dewey advocates that the dualism of mind-body is responsible for the insignificance of society and education. Like Dewey, Horne was critical of the liberalism of Rousseau, Herbert and Spencer. He has used Dewey's *"Democracy and Education"* as a text for his courses in philosophy of education ever since its appearance. Horne disagreed with Dewey's basic philosophical position, although he did grant that Dewey proposed the most significant change in educational theory since Plato. For students to have some basis for contrasting Dewey's educational philosophy with another system, Horne published a book titled *"The Democratic Philosophy of Education - Companion to Dewey's Democracy and Education.* In this volume Horne contrasted his philosophy of Idealism, point by point, with the philosophy of Dewey.

1. Naturalistic View: The naturalistic philosophers of education derive the aims and ideals, the means the methods of teaching and the principles of curriculum and school management from the nature. The ancient atomistic naturalism was presented by Democritus. Democritus explained the composition of universe in terms of innumerable, indivisible and indestructible atoms. What Rousseau thinks about the role of nature in the education of child is an outcome of his concept of nature, which is enjoyable, living, harmoniously balanced, useful, sympathetic and unexpressive methods of education for child development. Observation of nature therefore becomes an essential factor in education. Rousseau says, *"Observe nature and follow the way she traces for you; she is ever urging children to activity; she hardens them by presenting them with all kinds of difficulty; she teaches them very early what it is to suffer and know grief."*

2. Realistic View: The realistic philosophers of education give importance to scientific process and say that after scientific analysis of natural interests of the child and society, it is necessary to know which interest is common to both and is equally beneficial. Realistic view is directly related to life and society. It tries to bring all joys and happiness in society with the analysis of the real problem of the society. The supporters of realism are - Johann Friedrich Herbart and Herbert Spencer.

Spencer accompanied with the view that education teaches man to lead a complete life. A man has five types of duties – self-preservation, earning a living, fulfilling duties of regarding race preservation, fulfilling duties of a citizen and utilisation of leisure. For these above activities, Spencer feels the necessity of the study of science. For preservation of health, teaching of hygiene and for earning a living, teaching of mathematics, logic, physics and biology is necessary. This will enable children to make their knowledge practical and they will be able to use it in different situations of life.

3. Pragmatic View: Pragmatic philosophers of education consider the aim, nature, organisation and order of education should be such that it may do maximum good of man.

John Dewey argued that the mind-body (spirit-matter) dualism of classical philosophy is responsible for the unnatural cleavages in society and education such as labour-leisure, practical-intellectual, man-nature, culture-vocation, subject matter- method, ends-means and others. Dewey rejected the notion that the human mind is endowed from birth with reasoning power or that its origin is in the spiritual soul. Mind is not different from the body but one with it. All of man's functions are natural - none are supernatural. Dewey's denial of the validity of all kinds of dualism is the touchstone of his educational philosophy. For him, the removal of this unnatural dualism would give unity to education and life.

Dewey expected for a new system of education. In his *"My Pedagogic Creed"* he argued that the demands of social situations stimulated the child to act as a member of a unity, rather than as an isolated individual. This social stimulation presses him to act for the welfare of the group to which he belongs. Even the child's natural instincts and tendencies must be directed into social useful channels. In his own words Dewey wrote, *"Education must begin with a psychological insight into the child's capacities, interests, and habits. These powers, interests, and habits must be continually interpreted- we must know what they mean. They must be translated into terms of their social equivalents- into terms of what they are capable of in the way of social service... The child has his own instincts and tendencies, but we do not know what these mean until* we *can translate them into their social equivalents. We must be able to carry them as the inheritance of previous race activities. We must also be able to project them into the future to see what their outcome and end will be."* It is, therefore, impossible to determine the potentialities of an individual unless he is acting with others for the good of the group.

In rejecting the conservative notion that man is born with a readymade mind which absorbs stimuli and knowledge from an environment, he insisted that different people react to situations in different ways because of the social milieu. Therefore, Dewey believes that an individual derives his mental powers and other traits from society. Therefore, educational activities are of prime importance in making man what he is.

For Dewey social freedom has important implications for education. He believes that freedom consists in the ability to interact with others in the various social groups which make up human society. Man's choice are almost entirely determined by environment and training. Dewey's conception of human freedom tends to offset (do good or balance) the extreme emphasis on individual freedom found in the child-centered school of the early liberals. It attempts to harmonise individual freedom with social responsibility. It recognises that to a great intend, man acts in response to his environment but also possesses the power to improve that environment for himself and others. Dewey defended it in this way, "*social environment forms the mental and emotional disposition of behaviour in individuals by engaging them in activities that arouse and strengthen certain impulses that have certain purposes and entail certain consequences.*"

Rousseau, Pestalozzi and other early liberals had initiated the struggle against the conservative notion of education according to social classes. But they never adopted a thorough going democratic philosophy of education. Dewey's *"Democracy and Education"* is the first treatise in the history of education which set out to dethrone the *"Republic"* and *"Laws of Plato"* from their position of supremacy in educational thought. Whereas, Plato had taught that all men by nature fall into three distinct classes and only one of these classes is fit to rule, Dewey argued that all men have the potential to direct their own activities in association with other equals. He repudiated the view that there is any authority external to that of the people themselves. Each individual, then, in association and communication with others is equal to all others with respect to rights, privileges and responsibilities. Obviously, he concluded, a democratic society must see to it that equal educational opportunities are available to all so that proper direction may be given to all the affairs of individual and group living. Dewey advocates that a democracy is more than a form of government; it is primarily a mode of associated living, of conjoint communicated experience.

A.N. Whitehead did not consider that both reason and experience (including science) are valid modes of knowing. Whitehead added another dimension of knowing, that is the artistic. Man, he explained, is employing the artistic mode when he relies upon feelings, sensations, emotions, and intuition rather than upon abstract reasoning or the scientific method. In his own words, "*Culture is activity of thought, and receptiveness to beauty and human feeling...A merely well -informed man is the most useless bore on God's earth. What* we *should aim at producing are men who possess both culture and expert knowledge in some special direction. It is not what they are at eighteen; it is what they become afterwards that matters.*"

- **Marx and Lenin's view on Education:** In "*General Council of the First international*" Karl Marx was asked the question; what should be the purpose of the school? Marx responded that the schools should not concern themselves with developing a political, moral or religious outlook. Their sole purpose, he said, was to teach the "*natural sciences and those truths which are independent of all party prejudices*". In other words, Marx felt that the school's purpose was to impart objective knowledge and thereby develop the intellectual powers of the students. Marx felt that the development of communist morality should be accomplished through lectures, workshops, and seminars conducted for adults.

  The primary purpose of education in general is to prepare the young for conscious participation in world revolution, class struggle, and active roles in local and national government. Therefore, Lenin believes that the media is necessary for students.

4. Existentialist View: Existentialistic educators appreciated the Socratic Method as the humanistic approach to philosophy of education. Socrates neither established any school nor delivered lectures for the purpose of education or examination. His method of teaching was confined to asking questions and developing the issue till the conclusion is reached. He himself pleaded ignorance and sought enlightenment from those with whom he conversed. Existential philosophy seems to advocate Socratic Method as a model.

Keeping the aim of all round development of the children the existentialist philosophers of education suggested for the related curriculum. Only scientific knowledge is not sufficient for student. Science cannot help in inner realisation and achievement of peace. Besides science, the curriculum must include humanities, ethics and religion. It should vary according to the age level of the children. Humanities subjects are recognised as valuable and important by Sartre and Heidegger. Sartre believes that one should learn language before his own potentialities. "*I am what* I say" is the declaration of Heidegger. Sartre accepted aesthetic subject matter such as arts, music and myths as the sources of truth. Jaspers' importance was in genuine science along with anthropology and history. Modern science and technology is also recognised as the important subject matter of education.

(B) Philosophy of Education in Indian Perspective: Educational foundations in India are also found in the metaphysical, epistemological and axiological outlook of the philosophers. The Indian philosophy of education is distinct about aims, curriculum, methodology and other aspects of education.

(i) Vedic Period: In ancient India knowledge of sacred Veda is recognised as the second birth and the father of the birth is the teacher who imparted knowledge of *Vedas.* So teacher is respected as pivot of whole educational system. The ancient philosophy of education is especially spiritual or idealistic in nature. The basic aim of Vedic education is to attain liberation or *Moksha.* The *Samkhya* system also follows the Vedic view of liberation as the aim of education. The *Samkhya* philosophy of education believes that the deliverance or liberation is possible by understanding the difference between *Prakriti* or matter and the *Purusha* or soul. So education for *Samkhya* is to enable individuals to understand the difference between matter and soul in order that he may rid himself of the miseries of the world. And to attain this practice *yoga* is necessary.

Education in *Upanishadic* philosophy of education is related to social norms and it tried to conserve the cultural tradition of the society of those days. The society was divided on the basis of *'Varnas'* and *'Ashramas'*. It tries to bring about social change, not only conserve the social ethos. Aims suggested by *Upanishadic* philosophy of education are:

(a) Character building.
(b) Development of personality.
(c) Knowledge of social roles and status.
(d) Vocational efficiency.
(e) National integration.

Upanishadic aim of 'philosophy of education' is therefore not one sided. It emphasized all round development of a person. Its methods are discussion method, questioning, induction and deduction. It is also well known to commentaries, illustrations, descriptions, narratives and practical demonstrations. Education in the Vedic period was influenced and shaped by the *Ashramas,* the stages of a man's life: *brahmacharya* (as a student), *garhasthya* (as a householder), *vanaprastha* (as a recluse), and *shannyasa* (as a religious mendicant), the four stages were integrally woven into a path to liberation or *moksha.* The foundation of this path consisted in the *brahmachari's* entire approach to life and God. Hence the significance of his introduction to the Vedic scriptures and all the learning he did of the *brahminic* mantras and sutras (sacred formulae and texts). Education was thus not a thing to end with the first stage but was only an introduction to the other stages of life. It was a gradual and lingering process of unfolding the spiritual personality to the ultimate goal of self-realisation.

In Vedic philosophy the four *purusharthas* or aims of life have a determining influence on the human individual. They are: *Artha* (wealth), *Kama* (satisfaction of sense-desires), Dharma (righteousness), and *Moksha* (liberation). The *ashramas* and the *purusharthas* together provide the righteous direction for the common man to the ultimate goal of life. At the level of *brahmacharya,* education, the student under the teacher learns and practices the righteous and legitimate use of material wealth. Wealth is used as a means and not an end in itself. Again he is educated to make the righteous use the sense faculties and derive righteous enjoyment of life. Dharma designates the traditionally 'established order' which includes all duties, - individual, social or religious. Dharma includes all forms of righteous thought and deed. And these three leads to the *moksha.*

In Vedic education, it is accepted that knowledge can be gained by three steps, *Shravana* or hearing, *Manana* or memorising and *Dhyana* or meditation. That was a major contribution of the Vedic period to education. It was the primary duty of students to listen to recitation of the Vedic scriptures. *Shravana* had special Vedic significance. The fruits and the effect of the sacred rituals and sacrifices greatly depended on the nature of the recitation. As reading materials were rare the principal learning technique was listening.

But in this philosophy of education the method of gaining knowledge is theoretical. But *Yoga* system of philosophy of education is different from other ancient system as it is theoretical as well as practical. The aim of *yoga* is to control one's desires and aspirations. It is to remove ignorance and to achieve wisdom. Teaching and practice of *yoga* helps to acquaint students with the eight factors of yoga which are known as *Yama, Niyama, Asana, Pranayama, Pratyahara, Dharana, Dhyana* and *Samadhi.* Practice of *yoga* was necessary for one's general progress for the improvement of physical and spiritual aspect. It also helps to solve mental and other problems of life.

Educational amplification of *Gita* again shows that education is nothing but which enables one to see the existence of God in the soul of each living being. In *Gita* the ideals of education are as follows:

1. Development of virtuous knowledge.
2. Development of personality and its refinement.
3. Harmony between the individual and social aims.
4. Development of intellect and reasoning ability.
5. Establishment of importance of one's duty.
6. Development of Inner consciousness.

(ii) Medieval Period: *Jaina* and Buddhism accepted non-violence as the aim of education. Buddha emphasized on liberation as the ultimate goal and knowledge and law of Karma as the means of liberation. It is the liberation from the cycle of birth and death which is emancipation. Therefore, knowledge of the four supreme truths leads to emancipation. These truths *(aryasatyas),* known as four noble truths are

1. This world is full of miseries *(dukha)*
2. Ignorance is the cause of miseries *(dukhasamudaya)*
3. There are cessation of miseries (*dukhanirodha*) and
4. There are ways to get rid of miseries (*dukha-nirodh-marg).*

By advocating these four noble truths according to Buddha the ultimate aim of education can be achieved.

The religious aspirations and reaction of common men gave rise to Buddhism and Jainism whose founders attempted to bring religion down to the common men, place greater insistence on morality, self-control and good works, give more rational interpretation to human life and satisfy the aspirations of all common man to believe in a personal God.

During the Muslim ruling period in Indian history it was the mixed educational system of Vedic and Islamic education. The Islamic education flowed in India for a period of about five hundred years. This period continued till the advent of British in India who started the modem education.

The significance of reading, writing and teaching in Islam is obvious because the very first message of Allah to his Prophet *Muhammad* is in regard to reading, writing and teaching. Therefore, in *Koran* also the first priority is given to education and the attaining of knowledge. To seek knowledge is a religious duty for every Muslim.

In medieval period the philosophy of education was not influenced by secular education. The concept of secular education started in the British period of education. All education was influenced by religion since ancient to modern times. While the Hindus were instructed by Hindu scriptures and sacred books, Muslim, Jainism and Buddhism also followed their own scriptures.

The medieval period of philosophy of education had two aims, one, the propagation of the fundamental tenets and teachings of religion and the other to make the student practically successful in different vocations. The educational institutions therefore used to teach various arts and skills, such as sculptures, agriculture, medicine, painting, house building and various types of crafts. Military science formed an important part of curriculum everywhere since wars were usual phenomena. Again the humanist trend is also unavoidable in the medieval period. Some Muslim kings did try to propagate only Islamic teachings through education; others gave generous aids to Hindu *pathsalas* also. The syllabi of medieval institutions included literature, grammar, logic, philosophy, mathematics, law, astrology, history, geography, agriculture, medicine etc. The medium of instruction in Hindu institutions was Sanskrit or regional languages and in Muslim institutions Arabic and Parsi. The method of teaching had an important role on memorisation in addition to the three Rs' reading, writing and arithmetic.

(iii) Modern Period: In India, modern education started under the British rule. As the Indian people educated in Hindu and Muslim institutions were not useful for working of the British Government, therefore, Lord Macaulay drew up a plan of western oriented education in India. On February 8, 1835, Macaulay presented his historical 'minutes', making a bitter attack upon Indian literature and culture. He laid stress on what he called religious objectivity which meant the duty of England to teach Indians what was good for their health. The policy developed on the basis of Macaulay's educational views giving primacy to the propagation of European literature and science, suspension of scholarships for students, neglect of publication of Eastern literature and encouragement to propagation of English literature. This policy was accepted by Lord Bentinck. English education in India was useful and professional and vocational institutions started to provide education in medicine, engineering, law and other specialised areas.

The aim of British education was mainly creation of cogs for the British machinery in India. However, along with the study of Western language and literature, the study of oriental literature was also given a place in the curriculum. Both, English and Indian languages were accepted as the medium of instruction.

The British Educational system initiated Western influence of education in India. It created social and political awareness in the country. It inspired literary and cultural consciousness and developed nationalistic feelings. However, it was definitely British oriented, to serve British interest, colonial in aim and practice. The Christian missionaries and the British administrators encouraged Christian teachings in institutions.

All the traditionalists and the Western oriented Indian thinkers of education criticised the British philosophy of education. They could clearly see that its aims and means were against national interest. The philosophers of education of young India tried to reconstruct the values, ideals and systems of education in India suitable to their culture and philosophy. Therefore, long before India achieved freedom, illustrious thinkers particularly Swami Vivekananda, Sri Aurobindo and R.N. Tagore criticised the prevalent philosophy of education and presented alternative philosophies. The reformists including Raja Ram Mohan Roy, Annie Besant, M.G. Ranade and others asked for reforms in education. The philosophers of education suggested plans for national education. By education, Radhakrishnan means the process by which we conserve valuable elements in our culture and discard the wasteful.

Like ancient Indian philosophy of education traditional group of contemporary philosophers of education also drew inspiration from Vedanta philosophy. It only re-interpreted the ancient Vedanta philosophy in the light of new knowledge. Therefore, this is called *Neo-Vedantic* philosophy. It is new since it synthesises religion and science, ancient Indian wisdom and modern Western thought. It accepted the educational philosophy presented in different scriptures, suggesting modifications according to contemporary conditions. For example, Gandhi's philosophy of education is based on socio-economic condition of that time. He synthesises the *swadesi* and *svadharma* and world brotherhood and internationalism in the same field. But their thinking was not conservative, narrow or reactionary. They presented a philosophy of education founded upon man's status in the cosmos and the human nature.

Again contemporary Indian philosophers of education supported an integral approval in almost every field of education, the aims, the means, the curriculum, the teacher- student relationship, teaching methods, school administration etc. It gives equal values of all types of education. They also presented very pragmatic and practical scheme of education though rooted in Vedanta idealism.

The second group consists of J.L. Nehru and M.N. Roy; well-versed in western thought, they founded their educational humanism on the western naturalistic humanism. It is different from religious humanism and based on general ideas, social and political theory. They have firsthand knowledge of contemporary Indian politics and presented philosophies of education in the context of their general schemes of social and political reformation. Jawaharlal Nehru has accepted education as the most important means to social change. Education is the means to socialisation, the tool which trains citizens in the art of thinking. Education is the most important requisite, according to Nehru, to open up the individual. Freedom from ignorance is as essential as freedom from hunger. For economic and political reformation improved human relations are also required. Social development is inconceivable without mental development and broadening of mental horizon achieves the spirituality. So education aims for the victory of the mind and soul over lifeless matter. Nehru said, *"Unless this conflict of the spirit is solved there is going to be no peace in any country"*.

M.N. Roy is against any compulsion in education, because compulsion is against liberty. Education should help men and women to think rationally and to decide themselves, about the problems to be solved. General education by government is the mental slavery which promotes the masses to sing songs of patriotism, to salute the national flag, to study the history edited by government and to work collectively to achieve success of the state. This kind of national education is not true democratic education.

J. Krishnamurti believes that education helps in discovering the significance of life. He said, "*I*/we *may be highly educated, but if we are without deep integration of thought and feeling, our lives are incomplete, contradictory and torn with many fears; and as long as education does not cultivate an integrated outlook on life, it has very little significance*." For him to understand life, is to understand ourselves and that is both the beginning and the end of education. Intelligence is the capacity to perceive the essential, what *is* and to awaken this capacity, in oneself and in others, is education. The purpose of education is not to produce mere scholars, technicians, and job hunters, but integrated men and women who are free of fear; for only between such human beings can there be enduring peace. Education should not encourage the individual to conform to society or to be negatively harmonious with it, but help him to discover the true values which come with unbiased investigation and self-awareness.

(C) Philosophical divisions of Indian Education: The *Carvaka* philosophy of education is materialistic. Broadly it may be called Indian materialism, it believes that worldly pleasure is acquired through the acquisition of power and money. *Acharya Vatsyyayana,* the author of *Kamasutra* described only about the life style of Indian citizen, belongs to a very rich class. The citizen, described in *Kamasutra* goes on excursions, fond of hunting, loves singing and dancing, knows painting, music and other fine arts and usually has some girl friends who are cultured girl or women of the city. About women, *Kamasutra* prescribed that they should study 64 *katas* which includes *prahelikas* (riddles of words), *pustakavacana* (chanting from books), *Kavya samasya purty* (composing a suitable portion of a verse to fit in with a portion given), knowledge of lexicons and metres, singing, dancing, and other fine arts, various sorts of games, recreations and music were available to the girls. The ancient education is in forest and in natural environment but the contents were social morality and ultimately spiritual education.

Indian philosophy holds education as a sacred activity and best kind of charity. It always inspires to pray to God that he should direct us from untruth to truth, from darkness to light and from death to immortality.

It is generally said that Indian education is completely idealistic and religious. But it is not true. It is also criticised that ancient educational system has no relation with the real world. But the education of technical and vocational subjects like *Ayurveda* and *Dhanurveda* cannot be ignored. Students are taught all the subjects relevant to society that they can help the society with their best of practical knowledge and performance.

The above discussion shows that both the western and Indian philosophy of education is the guiding principle to fulfill the different aims of an individual and the social life. It deals with the questions which arise relating to the conditions, principles and norms of the individual and the social life. Education is a continuous process of learning and acquisition of knowledge in a systematic manner. It helps to achieve self-realisation and in the task of fullest expression of one's personality. Its aim is to train a person with a definite purpose and to give a particular direction to an individual and the society.

Character development is another aim of the philosophy of education for all the thinkers of west and east. For an ideal character, Bertrand Russell suggested for the education of the vitality, courage, sensitiveness and intelligence. Though the modern western system of education is materialistic, Indian philosophers of education always emphasized on spiritual attainment. In west also, Froebel mentioned about the spiritual development of the individual along with the moral, mental, physical, and social development. Froebel advocated that the main purpose of education is to lead and guide the child to clearness. This clearness is concerned with the child himself and that should be at peace and unity with Nature and God respectively. Gandhi modified the same view as follows, *"Education is that which liberates. It initiates one into the higher life of the spirit. Let education take you nearer to God.*"

Jawaharlal Nehru and M.N. Roy on the other hand, followed the western materialistic and scientific philosophy of education to develop the Indian spirit. According to Nehru, *"It is the scientific method alone that offers hope to mankind and an ending of the agony of the world"*. On the other hand, Radhakrishnan synthesized both the scientific and spiritual to emancipate the individual. While the western concept of education was influenced by their own philosophical thought and religious beliefs and social norms and values of that particular nation, Indian philosophy of education is also established based on the Indian culture, beliefs and norms. But the modern and contemporary philosophers of education are very liberal and democratic, when they accept the aims, methods and practice in the individual or social life.[36]

Having considered the Indian philosophy of education till about the pre and post-independence period we come to a stage of assessing the modern higher education system in India with its philosophical basis. The Indian education system from the ancient times was based on culturally scriptured pre-ordination of learning and vocations according to social status of communities in a stratified dominance-based social categorisation. In the British colonial period various commissions and committees on education defined the higher education system of the country.

The Woods Despatch 1854, prescribed establishment of universities at the presidency towns of Bombay, Calcutta and Madras on the model of London University in 1857. These universities were to be conferring degrees to such persons as would come from any of the affiliated institutions after passing some required examination. The universities commission of 1902 had made specific recommendations for fitting the youth for – commercial, vocational or non-literary pursuits but these recommendations were ignored by the then government. It can be understood that these were the seedling ideas of compartmentalisation between various disciplines of arts, commerce and technical education.

The Resolution of the Government of India on Education policy (1913) made recommendations concerning the inclusion of subjects of industrial importance in the curriculum and provision of facilities to the students desirous of prosecuting research work. This also indicates entry of technical education into higher education.

The Calcutta University Commission of 1917 recommended Intermediate classes to be separated from universities and a curriculum spreading over three years to be prescribed for the degree of B.A. The stage of admission to the university was to be Intermediate and not Matriculation examination. Another recommendation was for intermediate college to be established for completing the first stage. These colleges should conduct teaching in Arts, Science, Medicine, Engineering, Education, Agriculture and Commerce.

The Abbot-Wood report (1936-37) – On its revival in 1935, the Central-Advisory Board of Education recommended the appointment of a Committee to make recommendation for the reorganisation of education in view of the fact that a large number of graduates going out of the Universities were unable to secure employment of the kind for which the education qualified them. As a response the Abbot-Wood report of 1937, suggested a complete hierarchy of vocational institutions parallel with the hierarchy of institutions imparting general education. As a result of their recommendations "a new type of technical institution called the Polytechnic has come into existence."

This above mentioned historical evolution of higher education indicates the initiation of compartmentalisation of disciplines into those with employment potential and those without. The arts or social sciences without the potential and the technical or sciences with the potential of employment. These probably are the moorings of rigid compartmentalisation of disciplines into the social sciences, natural sciences and technology application. Another aspect of the Abbot-Wood report also clearly differentiates between general education and vocational education. General education for literary scholarship and vocational for skill based employment. These also are the seedlings of diversion between mental labour and manual labour. This whole discourse of knowledge building seems to have carried on to this day with all its strengths and failings.

It is very interesting that the framework of higher education of the present times has its roots in the policy developments of the colonial period. The question is after 70 years of independence in a democratic set-up why we have not radically changed the higher education framework for better implications. The question arises whether this continuity is convenient to perpetuate a system of education/higher education that is designed in favour of the socio-economic elites who are in position, traditionally and other wise, to exploit the higher education framework to their best interests. This continuance has an uncanny resemblance to the education/higher education system of ancient India. That was based on allocation of duties to social communities according to their social status in a descending order from the mental to the manual. The topmost Brahman represented by the mouth giving expertise of memorisation, speech – making and abstract thinking. The chest represented by the Kshatriyas with the duties of domination through rule with combat skills. The thighs representing the Vaishyas with the duties of business and trading. The feet representing the Shudras whose duties were to provide services to all the above social categories and the Atishudras/Antyaj or untouchables providing manual services of menial nature to the top three social categories.

The modern day higher education framework is far different from its ancient predecessor higher education system. But it uncannily reflects similar social implications of educational outputs to the socially and economically backward caste students of the day. The social sciences have least implications, employment-wise, while it changes as one moves to the natural sciences and technology education. And it is also co-incidental that to this day the scheduled castes and scheduled tribes students are forced in disproportionate numbers into the least return-giving social sciences.

The modern day higher education framework is also a manifestation of social stratification which can be understood as follows:

The prowess of mental skills of the then higher castes are today being utilised for better memorisation and presentation with little understanding, but with the great effect of securing very high marks at the secondary and higher levels examinations, which only prioritised memory skills, which are the entrance to higher professional education like engineering and medicine which give the best emoluments and status. This access to a dominating socio-economic position is an entrance to the consumption based capitalist economic model of the day. While the then manual skills of the lower castes is being forced into the social sciences, because of relatively lower mental and oral skills of which they did not have any cultural history. They are forced into the social sciences for abstract thinking, at which also they are not adept and to make matters worse the uni-dimensionality of social sciences, which lack in providing any skills, keeps them out of the modern employment domain. So the present system has reversed the roles of the then social categories of higher and lower order. The then mental prowess of the higher social categories has been utilised to enter into the financially and otherwise productive world of skills in the industry and corporate sector while the then manual skills or skill sets of the lower social categories are forced to be confronted with an examination system which tests their mental skills of which they never had any tradition and lack of educational history preventing them from mastering the examination techniques of the day.

In order to change the whole framework of higher education, to avoid the pitfalls of modern day higher education, especially for the scheduled castes and scheduled tribes students, this book attempts to create an indicative interdisciplinary curriculum of a science, rooted in the socio-economic contexts of the society.

Development of Higher Education in India- A Statistical Profile

Higher education in India has expanded enormously since independence. Not only this; it has also enlarged in size. The percentage of the students in higher education to the total population in the age group 17-23 has increased from 0.58 in 1950-51 to 4.8 in 1980- 81 and now it is around 6 percent. No doubt, this is an impressive quantitative growth in higher education. Despite such growth three aspects namely, access, quality and obsolescence have been causing great concern.[37]

(i) Number of Universities: India has the third largest higher education system in the world, next only to China and the United States. Before Independence, access to higher education was very limited and for the socio-economic elites, with enrolment of less than a million students in 500 colleges and 20 universities. Since independence, the growth has been very impressive over the years. The growth rate of universities after independence in India is indicated by the graph below:

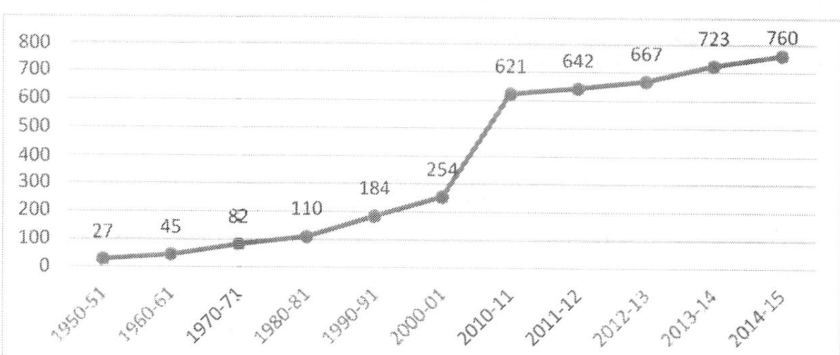

Source:- Educational Statistics at a Glance-2016.[38]

Graph 1.1: Number of Universities.

The number of higher educational institutions (HEIs) has increased from 27 universities in 1950-51 to 760 universities as of 2014-15. This growth rate is more than 28 times as compared to the number of universities before at the time of independence.

(ii) Type-wise Universities in India: Indian higher education sector is complex and multilayered. It can be hard for a layman to understand the different types of institutes and make the right choice. Student and parents have to make institute selection based on multiple factors like location, courses offered, fees, capitation fees or donations, placements, co-curricular activities.

The University Grants Commission (UGC) is the regulatory body for all the universities in India. Under the University Grants Commission (UGC) Act, 1956, "University" means a University established or incorporated by or under a Central Act, a Provincial Act or a State Act, and includes any such institution as may, in consultation with the University concerned, be recognised by the Commission in accordance with the regulations made in this behalf under this Act. The number of different types of universities in India are as follows:

Table 1.1: Type-wise distribution of Universities in India

Sr. No.	Type of Universities	Number of Universities	Percent
1.	Central Universities	43	5.66
2.	State Public Universities	316	41.58
3.	State Private Universities	181	23.81
4.	Deemed Universities	122	16.06
5.	Central Open University	01	0.13
6.	State Open University	13	1.71
7.	Institution of National Importance	75	9.87
8.	State Private Open University	01	0.13
9.	Institutions under State Legislation Act	05	0.66
10.	Others	03	0.39
	Total	**760**	**100**

Source:- Educational Statistics at a Glance-2016.[39]

Central universities are government run universities created by an act of the Parliament of India. There are 43 (5.66%) central universities all over India.

The State Government establishes and runs the State Universities. This is the most common type of university. These universities generally give affiliation to smaller institutes and various colleges. There are 316 (41.58%) state universities established by the various state governments in India.

Private universities are same as State Universities except that they are run by private organisations. Private universities are established by State government by an act in the Legislative Assembly. They are recognised by UGC and are empowered to award degrees, conduct examinations and design their own curriculum. There are 181 (23.81%) private universities all over India.

Deemed universities are private institutions that are empowered to grant degrees by the UGC. But, deemed universities are not established by the state government in the legislative assembly. There are 122 (16.06%) deemed universities in India.

There is only one (0.13%) Central Open University established in Delhi named Indira Gandhi National Open University (IGNOU). It was established in 1985 by an Act of Parliament with the dual responsibilities of (i) enhancing access and equity to higher education through distance mode and (ii) promoting, coordinating and determining standards in open learning and distance education systems. Since then, the IGNOU has undergone rapid expansion and emerged as an international institution in the field of Open and Distance Learning.

There are at present 13 (1.71%) State Open Universities set up by the respective states. They provide education only in the distance mode. These universities cater to people who are unable to pursue regular courses due to various reasons. These Universities are also instrumental in shaping the career growth of learners who are already employed.

Institutions of National Importance (INI) are a status that may be conferred to a premier public higher education institution in India by an act of parliament, an institution which "serves as a pivotal player in developing highly skilled personnel within the specified region of the country/state". There are 05 (0.66%) INI institutions all over India

There are 5 (0.65%) educational institutions established through the state legislation.

(iii) Types of Colleges in India: There are two types of colleges in India (i) Affiliated colleges and (ii) Autonomous colleges. The vast majority of colleges in India are Affiliated Colleges which follow their affiliated university's curriculum, examination structure and grading protocol. Transcripts and degrees are awarded by the university. Government, private aided and unaided are the types of affiliated colleges. The number of colleges in India in last five years is as follows:

Table 1.2: Number of Private and Government Colleges in India

Year	Private Un Aided	Private Aided	Total Private	Government	Total
2010-11	9735(59.00)	2344(14.21)	12079(73.21)	4420(26.79)	16499
2011-12	12265(57.97)	3136(14.82)	15401(72.79)	5757(27.21)	21158
2012-13	14042(58.22)	3584(14.86)	17626(73.08)	6494(26.92)	24120
2013-14	17721(60.42)	4379(14.93)	22100(75.35)	7230(24.65)	29330
2014-15	21710(63.02)	4857(14.10)	26567(77.11)	7885(22.89)	34452

Source: AISHE, MHRD, GOI (2010-11 to 2014-15).

The public expenditure in higher education remained close to 1% of the country's Gross Domestic Product (GDP) over the years, which has been quite low in proportion to the burgeoning requirements of this sector.[40] This has led to an exponential growth of private sector institutions. As evident from the above table the share of private higher education institutions (77.11%) is more than government colleges (22.89%) in the year 2014-15. The numbers of Private colleges are increasing constantly and on the other hand government colleges are decreasing continually. Over 4% private unaided colleges have increased in the year 2011 to 2015. At the same time near 4% government colleges decreased in this period.

(iv) Enrolment in Higher Education: Higher education in India starts after passing the higher secondary education or the 12th standard. Following table indicates the number of students enrolled for higher education between the years of 2010-11 to 2014-15.

Table 1.3: Enrolment in Higher Education (in Lakhs)

Year	SC	ST	All Category
2010-11	30	12	275
2011-12	36	13	292
2012-13	38	13	301
2013-14	42	15	323
2014-15	46	16	342

Source:- Educational Statistics at a Glance-2016.[41]

As evident from the above table all category students' enrolment in the higher education is increasing per year. In the year 2010-11 the enrolment of the SC students was 30 lakhs, ST students 12 lakhs and 275 lakhs were all category students in higher education. This increased in the year 2014-15 to SC-46 lakhs, ST-16 lakhs and all categories 342 lakhs.

(v) Discipline-wise number of students: Discipline-wise number of students for the year 2014-15, are enrolled at the undergraduate level as per follows:

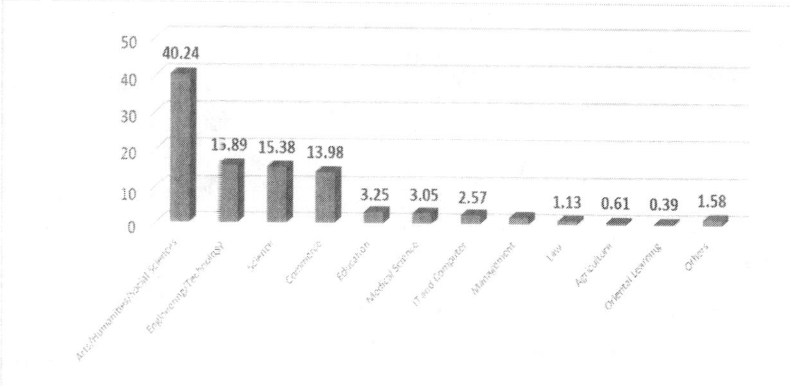

Graph 1.2: Percentage Enrolment in various Disciplines at under Graduate level in Higher Education 2014-15.

Total students enrolment is classified into 12 categories i.e. Arts/ Humanities/Social Sciences, Engineering/Technology, Science, Commerce, Education, Medical Science, IT and Computer, Management, Law, Agriculture, Oriental Learning and Others. Percentage share of students enrolment in these disciplines are shown in the above table. The highest number of students (40.24%) are enrolled at undergraduate level across India in the discipline of Arts/Humanities/Social Sciences. Engineering and Technology is second major stream with 15.89% students enrolled. After that is the science stream with 15.38% students enrolled and in the commerce field there were 13.98% students enrolled.[42]

It means a huge number of students were enrolled in the Arts/ Humanities/Social science faculty because the access of science and technological education is difficult and limited. Besides that students from the lowest income groups are still significantly under-represented in some of the popular professional courses like medicine, law or technical courses in IIT's and IIM's.[43] Lower academic performance due to socio-economic hindrances and lack of government technical higher education institutes in the rural areas forces the rural students to enroll into the social sciences. Besides this, the fees of the private science and technical education institutes is not affordable to poor people from rural India. These are the reasons, among others, that show the higher percentage of undergraduate students in the social sciences.

(vi) Percentage Enrolment in various Programmes: The programmes-wise percentage of the undergraduate students in the year 2014-15 was as follows:

Table 1.4: Percentage Enrolment in various Programmes in Higher Education (2014-15)

Programme	Male	Female	Total
B.A.	24.60	32.96	28.44
B.Sc.	11.44	12.22	11.80
B.Com.	10.96	10.77	10.87
B.Tech	8.68	3.78	6.43
B.E.	7.61	3.57	5.75
M.A.	3.27	5.36	4.23
B.A. (Honors)	3.31	4.23	3.73
B.Ed.	1.37	2.85	2.05
M.Sc.	1.33	2.15	1.70
M.B.A.	1.89	1.28	1.61
B.C.A.	1.53	1.25	1.40
B.Sc. (Honors)	1.37	1.25	1.32
B.B.A.	1.28	0.91	1.11
M.Com.	0.84	1.33	1.07
L.L.B.	1.05	0.54	0.82
Others	19.47	15.55	17.67

Source:- Educational Statistics at a Glance-2016.[44]

As regards the educational programmes, out of the total, the first 6 programmes have relatively higher enrolment. Others including Library and Information Science, Music, Performing / Visual Arts, Journalism and Mass Communication, Physical Education, Social Work, etc. have low enrolment rates. Among the higher education enrolment 28.44% students enrolled for the B.A. programme, which is the highest enrolment. The percentage of males is 24.60% and females is 32.96%. 11.87% students enrolled in the B.Com. programme and out of them 10.96% were male students and 10.77% were female. 11.80% students are enrolled in B.Sc. and out of them 11.44% are from male category and 12.22% are from female category. 6.43% students are enrolled in the B. Tech. programme, out of which 8.68% are males with females only at 4%. 5.75% students were enrolled at the B.E. programme out of which 7.61% students are from male category. At the M.A. level 4.23% of students were enrolled with 3.27% male and 5.36% female students. Among 67% students enrolled in the above mentioned six programmes the highest number of students were enrolled to the programme of Bachelor of Arts. Lower academic performance due to reasons explained earlier and lower access to the government science and technological education institutions, they being low in numbers, even if the performance of students from socio-economic backward categories is good enough the even higher fees of the private institutions is restricting access to science and professional programmes. These are the reasons for this higher enrolment in the arts faculty.

(vii) GER in Higher Education: Gross Enrolment Ratio (GER) in Higher Education in India is calculated for the 18-23 years age group. Total enrolment in higher education, regardless of age, expressed as a percentage to the eligible official population (18-23 years) in a given academic year. The GER is widely used to show the general level of participation in and capacity of higher education.

As per UNESCO estimates at least 20% GER is a prerequisite for rapid socio- economic development of a country. The government of India proposes to increase the GER from the present 12% to 15% by the end of XI plan (2007-2012) and to 21% by the end of XII plan (2012-2017). But, such a fast linear expansion of the system is likely to tell upon its quality which is already being questioned.[45]

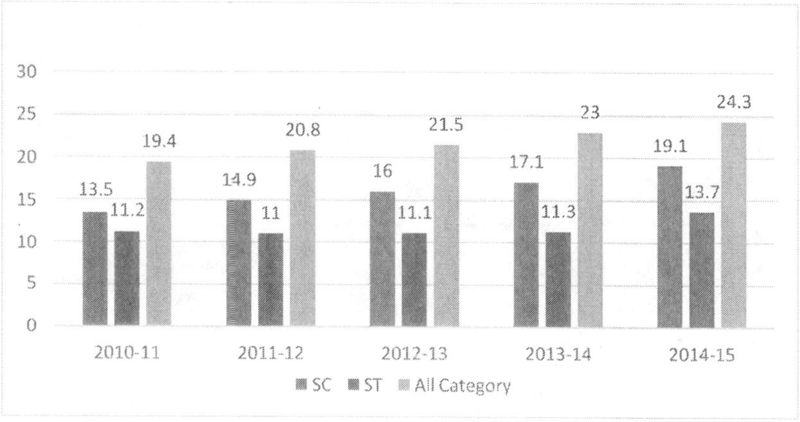

Source:- Educational Statistics at a Glance-2016.[46]

Graph 1.3: Gross Enrolment ratio in Higher Education.

Gross enrolment ratio in higher education of India has improved in the year 2014- 15 as compared to previous figures. Estimated Gross Enrolment Ratio (GER) in Higher education in India was 24.30% in the year 2014-15, which was calculated for 18-23 years age group. For Scheduled Castes it was 19.10% and for Scheduled Tribes it was 13.70%. From the year 2010-11 the researcher observers lack of improvement in the enrolment ratio.

Our GER (24.30) in higher education is lower as compare to world average GER of 34.45.[47] Developed countries worldwide possess higher GER with USA having 34%, UK 59%, Japan 55% and China 28%.[48] India needs to bring improvement in the education system and improve the number of institutes considerably by developing more institutions with accreditation. It will automatically increase the number of students being enrolled in the education arena, eventually promoting the progress and development of the nation. Additionally, it also needs to uplift the socio-economically backward students from the primary and secondary levels of education to the tertiary levels to increase the GER levels and achieve social inclusion at all levels of education.

(viii) Gender Distribution: In the issues of gender discrimination in all sectors we can notice the lower participation of women in all sectors. Education sector is also not excluded from gender discrimination. The researcher took a review of the participation of female students behind hundred male students from the primary to the higher education levels and the figures are as follows-

Table 1.5: Number of Female per hundred Male Enrolled by stages of Education

Year	Primary	Upper Primary	Secondary	Senior Secondary	Higher education
2010-11	92	89	82	79	78
2011-12	93	90	84	81	80
2012-13	94	95	89	87	81
2013-14	93	95	89	89	85
2014-15	93	95	91	90	85

Source:- Educational Statistics at a Glance-2016.[49]

Taking a look at the Male-Female ratio at each level in the above table, the trend is for higher males than females at every level. The proportion of females is decreasing with rising higher education levels. This trend is constant till the year of 2014-15.

Table 1.6: Average Annual Dropout rates in school education (2013-14)

Category	Primary	Upper Primary	Secondary	Senior Secondary
Scheduled Castes	4.14	4.38	18.66	1.81
Scheduled Tribes	7.98	8.43	27.20	2.94
All category	4.34	3.77	17.86	1.54

Source:- Educational Statistics at a Glance-2016.[50]

(ix) Pupil-Teacher Ratio: Pupil-teacher ratio is the number of students who attend a school or university divided by the number of teachers in the institution. Factors that can affect the relationship between student–teacher ratio and class size include the number of teachers with non- teaching duties, the number of classes per teacher and the number of teachers per class. On the other hand, if there are small classes with a small number of students, the teacher can concentrate on every student. The pupil-teacher ratio at all levels of education is given in the table below:

Table 1.7: Pupil-Teacher ratio by stages of Education

Year	Primary	Upper Primary	Secondary	Senior Secondary	Higher Education
2010-11	43	33	30	34	26
2011-12	41	34	32	33	24
2012-13	28	25	NA	NA	23
2013-14	25	17	26	41	25
2014-15	24	17	27	38	24

Source:- Educational Statistics at a Glance-2016.[51]

The pupil-teacher ratio is improving with the rising education levels. At the primary level the ratio was an average over 32 students per teacher in the year 2010 to 2015. The pupil-teacher ratio was 43 in the year 2010 which was decreasing with coming years. This is the result of right to education act, which proposed this ratio for primary education level at 40:1 and 35:1 for upper primary level. The average PTR at the upper primary level is 25:1 which is according to the RTE act. The average PTR at secondary and senior secondary level is respectively 28:1 and 36:1. At the higher education level the PTR is better than other educational levels, which is an average 24 students per teacher. This is good according to the students for better interactions with the teachers. This is good because of higher drop-out rates at primary and secondary levels leading to access for very few students to the tertiary levels. And incidentally the drop-out rates of the SC and ST students is comparatively much higher at the secondary level leading to far fewer number of these students entering the higher education domains. This is classic social exclusion from higher education. Further, even in the SC and ST numbers in higher education, most are absorbed, involuntarily, into the social sciences leading to far less productive outputs. This situational demand has led this book to relate higher education, interdisciplinarity and inclusiveness to come up with an indicative and modular interdisciplinary curriculum of a science integrating the social and natural sciences with applied implications in the larger socio-economic contexts.

(x) Budget Expenditure on Education of GDP: In India, over the last fifty years there have been major changes in the level of financing of education and in priorities attached to different sectors within it. Several commissions, committees, and policies were appointed after independence to deal with various issues in education. Many of them suggested higher investment in education and recommended expenditure of appropriate share of income of state and central government on education. In the post-independent era the expenditure on education by the education department and other departments viz (i) Revenue Account, (ii) Capital Account and (iii) Loans and Advances as % of GDP is as follows:

Table 1.8: Budget expenditure on Education by Education and other Departments as % of GDP

Year	Expenditure on Education by Education & other Departments as % of GDP
1951-52	0.64
1960-61	1.48
1970-71	2.11
1980-81	2.98
1990-91	3.84
2000-01	4.14
2005-06	3.34
2006-07	3.48
2007-08	3.40
2008-09	3.56
2009-10	3.95
2010-11	4.05
2011-12	3.82
2012-13	4.10
2013-14	4.13

Source:- Educational Statistics at a Glance-2016.[52]

Kothari Commission (1964-66) recommended that public expenditure on education should reach the level of 6 percent of GDP by 1986. But we could not reach the said percentage as observed in the above table. In the early decades after independence the government, for economic growth, emphasized on investment in the industrial sector. This among others, is the reason for low percentage of expenditure on education till 1960-61. After recommendations of Kothari Commission (1964-66) to extend the public expenditure on education up to 6 percent of GDP, we can notice the incremental improvement in the budget expenditure on education over the next decades. The percentage of GDP expenditure on education in the year

2013-14 was 4.13, which was very low compared to the expenditure on education among developed countries.

Further the researcher tries to give the actual breakup in the table below for the budget expenditure on education by education and other departments as a percentage of GDP.

Table 1.9: Budget expenditure on Education by Education and other Departments as % of GDP

Sector	Expenditure on Education		Expenditure as % of GDP	
	2011-12	2012-13	2011-12	2012-13
Elementary Education	149164.77	184650.63	1.71	1.86
Secondary Education	85572.91	102907.40	0.98	1.03
University and Higher Education	53900.98	60043.91	0.62	0.60
Adult Education	930.71	1084.26	0.01	0.01
Technical Education	44361.01	59735.50	0.51	0.60
Total	**333930.38**	**408421.70**	**3.82**	**4.10**

Source:- Educational Statistics at a Glance-2016.[53]

As evident from the above table, education level-wise expenditure as a percentage of GDP is very low. Government of India allocates more budget for elementary education compared to higher education. In the year 2012-13 the expenditure on elementary education as percentage of GDP was 1.86% and at the higher education level it was 0.60%, which is very low. The government has to improve budgetary allocation for quality, quantity and access to higher education for the educational inclusion of the socio-economically underprivileged students.

The continued neglect of the consecutive governments regarding raise in funding for education, higher education in particular, over the decades is indicative and significant. This highlights the lower priority given to education by the governing elites. India is a developing country with a huge socio-economic backlog especially with the scheduled castes and scheduled tribe communities. Education, especially higher education, is the greatest necessity for uplifting the socially backward masses to raise the overall index levels of the country. But the sheer neglect on lack of rise in funding to education is inexplicable especially when the dizzying development levels of the western and even some eastern countries is evident in relation to very high levels of GER in higher education. This situation has to be rectified urgently and also restructuring higher education in an interdisciplinary manner is to be undertaken for holistic knowledge building with social inclusion.

References

1. Hommadi, A. H. (1985), 'Higher Education in Third World', Delhi: Indian Bibliographies Bureau, Balaji Enterprises, p. 25.
2. Chauhan, C. P. S. (1990), 'Higher Education in India (Achievement, Failures and Strategies)', New Delhi: Ashish Publishing House, pp. 06-07.
3. *Ibid*, p. 06.
4. Halder, Santoshi (2011), 'Bridging the Gap: Education for All', paper published in the edited book titled 'Reforms in Higher Education' edited by Bawa, S.K. and Padhan, Ananda, Chandigarh: Abhishek Publication, p. 21.
5. Chauhan, C. P. S. (1990), 'Higher Education in India (Achievement, Failures and Strategies)', New Delhi: Ashish Publishing House, p. 03.
6. Chaube, S. P. and Chaube, A. (1999), 'Education in Ancient and Medieval India (A survey of the Main Features and a Critical Evaluation of Major Trends)', New Delhi: Vikas Publishing House Pvt. Ltd, p. 77.
7. Mane, Vikas (2013), 'Globalisation and Indian Higher Education', Pune: Scion Publication Pvt. Ltd, p. 90.
8. Choudhary, Sujit Kumar (2008), '*Higher Education in India: a Socio-Historical Journey from Ancient Period to 2006-07*' Journal of Educational Enquiry, Vol. 8, No. 1, p. 53.
9. Mane, Vikas (2013), 'Globalisation and Indian Higher Education', Pune: Scion Publication Pvt. Ltd, p. 91.
10. Choudhary, Sujit Kumar (2008), '*Higher Education in India: a Socio-Historical Journey from Ancient Period to 2006-07*' Journal of Educational Enquiry, Vol. 8, No. 1, p. 53.
11. *Ibid*, p. 54.
12. Ghosh, Suresh, C. (2007), 'History of Education in India', Jaipur: Rawat Publications, pp. 75-76.
13. Chauhan, C. P. S. (1990), 'Higher Education in India (Achievement, Failures and Strategies)', New Delhi: Ashish Publishing House, p. 03.
14. Choudhary, Sujit Kumar (2008), '*Higher Education in India: a Socio-Historical Journey from Ancient Period to 2006-07*' Journal of Educational Enquiry, Vol. 8, No. 1, p. 55.
15. Mane, Vikas (2013), 'Globalisation and Indian Higher Education', Pune: Scion Publication Pvt. Ltd. p. 92.
16. Dongerkery, S.R. (1997), '*University Education in India*', Mumbai: Manaktalas, pp. 8-9.
17. Ghosh, S.C. (2001), *The History of Education in Mediaeval India*, 1192 AD-1757 AD, Delhi: Originals, p. 22.
18. Chauhan, C. P. S. (2010), 'Higher Education in India: Issues and Challenges', in *Higher Education Quality and Management*, ed. Khurana, S. M., and Singhal, P.K., New Delhi: Gyan Publishing House, p. 77.
19. Laurence, James, C. (2010), 'Higher Education and Development', New Delhi: Rajat Publication, p. 252.

20. Biswal, A. and Agrawal, S. P. (1986), '*Development of Education in India: A Historical Survey of Educational Documents before and after Independence*' New Delhi: Concept Publishing Company, p. 464.
21. Bhatt, B.D. and Aggarwal, J.C. (1987), '*Educational Documents in India (1813- 1986) Survey of Indian Education*' New Delhi: Arya Book Depot, p. 34.
22. *Ibid*, p. 34.
23. Laurence, James, C. (2010), 'Higher Education and Development', New Delhi: Rajat Publication, p. 252.
24. Bhatt, B.D. and Aggarwal, J.C. (1987), '*Educational Documents in India (1813-1986) Survey of Indian Education*' New Delhi: Arya Book Depot, pp. 30-32.
25. *Ibid*, p. 34.
26. Bhatt, B.D. and Aggarwal, J.C. (1987), '*Educational Documents in India (1813-1986) Survey of Indian Education*' New Delhi: Arya Book Depot, p. 38.
27. *Ibid*, pp. 76-77.
28. Sharma, Shaloo (2002), 'History and Development of Higher Education in India' Vol. 5 perspectives on the History and Development of India Higher Education, New Delhi: Sarup and Sons, p. 51.
29. Biswal, A and Agrawal, S. P. (1986) '*Development of Education in India - A Historical Survey of Educational Documents before and after Independence*' New Delhi: Concept Publishing Company, pp. 474-475.
30. *Ibid*, pp. 477-479.
31. *Ibid*, pp. 479-480.
32. *Ibid*, pp. 480-484.
33. *Ibid*, pp. 484-487.
34. Power, K. B. 1995. Higher Education in India. In K.B. Power & S.K. Panda (eds), *Higher Education in India—in search of quality*, New Delhi: AIU, p. 39.
35. Sujit Kumar Choudhary, 2008, '*Higher Education in India: a Socio-Historical Journey from Ancient Period to 2006-07*' Journal of Educational Enquiry, Vol. 8, No. 1, p. 62.
36. http://shodhganga.inflibnet.ac.in/bitstream/10603/68349/7/07_chapter%202.pdf
37. Sharma, Shaloo (2002), 'History and Development of Higher Education in India' Vol. 5 perspectives on the History and Development of India Higher Education, New Delhi: Sarup and Sons, p.11.
38. GOI, (2016), '*Educational Statistics at a Glance*', MHRD, Department of School Education & Literacy, New Delhi, p. 17.
39. *Ibid*, p. 5.
40. ASHE (2013), '*Annual Status of Higher Education of States and UTs in India*', MHRD, Government of India, New Delhi, p. 09.
41. GOI, (2016), '*Educational Statistics at a Glance*', MHRD, Department of School Education & Literacy, New Delhi, pp. 19-23.
42. *Ibid*, p. 5.
43. G. Pankajam (2014), *Issues in Education*, New Delhi: Gyan Publishing House, p. 47.

44. GOI, (2016) '*Educational Statistics at a Glance*', MHRD, Department of School Education & Literacy, New Delhi, p. 6.

45. Chauhan, C. P. S.(2010), '*Higher Education in India: Issues and Challenges*', in *Higher Education Quality and Management*, ed. Khurana, S. M., and Singhal, P.K., New Delhi: Gyan Publishing House, p. 80.

46. GOI, (2016), '*Educational Statistics at a Glance*', MHRD, Department of School Education & Literacy, New Delhi, p. 31.

47. http://data.worldbank.org/indicator/SE.TER.ENRR

48. http://ireport.cnn.com/docs/DOC-1108407.

49. GOI, (2016), '*Educational Statistics at a Glance*', MHRD, Department of School Education & Literacy, New Delhi, p. 32.

50. *Ibid*, pp. 36-38.

51. *Ibid*, p. 40.

52. *Ibid*, p. 41.

53. *Ibid*, p. 16.

Chapter - 2

Higher Education – Interdisciplinarity and Inclusiveness

Concept of Interdisciplinarity

Interdisciplinarity involves the combining of two or more academic disciplines into one activity. It is about creating something new by crossing boundaries, and thinking across them. It is related to an interdiscipline or an interdisciplinary field, which is an organisational unit that crosses traditional boundaries between academic disciplines or schools of thought, as new needs and professions emerge.

The term *interdisciplinary* (ID) is applied within education and training pedagogies to describe studies that use methods and insights of several established disciplines or traditional fields of study. Interdisciplinarity involves researchers, students, and teachers in the goals of connecting and integrating several academic schools of thought, professions, or technologies—along with their specific perspectives—in the pursuit of a common task.

Interdisciplinary is most often used in educational circles when researchers from two or more disciplines, pool their approaches and modify them so that they are better suited to the problem at hand, including the case of the team-taught course where students are required to understand a given subject in terms of multiple traditional disciplines. For example, the subject of land use may appear differently when examined by different disciplines, for instance, biology, chemistry, economics, geography, and politics.

In order to understand 'interdisciplinarity' it is necessary to know about the 'discipline'. Academic discipline may mean a convenient division of knowledge into its component parts as well as the basis of organisation of a university.

(A) Definition of Discipline

1. According to Guy Michaud and C. C. Abt, a discipline is "A Specific body of teachable knowledge with its own background of education, training, procedures, methods and content areas."[1]
2. According to Marcel Biosot, "A discipline is concerned first with objects, methods and procedures and finally with laws. The objects are not isolated entities, they interact with other objects and give rise to phenomena. The aim of the discipline is to give coherent explanation of the phenomena generated by these interactions."[2]

(B) Definition of Interdisciplinarity

1. According to Garkovich, "Two or more disciplines..... Contributing their particular disciplinary knowledge on a common subject."[3]
2. According to Chettiparamb, interdisciplinarity is "filling the gaps that disciplinarity leaves vacant or in terms of transcendence surpassing what disciplinarity can ever hope to achieve."[4]

Interdisciplinarity is an approach where in more than one disciplines interact leading to non-unidisciplinary concepts in their own referential context. Interactions occur with respect to four features of disciplines viz. (a) Methods of enquiry, (b) Axiomatic or research paradigms, (c) Subject matter, (d) Concepts, generalisations and theories. Sharing of one or more features by more than one disciplines or interaction of more than one disciplines with respect to one or more features lead to different types of approaches or levels of interdisciplinarity.

Heckhausen (1972) identifies six types of interdisciplinarity. They are presented in an ascending order of maturation:

1. **Indiscriminate Interdisciplinarity:** This consists of encyclopedic endeavors that end up in curriculum mix-ups. Here introductory studies of various fields are thought to counteract disciplinarity. However, it mainly provides vocational training for pre-university practitioners, but is also found when an imperialistic discipline claims other discipline to be auxiliary.
2. **Pseudo-Interdisciplinarity:** While two different disciplines sharing the same analytical tools such as mathematical models or computer models are claimed to be interdisciplinary, this is then

called pseudo-interdisciplinarity. Topics such as pattern recognition, game and decision theory and models of social action may form the topics whereby and through which integration is claimed.

3. **Auxiliary Interdisciplinarity:** This happens when the method used by one discipline yields data that has an index-value for another discipline at its level of theoretical integration. If the level of theoretical integration is not achieved, it can lead to criticism and revision causing more sophistication and the development of more advanced interdisciplinarity.
4. **Composite Interdisciplinarity:** This happens when different disciplines are brought together to apply different techniques in an effort at problem solving. This type of interdisciplinarity is engaged in technological instrumentally, wherein hierarchical sequences of clear-cut goals are pursued which might change a person/environment system or even innovate one.
5. **Supplementary Interdisciplinarity:** This happens when disciplines in the same field develop a partial overlapping with certain subject matters. The overlaps come about by a correspondence between theoretical levels of integration. However, beyond that particular category there might not be an overlap. The overlap is seen, recognised, and established to provide more complete picture of the subject matter. This type of interdisciplinarity exists in the borderline of discipline.
6. **Unifying Interdisciplinarity:** This happens when there is a consistency between two disciplines in subject matter, levels of theoretical integration and methods. For example, in areas where biology reaches physics.

Interdisciplinarity in Higher Education

The knowledge economy requires an adept workforce and cadre of leaders to help address the many challenges and needs facing companies, governments and societies worldwide. Many of the challenges we face today are new and there will undoubtedly be others arising in the future that will require innovative approaches and solutions to overcome them. No longer are higher education institutions able to train graduates to address all of the current and emerging challenges from a singular disciplinary source. Interdisciplinary (ID) approaches to research and training are essential underpinnings to best meet the dynamic needs of today's higher education students.

Higher education disciplinary approaches often tend to focus only on a set of trees within a great forest. While disciplinary experts are essential for understanding particular ways of knowing within specific fields of study, their perspectives in addressing larger and more complex issues is often limited. ID approaches take a much broader view of the entire landscape, first by surveying the forest and afterwards drawing upon various tree experts depending on the needs, contexts and circumstances. Societal, environmental, economic, and philosophical issues and challenges are often so complex that it is impossible to fully understand them from a single perspective or knowledge framework. Multiple viewpoints can help draw from and leverage synergistic team efforts within higher education circles to address these broad and complex issues and challenges. Integrated efforts of researchers from multiple backgrounds and areas of expertise show the advantage of an ID approach to problem solving, innovation, training next generation leaders, and advancing research and development. ID practices in higher education refers to the integration of two or more disciplines or fields of study in relation to research, instruction and programme, certification and/or degree offerings. Interdisciplinarity can exist within a single higher education institution (HEI) or between two or more HEIs.

There have been consistent calls for an increase in ID activities in higher education, yet the traditional nature of the institutions have many barriers that in many ways discourage or prevent such activities from materialising. Higher education organisational cultures and structures often prevent researchers from collaborating. Funding streams and promotion and tenure criteria often perpetuate traditional cultural and structural norms within disciplinary departments and schools. The silo syndrome that permeates so many HEIs worldwide at the very least discourages ID practices and at the most eliminates them from happening all together. A paradigm shift is needed to help provide an ID enabling environment to encourage and facilitate ID research, pedagogy and degree offerings.

Interdisciplinary trends in higher education research

Some research topics like social, economic and political issues can only be addressed through a collaborative ID response. ID research in many areas enables stakeholders at all levels to draw on common synergies to provide optimal research and learning opportunities. Increasing recognition that the future of learning is multidisciplinary or cross-disciplinary, campus cultures are trying to break down silos, cross-pollinate as many efforts as possible and encourage students to collaborate and work together across disciplines.

There is also a trend in the increased amount of ID research among graduate students in many fields of study. Solutions to current and emerging challenges are often best answered through a talented and diverse team with strengths from multiple backgrounds recognise that many research projects could benefit from "interdisciplinary, international and inter-organisational" research partnerships. "Complex environmental problems inevitably require large teams to address them; graduate students must therefore be trained to work on such teams". On the basis of the National Science Foundation's Survey of Earned Doctorates from 2001 to 2008, 28.4% had dissertations which were considered ID.

(i) **Interdisciplinary (ID) trends for teaching in higher education:** Among the most notable areas of interdisciplinarity on higher education campuses occurs within traditional and online classrooms. Teaching in teams and to students from various departments is commonplace at the undergraduate level. Many teaching subjects are by nature ID. Research methods, gender, international development, organisational management, ethics and values, and environmental studies are some examples of such courses that attract ID students. Cross-cutting course themes and instructional topics often require team teaching to help provide the necessary content and training to class members. One of the most obvious advantages from a student's standpoint is the reality that multiple instructors enriches a student's learning experience through diversity exposure and multiple points of view. There are needs to bring faculty members from various backgrounds to provide instruction and training within fields of study that were previously taught by their own faculty.

(ii) **Increasing Interdisciplinary Degree Programme at higher education level:** The growth in the interdisciplinary degree courses at higher education level can be noticed in last few years. Among the most common ID fields include organisational behaviour, management, political science, public health, international studies, international development, human resource management, history, music, environmental studies, biomedical sciences, law, engineering, rural development, agro-physics, agro-chemistry and energy studies are increasing in recent years. These degree programmes are best offered through an integrated team teaching approach that provides students with the necessary ID under-pinnings required to perform well in both the private and public sectors. There is a need to draw from multiple disciplines to provide the necessary training required for many degrees, including at the master's and doctoral levels.

The rationale for increased ID higher education training is clear. Employment demands are drastically different today than they were in the past. Many employers recognise the need to hire recent graduates who are equipped with sufficient competencies, skills and an ability to adapt to change and diverse settings. Employers understand how important it is for graduates to be able to work as a member of a team as well as being able to understand certain core disciplinary competencies. In the post-Enron Scandal Era, there is likewise a renewed emphasis that business, accountancy and law graduates should have training and commitment to sound business ethics and character values.

The modern concept of interdisciplinary approach towards the unified knowledge is quite different from the older efforts in many respects. With the development of modern (Western) scientific approach to different phenomena there emerged different disciplines. This breaking up of knowledge into separate sectors or disciplines is characteristic of a particular approach to reality. This particular approach forms the core of western science as it has developed so far.[5]

While the Western scientific approach need not be superior to the older unified approach to reality. The technological and economical success of western civilisation has led to claim that western science is closer to truth than systems of knowledge central to other cultures.[6] Yet the empirically oriented scientific approach to the reality from western culture could make remarkable rapid strides in the field of human knowledge, resulting into emergence of a series of disciplines by the middle of nineteenth century.

Interdisciplinarity in Western Context

(i) Why interdisciplinarity?

'We are not students of some subject matter, but students of problems. And problems may cut right across the borders of any subject matter or discipline' (Popper, 1963)[7]

We may gain wrong information with one perspective but an integrated perspective gives you right knowledge. For example, six blind men identify the elephant by their own perspective shown in the image below.

In the following picture six blind men, each feeling a part of the elephant, unable to see what it is they are each touching, conclude they are

dealing with entirely different things. One of the blind men touches the tail of the elephant and concludes that the elephant is a rope. Another blind man hugs one of the legs and concludes it is a tree. Another, touching the side of the elephant, claims it is a wall. The others touching the elephant's tusk, trunk, and ear, claim the object is a spear, a rope, and a fan respectively. The analogy is meant to demonstrate that not one of the blind men was completely right, but that they had a partial view of the overall picture. They were all partially right, and thus, it is supposed that exclusive claims to truth are to be avoided on the basis of the blind men and the inability of any of them to be able to give us the full picture of what they were dealing with. The parable is meant to demonstrate the difficulty in deciphering truth through the limitations of our perceptions. Only when they worked together, sharing their different ideas and experiences, were they able to discover the truth.

In research we cannot get holistic knowledge with the help of only one perspective. All the sciences have their own limited perspectives about the fact. But now it seems that scientists across the world are increasingly getting the point of this story. They are expanding their communication across fields, telling one another about their part of the elephant. The result is the formation of new, interdisciplinary scientific fields, such as bioinformatics. Interdisciplinary study allows for synthesis of ideas and the synthesis of characteristics from many disciplines.

The breaking up of knowledge into separate sectors or disciplines is characteristic of a particular approach to reality, a specific system of relations which humans form with the world around them. This particular approach forms the core of Western science as it has developed so far. There is nothing in reality which favours such an approach over others or gives it an exclusive right to truth. But the technological and economic success of Western civilisation has led to claims that Western science is closer to truth than system of knowledge central to other cultures and equally successful in their own way. It is important to understand the quest for knowledge as a form of interaction between living systems and their environment, no less essential than, say, breathing or feeding, and in the same sense subjective and objective at the same time.[8]

- **Definitions of Interdisciplinarity:** There is at present considerable confusion as to the use of terms such as multi-, inter- and transdisciplinarity. But there is also a need for different terms to distinguish different degrees of overcoming disciplinary separation. In this article, the terminology is structured according as a widely accepted usage which is aware of these distinctions and needs well-defined words to address them. They may be arranged in a hierarchy of nations:

> Interdisciplinarity is the juxtaposition of various disciplines without an attempt at their synthesis. The French multidisciplinary university, after the reform following the student rebellion of 1968, has settled at such a scheme. Multidisciplinary, in this sense stands for an administrative reform which preserves the old disciplinary structures and contents of science. The synthesis is at the discretion and creative ability of the student.

Multidisciplinarity, is the synthesis of two or more disciplines which establishes a new level of discourse (a metalevel), characterised by a new language of description and new structural relationships. It may be compared to the dialectical synthesis of opposites (although in interdisciplinarity the disciplines need not contradict each other- rather, their language and structures are different so that they do not speak to each other). Such a synthesis implies the dynamics of moving towards a new level.

Transdisciplinarity is the recognition of the interconnectedness of all aspects of reality. Since this interconnectedness becomes manifest only through interactions, transdisplinarity implies an overall dynamics of a dialectical synthesis and corresponds to an overall attempt at grasping the total dynamics of reality as a whole. Transdisciplinarity may be viewed as the ultimate result of interdisciplinarity penetrating the entire system of science. It is an ideal that will always be beyond the complete reach of science, but which may guide in important ways the direction of its evolution.

Interdisciplinarity, as the intermediate concepts in this hierarchy, is furthered in different ways which may be termed in accordance with pushes and pulls exerted to achieve the dynamics required for bringing about interdisciplinary synthesis.

- **Push/ Pull:** The push/pull inherent in the evolution of science itself stems from the generation of new opportunities which are not limited in their application to the area of scientific activity that has generated them. As concept and paradigms – that is to say, mental structures of interaction with reality- change in one field of endeavour, they link up naturally with specific concepts and paradigms acting as force coordinating the activities in various fields.

- **Social Pull:** The application of science towards techno-social ends which, in turn, are generated to serving human needs has always exerted a strong pull on interdisciplinary synthesis. Technology is a prime example of interdisciplinarity. The generation of electricity, for example, may involve such diverse scientific fields as thermodynamics, chemistry, nuclear physics, electromagnetism, metallurgy and others. Their synthesis in technological design clearly establishes a new level of description and rules. Empirically calibrated microscopic relationships, such as formulae for the calculation of heat and matter transfer of the formulae for nuclear reactor design, ultimately deal with the effects of highly complicated microscopic processes never entered explicitly. The technology designer may even be largely unaware of them, and yet be capable of designing elaborate chemical-engineering plants or nuclear reactor by relying on a combination of macroscopic relationships.

(ii) International framework for interdisciplinarity

It was perhaps a mistake to expect that the discipline-oriented university would be able quickly restructure itself to become a leader in inter-disciplinarity. The structure of university is interests and skills, beliefs and ambitions. The rapid quantitative expansion of higher learning- in the United States rounded half of population now passes through college –has generated an academic problem of narrow-minded, highly specialised and frightened faculty members who are concerned mainly with their static security and are too unlikely to take up the challenges of new views and synthesis. The focus of the university has become teaching instead of learning and as long as curricula are shaped by discipline oriented departments, this defensive attitude further strengthened by a collective security thinking which prescribe uniform themes and even methodologies.

The situation in the university is significantly different from the situation in industry and non-academic research where the disciplinary truly serves as an administrative skeleton only. Physicists are then administrated and ….. by the physics division, etc., but the units in which they work are interdisciplinary groups, set up .....and for a limited life-time only, and structure according to tasks. On the other hand, relatively independent research establishment lacked the social pull towards interdisciplinary synthesis.[9]

In The University in Ruins (1997), Bill Readings argues that liberal arts education - and the university in general - has undergone a profound change in its mission and identity as it has been transformed from a site designed to foster a unified national culture into a corporate-style service industry selling a vacuous and indefinable nation of excellence. The shift to university-as-service-industry has led to a need for increased specialisation to provide specific marketable skills or sites of interests that can attract the student/customer. This most cynical reading sees institutional support for interdisciplinary studies as an attempt to create and foster niche markets. Furthermore, in striking this deal, interdisciplinary studies become complicit, if not responsible, for the fragmentation of the university into a series of localised specialisations isolated from, and in competition with one another to attract niche customers/students. Thus, the interdisciplinary departments, programmes, and centers found willing partners but at a price: their interdisciplinarity. Far from marking the dawn of an interdisciplinary era, this pact with the devil has marked the end of real interdisciplinarity.

Is the very success of interdisciplinary studies leading to its demise? And are they displacing and discrediting the traditional disciplines along the way? Not yet, but these are real and pressing possibilities. Then again, if Reading's diagnosis of the contemporary university system is correct, one might be tempted to regard these questions as moot and admit defeat in the face of a higher educational system rendered ineffective and obsolete by current political and market forces. The alternative is to take the threat seriously and use these questions as a springboard to think through the past, present and future of interdisciplinary studies in an attempt to find productive and substantive ways for it to work and flourish within the current university system.

(a) **The American university experiment in Interdisciplinarity:**In December 1958, Wesleyan University President Victor Butter-flied and the university's educational policy committee called for doing away entirely with the traditional departmental structure of the American university system. They proposed instead to reorganise Wesleyan University into a collection of semi-autonomous interdisciplinary colleges and divisions. The proposal was presented in response to the perception that existing educational structure had led to an intellectual malaise and the hope that this interdisciplinary reorganisation would revitalise the curriculum, the faculty and the students. The goals were idealistic and noble; to paraphrase Butterfield in The College Plan in Perspective, the plan would break through the artificial barriers of specialised subject and instead allow these various fields (such as literature, philosophy, art, and science) to shed light on one another so as to extend the body of knowledge and ideas common to teachers and students alike. This in turn, would force established scholars and teachers to rethink their own approaches and assumptions. Perhaps most striking is that this plan sought to destabilise the authority of the faculty and the disciplines themselves by asking instructors to move away from disciplinary pronouncements based on past success and formulations and instead, to extend themselves beyond the areas of their authority and expertise in pursuit of innovation. For its time it was a radical plan. Indeed, it was so radical that it was not implemented. Wesleyan was not reorganised, although in 1959 it did create three interdisciplinary teaching colleges: the College of Letters, the College of Social Studies, and the College of Quantitative Studies- of which the first two are still active.[10]

(b) **The Polish experiment in Interdisciplinarity:** The passing of time since the 1990s has verified realisation of the newly implemented ideas. Two levels of education (engineer and masters of science) have been implemented in almost every higher education institution in Poland. Since the 1990s, humanities courses have been implemented as a necessary element of technical study. These requirements were made by the Ministry of Higher Education. The Ministry stated the minimal (study standards) for each course of study. It should be pointed out that the idea of the humanisation of engineering study comes from the early 1960. After World War II, engineering studies were generally dehumanised - in Poland, too. Professional courses were stressed and the humanity courses (present in the curricula before) were found to be old-fashioned and then abandoned. One of the earliest ideas of humanisation of technical curricula appeared in the 1960s, thanks to Professor Bugiel at AGH University of Science and Technology in Krakow and it was also accepted at Warsaw Polytechnic. Courses dedicated to Sociology, Psychology, Management and interpersonal relations, were implemented in the curricula of engineering study. In 1995, the idea of creating a Department of the Humanities was raised in AGH in Krakow and 2001 the Social Applied Sciences Department was created there. Dziewulski expressed an opinion that the most important subject in humanities studies is philosophy, because it deals with creating the human spirit, in such things as truth, goodness and beauty. He represents an opinion that says only philosophy is the humanities science. Other courses/sciences also could be treated as humanities science if they correspond to philosophy - contrary to para-humanities studies (or courses). The para - humanities courses only deal with the statistics of social life. Courses in the Humanities in fact influence personality and intellectual development of society. They are creating people criteria and moral estimations. They also teach how to live in accordance with nature. Studies in Humanities develop intellectual sensitivity in the youth, leading to distinguishing between values and valueless things.

For more than 10 years the Polish Ministry of Higher Education has stressed the implementation of humanities of natural science courses into engineering studies curricula. These courses mostly are electives (optional courses). The humanities courses, as implemented in to the engineering study plans, have produced in recent years: an increased number of interdisciplinary science research projects; interdisciplinary diploma projects; engineering research and projects in collaboration with institution from non-engineering branches; and even interdisciplinary study curricula. It has also resulted in student personal development and individual talents and hobbies. In this paper the authors discuss the role of humanities and natural science courses in engineer's education; examples, both good and bad; and the opinions of students and teachers, ideas, especially in pop-culture and the mass-media. At present, the humanisation of engineering studies does not only mean the contents of courses or curricula, but also methods of teaching and studying.

At present, in Poland, for every engineering study course, as well as for most of the non-humanities study courses, the number of hours dedicated to humanities courses must be planned into the study curricula. Sometime it is described in the standards that such blocks of course/electives should include particular subjects (as, for example, ethics for medical of healthcare courses). For some engineering courses, requirements may be management, law, or natural science. Such courses should be offered by the university as optional and it should be the student's decision as to what he or she prefers.

Present demands for professional engineers mean the humanities courses in the study curricula are not enough. People in accordance with market labour demands are seeking interdisciplinary engineering or master's courses, as well as interdisciplinary postgraduate courses. More than 60% of European universities questioned declared they offer interdisciplinary courses for postgraduate curricula.

Incorporated into the curriculum for IT are courses dedicated to law, copyright, and sociology. In the curricula for electronics, materials engineering and electrical engineering are courses dedicated to sociology, psychology, low philosophy, and natural science (as optional or elective courses). For the natural sciences, courses dedicated to Ecology are offered at present, as well as Ecology and environmental management.

All of the students were interested in the ecology courses for engineers. This might suggest the teachers interests influenced in the student. The ecology course for engineers was organised into lectures/or tutoring (15 hours per semester); or lectures plus tutoring (30 to 45 hours per semester). Even if the course was made up of only lectures, it was organised more in the manner of seminars: the students were frequently questioned, and pushed to discuss and solve a problem. Also one or two lecturing hours were dedicated to excursions (even then it was just 15 hours of meetings in total). The main educational aspects of the course, Ecology, for engineers were to: present the main problems that may happen in engineering, caused by environment (with good and bad examples); impact of the people on the environment, as well as impact of the environment on people; improve the knowledge of dangerous (for human beings) physical and chemical factors in the natural environment, and especially in the work environment; present the case that engineering is mainly applied science; improve general knowledge of the natural environment. Also, the course conveys the general idea that science and engineering may be interesting and even funny, and gives a chance for student to develop individual skills and hobbies, as well as to present their individual achievements. Subjects dedicated to the main problems that could happen in engineering (caused by the environment) are electrical engineering, mechanical and civil engineering. This is because large construction projects and the important impact of engineering investments/technologies on the environment are within these areas of the profession. When student recently were asked to solve the problem, examples were arranged to show that, usually, it is possible to solve the problem simply or cheaply (or just not to cause the problem in the first place). The main aspects of the part of the course dedicated to physical and chemical factors in the natural environment and especially in the work environment, were: toxins and poisonous substances; heavy metals; electrical and magnetic fields. Also, engineering problems, such as sustainable development, clean production and the necessity to use best available technology, were presented where there was an adequate knowledge base. Students were interested also in applying engineering to medicine and environmental technologies.

Structural Settings for Interdisciplinarity

As Simon Goldhill, director of the Cambridge Center for Research in the Arts, Social Sciences and Humanities (CRASSH) states, we have people who know more and more about less and less. That's the definition of a PhD, isn't it? This intense specialisation prevents us from seeing the forest among the trees. So it is completely unsurprising that cross-disciplinary efforts and inter-departmental initiatives often fail and do not go beyond initial superficial connections. I have heard gripes at more than one prestigious institution about the impenetrable silos that separate departments and communities within the university.

A common reminiscence about college concerns the spontaneous philosophical conversations that occur in dorm hallways at 3 am. It is unfortunate that in most institutions of higher learning, we stop talking to each other after undergraduate level. Instead, we compartmentalise ourselves off in our departments, talking to people who think the same way we do. We being preaching to the choir and feel affirmed that our style of thought is the only right way. The way in which we are trained and specialise shapes our identity and how we process the world beyond pure academic disciplines.

Not only do we develop specialised knowledge, but we also become inculcated in a particular way of examining and talking about the world that breeds distrust against others approaches and a belief that our methodology is the best. I have felt, for example, that some academic physicians on the surface embrace the concepts of applying social sciences to medicine, but are unable to accept non-positivist ways of understanding the world and dismiss it as insufficiently rigorous.

I think a key aspect to achieving interdisciplinarity is through the design of physical and social spaces. Creating spaces where people continuously come into contact with people outside their discipline in natural, casual social settings over and over again, helps develop social networks that eventually become the source of intellectual inspiration and creativity.

Stanford has been a pioneer in designing physical spaces to foster mixing of ideas and philosophies. The Center for Clinical Sciences Research (CCSR) building has few walls. Instead of lab bench space being allocated by research group, where all members of a lab are grouped together, scientists are interspersed around the entire building, promoting collegiality and discussion among members of different labs and disciplines. Their intentions were clear from the start, its design responds to emerging trends for interdisciplinary biomedical research, [where] interaction between disciplines and individuals is encouraged.[11]

Interdisciplinary Education and Humanistic Aspiration

The education I propose includes all that is proper for a man, and is one in which all men who are born into this world should share. Our first wish is all men should be educated fully to full humanity; not only one individual, nor a few, nor even many, but all men together and single, young and old, rich and poor, of high and lowly birth, men and women in a word all whose fate it is to be born human beings; so that at last the whole of the human race may be educated, men of all ages, all conditions, both sexes and all nations. Our second wish is that every man should be wholly educated, rightly formed not only in one single manner or in a few or even in many, but in all things which perfect human nature. - John Amos Comenius, the Great Didactic (1632)

While specific conceptions of interdisciplinarity and hence of interdisciplinary education vary considerably, the arguments advanced in favour of virtually all of these forms appear to share a common conceptual structure, insofar as they draw upon a common body of general desiderata.

1. **Integration of knowledge:** Interdisciplinary education aims at being an intrinsically integrative learning experience for the student; i.e. it encourages the student to perceive the various

components of human knowledge within some larger holistic framework. As Kockelmans puts it in 'Why Interdisciplinarity?' Interdisciplinarity aims at contributing to the restoration of the unity of the sciences, and in the long run, of the unity of our world view.

2. **Freedom of inquiry:** Interdisciplinary education stimulates greater freedom of inquiry than conventional disciplinary education, since the student is not confined to a single field in pursuing an idea, theme, or problem, but rather is encouraged to range over several different ones.
3. **Innovation:** Partly because of these two considerations, interdisciplinary education is thought to have a greater chance of getting students to break out of narrow, conventional lines of thinking and to attain something akin to original insights. The assumption underling this view seems to be the following: since the overwhelming preponderance of intellectual investigation and research is done within separate disciplines, with consequently far less effort expended in looking at the intersection of the disciplines, it seems plausible that there is greater opportunity for fresh knowledge to emerge from integrated inquiry and making connections between disciplines.

Viewed in the light of these three desiderata, the call for inter-disciplinary education in institution of higher learning appears to constitute a call for educational reform. In particular it appears to demand renewal of the traditional humanistic values of intellectual wholeness, freedom, and academic and vocational, has become the order of the day. Interdisciplinarity resolutely resists the fragmentation of education into a series of separate and isolated fields, each autonomous and presided over by a group of narrow specialists. As Kockelmans' "Why Interdisciplinary?" makes clear, the majority of interdisciplinary advocates, both in research and in education do not object to specialisation per se-indeed they grant that the complex state of contemporary knowledge requires it; rather they object to the fact that specialisation today is divorced from a broad, unifying framework of thought founded on genuine human concerns. The call for interdisciplinary education in our colleges and universities therefore constitutes a call for an authentically humanistic education, one which situates technical expertise and specialisation within a broad framework of thought that encourages integration of knowledge, wide ranging freedom of inquiry and individual innovation.

In what follows, however, I will argue that this essential humanistic promise contained within the core of interdisciplinary is threatened not only by extrinsic barriers (e.g. the institutional, psychological and cultural obstacles discussed by Kockelmans) but also by an intrinsic barrier that lies as a hidden presuppositions at the conceptual foundation of interdisciplinarity itself.[12]

Barriers to Interdisciplinary Research and Training

(i) **Attitudinal Barrier:** Most scientists recognise a need for interdisciplinary research, many are reluctant to abandon their disciplinary focus. In the 1980s, Sigma Xi, The Scientific Research Society, surveyed its members as to whether they agreed with the statement that "more interdisciplinary research should be funded because many of the most significant scientific problems cannot be accommodated within arbitrary disciplinary structures." Almost three- fourths (2,995 of 4,071) of the responding society members reported that they "agreed" or "agreed emphatically." The perception exists, however, that interdisciplinary science is viewed as second-rate. At the committee's workshop (IOM Workshop, 1999), Dr. Paul Smolensky pointed out that disciplines have been able to investigate a given subject in depth. But when research bridges disciplines and this same depth cannot be attained, the quality of the research is perceived as poor. In another survey of its members, "Removing the Boundaries: Perspectives on Cross-Disciplinary Research," Sigma Xi received responses from over 120 members representing seven scientific disciplines, including psychology and medicine who expressed opinions on obstacles to interdisciplinary research. Some of the comments indicated concerns: working in interdisciplinary research was not "pure"; it was "less challenging" or "high risk"; those who do collaborative work could not succeed in their own discipline; they would be lost in a team effort and "lose their professional identity." Others have expressed similar views:

> While they pay lip service to the principle [of interdisciplinarity], most scientists look upon their own discipline as either too incomplete or too immature to be coupled with another one.—De Mey, as cited in Bechtel.

Despite the hesitation of some about venturing into an interdisciplinary effort, many have embraced it enthusiastically. The motivation for moving into interdisciplinarity is varied. Some scientists working in their own disciplines might see, after working on a problem for some period, that their scientific approaches are insufficient to answer their questions. Scientific interactions can stimulate ideas that are new and exciting but require additional expertise or techniques to pursue. Funding opportunities might provide an impetus to seek out collaboration to answer broad scientific problems identified by funding agencies. Some might be attracted by the challenge and the need for answers to a larger problem and the satisfaction that would come from making progress.[13]

(ii) Communication Barrier

(a) Jargon: Scientists trained in a discipline learn to speak a specific language and adopt the analytical and methodological constructs that have accumulated in that discipline. This constitutes a form of professional socialisation that serves as an important part of the training experience, but it can present obstacles to interdisciplinary research.

We speak the language of our discipline, which raises two problems: first, we may not understand the languages of the other disciplines; second, more dangerously, we may think that we understand these, but do not, because although the same terms are used in different disciplines, they mean something very different in each. — Margaret A. Somerville.

In addition, the problem exists that "different disciplines are continually rediscovering one another's discoveries, because they all have different names for them".

Communicating with another discipline requires time and work. An extensive effort must be made to learn the language of another field and to teach others the language of one's own. Many have recognised that this barrier must be overcome before successful collaboration can occur.

(b) Intellectual Turf: By definition, interdisciplinary efforts bring together researchers who have different expertise. Pride in one's discipline and its methods can be instilled during graduate school. As a consequence, other disciplines might be viewed as less rigorous or important. To work together, people must understand and appreciate the value and limitations of both, their own and others' methods. Groark and McCall have written about the distrust between researchers and clinical providers: each group believes in its own superiority. The same can occur between disciplines. Heated discussions can result when people with different backgrounds try to assert the correctness of their views.

(c) Team Building: Teamwork requires trust in another's skills and expertise. If these are outside one's field, as implied in interdisciplinary research, they might be difficult to evaluate. Interdisciplinary team members sometimes have difficulty in evaluating each other's performance on a given project because the criteria that are appropriate for such an evaluation are not familiar. Moreover, reward systems and practices regarding authorship differ among disciplines. Good communication skills are helpful in alleviating such problems, but most members of interdisciplinary teams lack training and proficiency in such skills.

Relationships among team members affect productivity. Team members need to be able to compromise and cooperate. A feeling of community can facilitate interactions in an interdisciplinary team. Many stress that good communication among team members is essential for the process to succeed.

In building an interdisciplinary team, clarity regarding roles, expectations, and authority—particularly with regard to sharing of data and resources—is important for success. Mutually acceptable policies for disseminating research results (including authorship) and facilitating achievement of team members' personal and professional goals need to be developed. A possible consequence of not having a team process is that crucial voices will be missing in defining and solving the research problem. All this suggests that it takes interpersonal skills to conduct interdisciplinary research and that expertise in disciplinary methods alone might not be sufficient.

(d) Leadership: Interdisciplinary research teams need leaders who understand the challenges of group dynamics and who can establish and maintain an integrated programme. Leaders need to have vision, creativity, and perseverance. To establish a successful interdisciplinary programme requires education of scientific colleagues and administrators about the potential value of interdisciplinary research. To coordinate the efforts of a diverse team requires credibility as a research scientist, skill in modulating strong personalities, the ability to draw out individual strengths, and skill in the use of group dynamics to blend individual strengths into a team. Some have suggested that the best persons to direct interdisciplinary teams are mature scientists with well-established research careers who have conducted interdisciplinary research of their own.

(e) **Facilitating Interactions:** In the experiences of the committee members, chance interactions can promote interdisciplinary collaborations. The casual discussion of research at the coffee machine, the fortuitous meeting in the corridor with a colleague from another department, an interesting seminar, or interactions among students and postdoctoral scientists—all can trigger collaboration. Buildings that isolate laboratories and research groups from one another can limit this type of interaction. But, bringing people together through the creation of central facilities or common areas can increase its probability.

Common location of faculties leads to interactions, scientific discussions, and possibly new insights on research data. For example, Washington University invested $28 million in a new laboratory building to house a shared imaging facility, animal facility, and psychology laboratories with the intent of encouraging interdisciplinary collaboration. More recently, the University of California, Berkeley launched an interdisciplinary "Health Sciences Initiative" that includes the construction of two buildings that will house laboratories of researchers from several departments. The intent is to encourage daily interactions among the investigators in a variety of fields, such as physics and molecular biology. Similarly, in an effort to integrate the intramural neuroscience research, the National Institute of Health (NIH) is planning a center that will co-localise the basic and clinical neuroscientists from nine institutes.

Architectural design can promote interactions, but virtual proximity, through the Internet or videoconferencing, provides another opportunity for achieving intellectual proximity as needed and deserves further research and consideration.

(iii) Academic and Professional Barrier

(a) **Academic Structure:** A 1998 editorial in *Science* asserted that the modern university is "partitioned along academic lines that no longer truly reflect today's intellectual life. These academic groupings are now just categories that accountants and business managers use to build a budget. The issue is most pronounced in the scientific disciplines." Others have written about the conflict between the scientist's professional need for autonomy and identity and the organisation's need for an efficient bureaucratic structure. Despite some pioneering approaches (e.g., Rockefeller University's absence of departments and the University of California, Berkeley Health Science Initiative, which coordinates hundreds of scientists in multiple schools), institutions change slowly. Thus, in considering interdisciplinary research and training, the continued presence of some system of academic departmentalisation must be acknowledged.

(b) **Publication and Professional Organisations:** Professional organisations and journals are key ingredients of disciplinary identity. Their major impact is in providing an outlet for dissemination of information. Whitley commented that "the existing set of journals in a science constrain and direct research topics and ways of working on them." Although some societies (e.g., the Society for Neuroscience) are interdisciplinary by design, many are discipline-specific. Similarly, some journals (e.g., *Science, Nature,* and the *New England Journal of Medicine*) are broad- ranging, but the vast majority are discipline-specific. Multidisciplinary researchers, as opposed to more discipline-identified professionals, face problems of professional identity and outlets for publication in prestigious journals.

Research reputation is essential to obtaining support for research, gaining employment, getting promotions, and winning grants. Authorship of papers is perhaps the most important predictor of one's success in these activities. The size of collaborative groups can limit the frequency of first-authorship and thereby pose problems for interdisciplinary researchers. New editorial policies on authorship are arising out of ethical concerns about multi-author papers. To protect against fraud, there is a growing call to define the contribution of each author. Acknowledging individual contributions to a research effort might provide a means to provide credit to people involved in interdisciplinary research, above and beyond senior authorship.

(iv) Funding Barrier

(a) Federal Funding: Scientists perceive that they will encounter difficulties in obtaining support for and conducting successful interdisciplinary research because funds for such research come from many agencies with different programmatic emphases. In contrast with that perception is the apparent consensus among federal research sponsors that interdisciplinary research and training are essential.

(b) Peer Review: Although strong peer review is considered to be the basis of a successful funding system, it is a long-held perception that it puts interdisciplinary research proposals at a disadvantage. Many have suggested that the traditional proposal evaluation by discipline-specific study sections makes it difficult for interdisciplinary proposals to compete successfully. In an "open letter" to NIH, Howard Morgan wrote that, "peer review of cross-disciplinary research presents the problem of the definition of a peer." Even if all disciplines covered by a proposal are represented in a review committee, unless the committee members themselves have tried to do interdisciplinary research in the field in question, they might not appreciate the issues. Morgan called on NIH to correct the problems associated with the review of interdisciplinary grants. In their responses, representatives of NIH acknowledged the legitimacy of the concern.

(v) Career Barriers

(a) Duration of Training: The length of time required to complete training in more than one field—whether in the basic or clinical sciences or in a combination of the two—can be discouraging. The explosion of information in each scientific discipline raises concerns about how long it would take to attain expertise in one, let alone two or more, fields. The requirement for depth of knowledge in one field during graduate school might seem to preclude obtaining breadth in other disciplines within a reasonable period. The length of graduate training is increasing and the time spent in postdoctoral positions is also on the rise. Interdisciplinary requirements might worsen the delay in starting a career.

(b) **Debt:** Educational costs are increasing. To pay for their training, many students are taking loans for their undergraduate or professional education.

(c) **Job Opportunities:** There is a concern among junior scientists that training in interdisciplinary fields will not prepare them for careers. "Jack of all trades, master of none" is a refrain that is often heard when interdisciplinary training is proposed. It raises the question, is there a market for people trained with an interdisciplinary perspective? Some have reported difficulties in finding positions for graduate students who received interdisciplinary training.

(d) **Staying Current:** As the volume of information grows in a given subspecialty, the number of publications that a person needs to read to stay current in his or her own field forms another deterrent to becoming more interdisciplinary.[13]

Interdisciplinary trends in higher education

There have been consistent calls for an increase in ID activities in higher education, yet the traditional natures of the institution have many barriers that in many ways discourage or prevent such activities from materialising. Higher education organisational cultures and structures often prevent researches from collaborating. Funding streams and tenure criteria often perpetuate traditional cultural and structural norms within disciplinary departments and schools. The silo syndrome that permeates so many HEIs worldwide at the very least discourages ID practice and at the most eliminates them from happening all together. A paradigm shift is needed for an ID enabling environment to encourage and facilitate ID research, pedagogy and degree offerings. In many instances higher education policies and management bureaucracies discourage or prevent ID practices.

While there are generalists, or interdisciplinarian scholars who may have expertise from multiple disciplines, the vast majority of ID activities are grounded by faculty members with expertise in a specific field of study. Combining two or more faculty members from at least two fields of study constitutes an ID team for research of instructional purposes. There are often tensions that exist when combining experts from multiple fields, and it always helps to consider chemistry and fit in ID team building. This helps achieve collaborative or Tuckmans (1995) performing status much quicker than if a hodgepodge of scholars are randomly identified and brought together with title thought considering organisational fit and the various assignments each team member will play. Based largely on the work of Nancarrow, the following list provides 10 key characteristics essential for successful ID teams:

1. Leadership and management
2. Effective communication
3. Personal rewards, training and development
4. Appropriate resource and procedures
5. Appropriate skills mix
6. Positive and enabling climate
7. Individual characteristic
8. Clarity of shared vision
9. Quality and outcomes
10. Respecting and understanding roles.[14]

Interdisciplinary approach in higher education in India

Interdisciplinarity as an approach to reality is relatively recent in academic discussion and much scarce in practical application so far as problem solving is concerned. However, this is not to suggest that there were no such attempts in history that could transcend the narrow disciplinary boundaries to 'synthesize' elements of two or more branches of knowledge to arrive at a comprehensive solution for any recurrent or urgent problem. Even a cursory look at the vast cultural heritage we had in past and divergent socio-cultural customs we have had until recent years give full testimony to the 'integrated' approach followed by our social thinkers and policy designer. Chanakya's "Kautileya Arthashastra" for instance is an integrated and comprehensive view of the contemporary economy, polity, society and ethics. We have many such evidences in almost all societies and cultures indicating "interactive" efforts put in to reveal the essence of "unified" knowledge.[15]

India has made appreciable progress with regard to creation of infrastructure for education. But, employers have complained that they are unable to find required talent. In their drive to become world class, owing to the pressure of competition as a result of globalisation, Indian industry finds a serious shortage of skills. The gap between institutional input and industrial requirements can be filled only by inculcating two capabilities in students. The first is task performance capability focused on acquiring skills required by employers. The second involves building conceptual performance which is not job-related but behaviour-related. These can be obtained not from the curriculum but by application of knowledge through skills. Skills and knowledge are the engines of economic growth and social development.

Therefore, the need of the hour for the regular colleges is to ensure knowledge construction by designing employable curricula, knowledge dissemination through effective teaching, knowledge use by application of knowledge and knowledge embodiment by making the student as a needed product.[16]

The higher education system has isolated itself from the ground reality and grooming young students in an artificial atmosphere. Students of different disciplines consider it as a taboo to even go beyond the confines of their respective department.

The Yashpal Committee report on Renovation and Rejuvenation of Higher Education laments that what we have currently is a steel box of a system within which there are smaller boxes with no interaction with the outside or with each other. The report emphasizes the need for interdisciplinary experiences and this should help students sustain themselves "when the demands of a particular job market change." It would mean that students would be exposed to multiple subjects under the aegis of one university or college.[17]

Besides knowledge, students should pick up transferable skills and it should be incorporated in the curriculum. There was a time when a person would remain in one profession for a lifetime. Now a U.S. survey has shown that on an average a person changes at least 10 professions in his lifetime. Instead of preparing a career for life, we have to prepare for a life of careers.

"Making graduates and postgraduates more employable" is the new 'mantra' of educational administrators. Though the think-tank of the higher education system has taken a small step in the right direction, we have a long way to go. And an interdisciplinary approach would be essential to its success.[18]

According to the recent economic survey of India, the unemployment rate is monstrous to say the least. There are more than 6 crore well-educated youth who are unemployed.

Employers have complained that they are unable to find required talent to help their drive to become world class, owing to the pressure of competition as a result of globalisation. A leading software company's experience in this context is quite interesting: in 2005-2006, the company screened 14 lakh applications of graduates, tested 1,64,000 applicants, interviewed 48,700 candidates and appointed only 21,000 that too for the purpose of undergoing training. There are apparent limitations in the present regular college since they look only at the traditional and the theoretical.

Higher Education and Inclusion

'Inclusion' is a term that can be used to describe a series of positive actions to achieve equality of access to goods and services, to assist all individuals to participate in community and society, to encourage the contribution of all persons to social and cultural life and to be aware of and to challenge all forms of discrimination. By ensuring that the marginalised and those living in poverty have greater participation in decision-making, which affects their lives, will allow them to improve their standard of living and overall well-being.

Social inclusion is a proactive strategy to put the vulnerable groups and communities on par with other groups that are better placed in accessing benefits. It seeks to render justice to these vulnerable groups by being fair to them in a way that they will have equal access to the opportunities, resources, services and institutions to develop themselves and be mainstreamed.

By the year 1990 the term was theorised by scholars like Bourdieu and Luhman. The latter clarified the concept in the following terms:

> The concept of inclusion means the encompassing of the entire population in the performances of the individual function systems. On the one hand this concerns access to these benefits and, on the other dependence of individual modes of living on them. To the extent that inclusion is achieved, groups disappear that do not or only marginally participate in social living.[19]

(a) **Definition of Inclusion:** Inclusion is a broad social model of adapting organisational or community facilities and processes to diversity, thus including vulnerable or oppressed groups. Social Inclusion is defined as follows:

(1) **General Definition** – 'A socially inclusive society is defined as one where all people feel valued, their differences are respected, and their basic needs are met so they can live in dignity'.

(2) **According to the Twelfth Five Year Plan (2012-17)** - 'Inclusiveness means many different things and each aspect of inclusiveness poses its own challenges for policy'.[20] Different facets of inclusiveness are inclusiveness as poverty reduction. inclusiveness as group equality, inclusiveness as regional balance, inclusiveness and inequality, inclusiveness as empowerment and inclusiveness throw employment programmes. As per Twelfth five year plan (2012-17), inclusiveness as group equality is also about a growth process which is seen to be fair by different socio-economic groups that constitute our society. Inclusiveness must also embrace the concern of other groups such as the Scheduled Castes (SCs), Scheduled Tribes (STs), Other Backward Classes (OBCs), Minorities, the differently abled and other marginalised groups.

(3) **According to Luhman**, "The concept of inclusion means the encompassing of the entire population in the performances of the individual function systems. On the one hand, this concerns access to these benefits and, on the other, dependence of individual modes of living on them. To the extent that inclusion is achieved, groups disappear that do not or only marginally participate in social living".[21]

(4) The World Bank defines social inclusion as the process of improving the terms for individuals and groups to take part in society. Social inclusion aims to empower poor and marginalised people to take advantage of burgeoning global opportunities. It ensures that people have a voice in decisions which affect their lives and that they enjoy equal access to markets, services and political, social and physical spaces.[22]

(5) An inclusive society is a society that over-rides differences of race, gender, class, generation, and geography, and ensures inclusion, equality of opportunity as well as capability of all members of the society to determine an agreed set of social institutions that govern social interaction.[23]

Inclusiveness is the catchword of the twelfth five - year plan signifying the nation's urge to include the socio-economic uplifment of the SC, ST and OBC to the pedestal of the main agenda of planning and growth. Inclusiveness is a process of addressing and responding to the needs of the socio-economically underprivileged sections of the society in order to bring them at par. Inclusive education is a process of addressing and responding to the socio-economically and psychologically tugged learning abilities and educational opportunities of the underprivileged sections of our society. Inclusive education incorporates the principle of access which should go to became access to quality education. And at the core of inclusive education is the right to education.

(b) **Social context of inclusion:** We need to understand inclusion as a concept since it has been a government policy issue for last few years. Inclusion is being used alternatively for the term social justice in the last few years. Which underlines importance giving for mainstreaming of the excluded. The substance and credibility of the main stream is an issue to be discussed later. Now inclusion of the underprivileged communities in to the mainstream is of urgent significance. Inclusion means inviting those who have been historically locked out. But the question arises as to who has the authority or right to invite others in it. It is high time to recognise and accept that all are born "in". So inclusion is recognising our universal "oneness" and "interdependence". Inclusion is recognising that you are 'one' even though we are not the same. Inclusion means fighting against exclusion and all the social diseases exclusion gives birth 'to'. i.e. Casteism, communalism, gender discrimination and handicapism. The fighting for inclusion involves assurance or support system to the excluded as a state policy.

Inclusion can only be brought about with change and change brings anxiety and fear and social instability so to change we need to overcome fear.

This theoretical understanding of inclusion applies to Indian social context. The Indian stratified social system has been built on rigidity and lack of dynamism, so is an extraordinary system of exclusion of the downtrodden sections of the society including women. The highlight of this stratified social system has been in the acceptance of assigned duties ordained by divine scriptures. The divine interpretation made communities accept exclusion voluntarily. The Shudras and the Atishudras, who were the so called untouchables, worked in a pre-ordained manner to serve and clean for the upper social categories.

Western colonial intervention and enlightened Indian socio-political leadership armed with exposure to western liberal thought, initiated dynamism in Indian culture and especially in the education system of the country. Inclusion required change and change could be brought about by raising questions. To raise questions one needed to have deeper understanding and analytical acumen. This could only be brought about through education, especially education for the masses, the down-trodden and women. So education has become a necessity for social inclusiveness in society.

Education is about information, understanding, awareness, analysis, skill- sets and sensitivities of social relationships. It is an empowerment, especially for the downtrodden who desire social mobility to enter the mainstream in pursuit of financial gains and new found social status.

The primary vehicle of education is the state sponsored formal education along with the private endeavour. The formal initiative has taken the form of right to education in India to cater to the children aged between 6 to 14 years. The RTE is free and compulsory with emphasis on evaluation, variation, outreach to the last child, private school participation, community participation and no-detention policy.

(c) **Constitutional Provisions regarding Social Welfare and Social Inclusion:** The Indian Constitution guarantees all citizens basic civil and political rights and fundamental freedoms. Constitutional provisions regarding social welfare and social inclusion are as follows:

- **Right to Equality**- Constitution has provision prohibiting discrimination based on caste, these provisions are found under Articles 15, 16, and 17
- **Right Against Exploitation** – Article 23
- **Cultural and Educational Rights** - Article 29:2
- **Prohibition against disenfranchisement in elections based on one's religion, race, caste or sex** - Article 325
- **Reserve seats for SC and ST in Union and State legislature** – Articles 330 and 333
- **National Commission for SC and ST** – Article 338

(d) **Legislative Enactments:** India has passed various laws to protect the rights of the Scheduled Castes to fulfill the constitutional provisions pertaining to them. These include the following[24]:

- Protection of Civil Rights (Anti-Untouchability) Act (1955);
- The Bonded Labour (Abolition) Act (1976);
- The Scheduled Castes and Scheduled Tribes (Prevention of Atrocities) Act (1989) and Rules (1995); and
- The Employment of Manual Scavenger and Construction of Dry Latrines (Prohibition) Act (1993).

Moreover, government legislated various land reform laws to redistribute community land to the landless. Finally, to monitor enforcement of some of these laws, the Central Government established the National Commission for Scheduled Castes and Scheduled Tribes and the National Human Rights Commission in the early 1990s.

This book is attempting to underline the significance of social relationships for community living not just at the individual or group level living but also at the humanity level for the sheer survival and future of social living which are at stakes. We are trying to underline that tools and consumables, which are manifestations of science and technology, are just the means of living an enriched and prosperous community lives. To understand social living and to give priority to social relationships we have to enhance the significance of the social sciences. Because only the social sciences paradigm of knowledge building will keep the sciences and technology in the best perspectives. So knowledge building has to be interdisciplinary among the natural and the social sciences for best technology tool applications in public interest.

Interdisciplinarity and Inclusion

Interdisciplinary approach is a process of giving and taking in the context of particularistic limitation that need to be filled up for holistic understanding of enhanced productivity. The process of interdisciplinarity reflects flexibility and consent for change. Change is a permanent process and interdisciplinarity represents change. With modernity have come human social sensitivity through human rights via. democracy and welfare state. It is the acknowledgement of social diversity that represents human sensitisation to humanity along with nature. This also reveals the human will for accommodating the socio-economic and political rights of the underprivileged community of the society. All this represents inclusiveness. The reality of Indian schooling and higher education shows a disproportionate number of underprivileged students in the social sciences that are employably less productive. This reality forces us to find the lacunae in the education system especially the higher education system. The solutions probably lie in the interdisciplinarity of higher education for inclusion which is the primary hypothesis of this book that is tested and represented by the fieldwork data.

References

1. Report on "*Interdisciplinarity*" (Problems of teaching and Research in Universities) Paris, Centre for Educational Research and Innovation (CERI), Organisation for Economic Cooperation and Development (OECD) 1972, p. 25
2. *Ibid,* p. 90.
3. Garkovich, L. (1982), '*A proposal for Building Interdisciplinary* Bridges'. Teaching Sociology, p. 154.
4. Chettiparamb, A. (2007), '*Interdisciplinarity: a literature review*', The Interdisciplinary Teaching and Learning Group, Subject Centre for Languages, Linguistics and Area Studies, School of Humanities publication, University of Southampton.
5. Jantsch, Erich (1980), '*Interdisciplinarity: Dreams and reality*' Prospects, Vol. X, No. 3, p. 1.
6. *Ibid*, p. 1.
7. Popper, K. R. (1963), 'Conjectures and Refutations: The Growth of Scientific Knowledge'. New York: Routledge and Kegan Paul, 1963, pp. 88.
8. Jantsch, Erich (1980), '*Interdisciplinarity: Dreams and reality*' Prospects, Vol. X, No. 3, p. 1.
9. Jantsch, Erich (1980), '*Interdisciplinarity: Dreams and reality*' Prospects, Vol. X, No. 3, pp. 304-312.
10. Kleinberg, Ethan (2008), '*Interdisciplinary Studies at a Crossroads*' Association of American College and Universities, Washington D.C. http://wesscholar.wesleyan.edu/div1facpubs/99/
11. Lisowska, A., Wojciechowska, E. and Mitkowski, S. A. (2010), '*Interdisciplinarity in higher education- natural science electives for engineering students*' 1st World Conference on Technology and Engineering Education, Krakow, Poland, 14-17 September 2010.
12. Kockelmans, Joseph J., Ed. (1979), '*Interdisciplinarity and Higher Education*' The Pennsylvania State University Press, 215 Wagner Building, University Park, PA 16802, pp. 224-243.
13. https://www.ncbi.nlm.nih.gov/books/NBK44876/
14. W. James Jecob, http://www.palgrave-journals.com/articles/palcomms20151
15. Sorokin (1956), '*Fads and Feables in Modern Sociology and related sciences*', Chicago University Press.
16. http://www.thehindu.com/features/education/Interdisciplinary-approach-in-higher- education/article16811839.ece
17. Pramanik, Auditi (2014), '*Role of Interdisciplinary Studies in Higher Education in India*' Journal of Education and Human Development June 2014, Vol. 3, No. 2, pp. 589-595.

18. Thiruvasagam, G. (2010), '*Interdisciplinary approach in higher education*' article published in the Hindu paper dated 2 Feb. 2010.
19. Sonowal C.J. (2008), '*Indian Tribes, and Issue of social inclusion and Exclusion*', Article published in stud Tribes, Tribls, 6(2) pp. 123-124.
20. Twelfth Five Year Plan (2012-17): '*Faster, More Inclusive & Sustainable Growth*', Volume I.
21. Mohapatra, Tanuja (2011), '*Tribes of Odisha: Issues of social inclusion, exclusion and cultural assimilation*' article published in Bodhy: An interdisciplinary Journal, 5, ISSN: 2091-0479.
22. http://www.worldbank.org/en/topic/socialdevelopment/brief/social-inclusion
23. Department of Economics and social Affairs (2009), Report published on '*Creating an Inclusive Society: Practical Strategies to Promote Social Integration*'.
24. Arvind Kumar, '*Law and Dalits Social Inclusion in India*', article accessed from - http://focusglobalreporter. com/article17.asp

Chapter - 3

Research Methodology

Introduction

Indian higher education is a developing system but rigidly compartmentalised into the sciences, social sciences and applied-professional disciplines. Entry into particular disciplines is decided by the number of marks scored by the students at the secondary or higher secondary level schooling. The average or mediocre students are forced to go to the social sciences or commerce disciplines which do not carry sufficient scope for employment or self-applicatory skills. While the better and the brilliant students get access to the sciences and the professional disciplines ensuring better employment prospects and self-skills applicability. It is a fact that the dropout rates of schooling in India are much higher for the schedule castes, schedule tribes students. As a result, fewer number of SC and ST students move into higher education and especially into the social sciences and commerce disciplines, as they are unable to crack the secondary and higher secondary, memory based examinations, with flying colours. This vicious education process plays out as a huge social exclusion presentation.

Schooling excellence through rote memorisation gives extra advantage to those students coming from a social precedence of oral presentation skills. While the others carried history of manual exertions and servitude finding the oral -memory based skills, difficult to handle. So interdisciplinarity at the higher education level between the sciences, social sciences and technology, complimenting the dynamics of the mental and the manual, learning to holistic and productive educational output and inclusion of the historical strength of the deprived sections of the society. In this project the researcher studied the Indian higher education system along with interdisciplinarity for social inclusiveness.

Objectives

1. To identify the social and educational among other, shortcomings of traditional system of Indian higher education.
2. To determine interdisciplinarity and assess its need.
3. To compare nature and status of interdisciplinarity in Western countries.
4. To analyze whether interdisciplinarity has a broader canvas and is it socially and educationally inclusive.
5. To determine whether the traditionalists are ready to accept the new interdisciplinary approach.
6. To determine whether a new interdisciplinary curricular model shows holistic and quality higher education outputs.

Scope of the Research

The scope of this research is at the discipline level and also at the individual level. Exploration requires more than one discipline, but due to compartmentalisation, every discipline works in a limited area of knowledge. That is why it does not suffice to meet the requirement of the problem with a single or compartmentalised system of knowledge. In order to give justice to the issue undertaken interdisciplinary approach is always feasible and appropriate.

At the individual level more and more people will be inducted or accommodated in the interdisciplinary system of approach. The overall benefits of interdisciplinary kind of system of knowledge will have a comprehensive and elevated scope.

In the name of specialisation, less and less inclusiveness is achieved whereas, in case of interdisciplinarity it moves in reverse order, from narrow to greater and higher state. Hence, more and more people will be accommodated in the stream of knowledge, leading to inclusiveness of the individual and the system.

This research project has studied the higher education system in India, at a macro level, leading to the studies of streams from the social sciences to the professional. It has ultimately come up with a curricular fabric integrating the social sciences and pure sciences including technology, to come up with a curricula that creates holistic human resources with a balance between the mental and the manual and thus leading to inclusiveness of the individual and social variety.

Research Questions

(7) What are the social and educational, among other, short-comings of traditional system of Indian higher education?

(8) What and why Interdisciplinarity?

(9) Nature and status of interdisciplinarity in Western countries.

(10) Does Interdisciplinarity have a broader canvas and is socially and educationally inclusive?

(11) Shall traditionalists be ready to accept the new interdisciplinary approach?

(12) Will a new interdisciplinary curricular model show holistic and quality higher education output?

Research Methodology

(a) Universe: This research project has studied the higher education system in India, at a macro level, leading to the studies of streams from the social sciences to the natural sciences and the professional. So, higher education institutions all over India is the universe of this study.

(b) Research Design: The study is based on survey method with an exploratory and analytical design to fulfill the set objectives. Exploring innovations mainly at the research level and the applied level.

- **(i) Research:** Library work and consultation with expertise.
- **(ii) Applied:** Mainly comparing and contrasting and examining various curricula at the higher education level in various universities and research institution. The project has formulated an indicative curriculum of a science discipline in an interdisciplinary mode rooted in the larger social and economic canvas.

(c) Units of analysis: The study has used multiple units of analysis including Academician, research scholar and students of graduation and post-graduation.

(d) Sampling: Out of an all India total of public and private, 760 Universities, 34,452 colleges, the researcher selected 20 renowned higher education institutions all over India. The sample number of institutions has been identified by the purposive sample method. The higher education institutions selected had interdisciplinary courses or courses with scope for interdisciplinarity. The researcher visited institutions from Delhi, Bengaluru, Hyderabad, Dharwad, Mumbai and Pune.

(e) **Selection of respondents:** The researcher interacted with two professors, two associate professors, one assistant professor along with five research students and five students from the graduation and post-graduation levels. But on the fieldwork proper, the researcher collected a sample of 331 respondents due to conditions beyond control. The selection of the respondents was by purposive sampling. The sampling of the three types of respondents consisted of professors, associates professor, assistant professor according to seniority. The sample selection of the research, graduation and post-graduation students was done in a way so as to accommodate students from different social categories including scheduled castes and scheduled tribes facilitating comparative participation and performance.

Table 2.1: Educational Institution-wise number of respondents

Sr. No.	Educational Institution	Academician	Research Student	Student
1.	IIT Delhi	04(3.40)	03(2.20)	00(00)
2.	JNU Delhi	13(11.20)	16(11.80)	02(2.50)
3.	Delhi University	04(3.40)	03(2.20)	00(00)
4.	Bangalore University	10(8.60)	19(14.00)	13(16.50)
5.	NIAS Bangalore	05(4.30)	3(2.20)	00(00)
6.	ISEC, Bangalore	17(14.70)	23(16.90)	01(1.30)
7.	Hyderabad Central University	04(3.40)	09(6.60)	01(1.30)
8.	CESS, Hyderabad	06(5.20)	04(2.90)	00(00)
9.	CMDR, Dharwad	05(4.30)	01(0.70)	00(00)
10.	Adarsh College Pune	03(2.60)	02(1.50)	11(13.90)
11.	College of Agriculture	09(7.80)	12(8.80)	09(11.40)
12.	COEP, Pune	10(8.60)	04(2.90)	6(7.60)
13.	Symbiosis Health University Pune	05(4.30)	00(00)	00(00)
14.	ILS Law College, Pune	00(00)	08(5.90)	10(12.70)
15.	Bharati Vidyapeeth University, Pune	05(4.30)	00(00)	10(12.70)
16.	IISER, Pune	02(1.70)	02(1.50)	04(5.10)
17.	Savitribai Phule Pune Uni. Pune	04(3.40)	00(00)	00(00)
18.	Symbiosis Management University Pune	03(2.60)	00(00)	5(6.30)
19.	TISS, Mumbai	02(1.70)	15(11.00)	7(8.90)
20.	Other than Selected	05(4.30)	12(8.80)	00(00)
	Total	**116(100)**	**136(100)**	**79(100)**

(f) Units of Observation and Sampling size: Total type-wise selected sample respondents

Table 2.2: Selected sample for the study

Sr. No.	Type of respondent	Total	Percentage
1.	Academician	116	35.04
2.	Research Student	136	41.09
3.	Student	79	23.87
	Total	**331**	**100**

The sample size of the research project is 331. The researcher collected primary data from 331 respondents. In all 116 (35.04%) were academicians including professors, and associate professors and assistant professors. 136 (41.08%) were research scholars and 79 (23.87%) were students of graduation and post-graduation levels.

Among 136 research students 43.40% from general category, 22.10% from SC, 5.90% from ST, 24.30% from OBC and 2.90 from Minorities (Jain, Muslim, Sikh). Two research students did not mention there social category. Among 79 students of graduation and post-graduation levels 62.00% were from the general category, 17.70% from SC, 2.50% from ST, 15.20% from OBC and 2.50% from NT category. The variation in social categorisation of the respondents students (Research, graduation and post-graduation) was achieved in a random manner.

The school/department-wise classification of the respondents is as follows:

Table 2.3: Department/School-wise respondents

Sr. No.	Department/School	Academician	Research Student	Student
1.	Social Sciences	69(59.50)	90(66.20)	52(65.80)
2.	Natural Sciences	26(22.40)	31(22.80)	16(20.30)
3.	Women Studies	01(0.90)	02(1.50)	00(00)
4.	Professional Courses Engineering, B. Ed, M. Ed, Law	12(10.30)	09(6.6)	11(13.90)
5.	No Response	08(6.90)	04(2.90)	00(00)
	Total	**116(100)**	**136(100)**	**79(100)**

The researcher selected a department, which was interdisciplinary or with scope of interdisciplinarity with other subjects or streams. Most of the respondents were from the social sciences among which 59.50% were academician, researcher students 66.20% and the students of UG/PG were 65.80%. There were 21.83% respondents were from the natural sciences, about 1% respondent from women studies and 10.27% respondents from the professional courses. 3.62% of the respondents did not give any response to the department column.

The course/programme-wise number of respondents are as follows:

Table 2.4: Course/Programme-wise student respondents

Sr. No.	Course/Programme	Student	Research Student
1.	MA	09(11.40)	00(00)
2.	M. Sc	05(6.30)	08(5.90)
3.	M. Ed	18(22.80)	00(00)
4.	B. Sc.	14(17.70)	00(00)
5.	MSW	10(12.70)	00(00)
6.	MBA	05(16.30)	00(00)
7.	B. Tech./ M. Tech	06(7.60)	05(3.70)
8.	LLB/LLM	10(12.70)	08(5.90)
9.	M. Phil.	00(00)	17(12.50)
10.	Ph. D.	00(00)	89(65.40)
11.	Post-Doctoral	00(00)	01(0.70)
12.	No Response	02(2.50)	08(5.90)
	Total	**79(100)**	**136(100)**

The researcher covered 13 course/programmes and interacted with 79 students from the graduation and post-graduation levels and 136 research students pursuing LLM, M.Sc., M. Tech, M. Phil, Ph.D. In all the 215 student respondents composed of 4.18% from M.A., 6.05% from M.Sc., 8.37% from M.ed.,6.51% from B.Sc., 4.65% from MSW, 2.32% from MBA, 5.11% from B. Tech and M. Tech, 8.37% from LLB and LLM, 7.90% from M. Phil, and 41.40% from Ph. D students. There was one student pursuing post-doctoral fellowship.

(g) **Data collection:** Researcher collected the data from both - primary and secondary sources. The data was collected both quantitatively and qualitatively. Questionnaire was the tool for primary data collection.

The questionnaire was made by the researcher himself with expert guidance from honourable advisory committee members and valuable inputs from the project associate. For this research project a pilot study was conducted to understand the fieldwork difficulties, especially regarding implementation of research tools. The pilot study was conducted in Savitribai Phule Pune University. It was realised that the social sciences respondents were comfortable filling the questionnaire but those from the natural sciences and professional streams were not. They were not understanding the essentially education and social sciences question constructions or terminology. To resolve the problem the researcher revised the questionnaire with simple language and giving optional choice of answers, along with the space for free expression, to all the research students and students of graduation and post-graduation levels. The pilot study helped refine the questionnaire for easy understanding and responses to fulfill the aims and objectives of the research project.

(i) **Primary Data:** The researcher used the questionnaire for collection of the primary data. The researcher used both closed-ended and open-ended questions to collect the data. In the close-ended questions the researcher gave multiple options for response and in the open- ended questions he gave space for the respondent free expression.

(ii) **Secondary Data:** The researcher also used the secondary data to prepare the report. Studies and literature on higher education as well as interdisciplinarity and social inclusion were used as secondary source material. In the secondary sources the researcher used reference books, research papers, working papers, published/unpublished documents, reports on higher education, unpublished M. Phil and Ph.D. thesis and e-material.

(h) **Data Analysis:** Both descriptive as well as inferential statistical procedures were adopted to analyze and interpret the data collected for the study. And a new interdisciplinary indicative curriculum integrating the social sciences and pure sciences including technology of the first year undergraduate programme is arrived at.

Ethical Consideration

The informats from different universities, research institution and national technology institutes voluntarily participated in the research inquiry.

Two medical colleges from Pune did not participate in the research inquiry. So I drop them from the sampling.

Assurance of the information gathered, not to be disclosed or shared for other than this research project was given to the respondents.

Finally, the inquiry questions in the questionnaire were related to aims and objectives of the study and not related to the personal life of the informats.

Limitations of the Study: The data analysis is based on the responses of the informats. Another limitation included the denial of participation as respondents of two Medical colleges of Pune.

Delimitation of the Study: To make research manageable only twenty universities, research institutions and national institutes of technology were selected. Only interdisciplinary or departments with interdisciplinary scope were selected for responses.

Conceptual Definitions

(a) Discipline: Academic discipline may mean a convenient division of knowledge into its component parts as well as the basis of organisation of a University.

6. According to Guy Michaud and C. C. Abt, a discipline is "A Specific body of teachable knowledge with its own background of education, training, procedures, methods and content areas."[1]
7. According to Marcel Biosot, "A discipline is concerned first with objects, methods and procedures and finally with laws. The objects are not isolated entities, they interact with other objects and give rise to phenomena. The aim of the discipline is to give coherent explanation of the phenomena generated by these interactions." [2]

(b) Interdisciplinarity

3. According to Garkovich, "Two or more disciplines….. Contributing their particular disciplinary knowledge on a common subject."[3]
4. According to Chettiparamb (2007), interdisciplinarity is "filling the gaps that disciplinarity leaves vacant or in terms of transcendence surpassing what disciplinarity can ever hope to achieve."[4]

(c) Social Inclusion

1. According to Bourdieu and Luhmann, "The concept of inclusion means the encompassing of the entire population in

the performances of the individual function systems. On the one hand this concerns access to these benefits and, on the other dependence of individual modes of living on them. To the extent that inclusion is achieved, groups disappear that do not or only marginally participate in social living."[5]

2. **According to the Twelfth Five Year Plan (2012-17)**, 'Inclusiveness means many different things and each aspect of inclusiveness poses its own challenges for policy'.[6] Different facets of inclusiveness are inclusiveness as poverty reduction, inclusiveness as group equality, inclusiveness as regional balance, inclusiveness and inequality, inclusiveness as empowerment and inclusiveness throw employment programmes. As per Twelfth five year plan (2012-17), inclusiveness as group equality is also about a growth process which is seen to be fair by different socio-economic groups that constitute our society. Inclusiveness must also embrace the concern of other groups such as the Scheduled Castes (SCs), Scheduled Tribes (STs), Other Backward Classes (OBCs), Minorities, the differently abled and other marginalised groups.
3. The World Bank defines social inclusion as the process of improving the terms for individuals and groups to take part in society. Social inclusion aims to empower poor and marginalised people to take advantage of burgeoning global opportunities. It ensures that people have a voice in decisions which affect their lives and that they enjoy equal access to markets, services and political, social and physical spaces.[7]

References

1. Report on "*Interdisciplinarity*" (Problems of teaching and Research in Universities) Paris, Centre for Educational Research and Innovation (CERI), Organisation for Economic Cooperation and Development (OECD) 1972, p. 25.
2. *Ibid*, p. 90.
3. Garkovich, L. (1982), A proposal for Building Interdisciplinary Bridges. Teaching Sociology, p. 154.
4. Chettiparamb, A. (2007), '*Interdisciplinarity: a literature review*' The Interdisciplinary Teaching and Learning Group, Subject Centre for Languages, Linguistics and Area Studies, School of Humanities publication, University of Southampton.
5. Sonowal, C.J. (2008), '*Indian Tribes, and Issue of social inclusion and Exclusion*', Article published in stud Tribes, Tribls, 6(2) pp. 123, 124.

6. Twelfth Five Year Plan (2012-17): Faster, More Inclusive & Sustainable Growth, Volume I.
7. http://www.worldbank.org/en/topic/socialdevelopment/brief/social-inclusion
8. Thorat, Sukhadeo (2006), '*Higher Education in India Emerging Issues to Access, inclusiveness and Quality*' Nehru Memorial Lecture, University of Mumbai.
9. Jandhyala, B.G. Tilak (2015), '*How Inclusive Is Higher Education in India?*' Social Change 45(2) 185–223, SAGE Publications sagepub.in/home.nav
10. Oommen, T. K. (2015), '*Social Inclusion in Independent India*' http://uohherald.commuoh.in/social-inclusion-in-independent-india/
11. Deepika Kumari (2014) '*Social Inclusion in Indian Higher education- Equity in Access*', Centre for Civil Society, Researching Reality Summer Internship 2014, Working paper: 313.
12. Rachel, Westfall (2010) *'Dimensions of Social Inclusion and Exclusion in Yukon'* Yukon Bureau of Statistics, December 2010.
13. Stirling, J. and McGloin, C. (2015), '*Critical pedagogy and social inclusion policy in Australian Higher Education: Identifying the Disjunctions*', Radical pedagogy, 12 (2).
14. Ingole, K. S., '*A Critical Study of Social Exclusion and its Implication*' http://www.ambedkar.org/research/SOCIAL_EXCLUSION_and_ITS_IMPLICATION.pdf
15. Neelakandan, Sanil and Patil, Smita (2012), '*Complexities of inclusion and exclusion: Dalit students and higher education in India*' Journal of Social Inclusion 3(1) 2012.
16. Kirpal, Viney and others (1985), '*Scheduled Caste and Tribe Students in Higher Education: A Study of an IIT*', article published in Economic and Political Weekly Vol. XX, No. 29, July 20, 1985.

    http://www.epw.in/system/files/pdf/2015_50/25/special_articles_scheduled_caste_ and_tribe_students_in_higher_education.pdf
17. Brahmanandam, T. and T. Bosu Babu (2016), '*Educational Status among the Scheduled Tribes: Issues and Challenges*', The NEHU Journal, Vol. XIV, No. 2, July-December 2016, pp.69-85. https://nehu.ac.in/public/downloads/Journals/NEHU-Journal-July-Dec-2016- A5.pdf
18. George, K. K. (2011), '*Higher Education in Kerala: How Inclusive is it to Scheduled Castes and Scheduled Tribes?*', Education Exclusion and Economic Growth Working Paper Series, Volume 1, Number 4, 2011, Centre for the Study of Social Exclusion and Inclusive Policy, http://csesindia.org/admin/modules/cms/docs/publication/28.pdf
19. Solomon Arulraj David (2016), '*Social Responsiveness of Higher Education: Access, Equity and Social Justice*', Rupkatha Journal on Interdisciplinary Studies in Humanities, Vol. VIII, No. 4, 2016, 0975-2935.

    http://rupkatha.com/V8/n4/v8n420.pdf
20. Mahadevaswamy, M, Dr. Sajan C.P., and Dr. G. Kotreshwar (2013), '*Perception of SC/ST students participating in higher education with special reference to Mysore, Karnataka*' IOSR Journal of Economics and Finance (IOSR-JEF)

e-ISSN: 2321- 5933 p-ISSN: 2321-5925.Volume 1, Issue 4 (Sep. – Oct. 2013), pp. 39-42, http://www.iosrjournals.org/iosr-jef/papers/vol1-issue4/F0143942.pdf

21. Abdul Salim (2004), '*Opportunities for Higher Education: An enquiry into entry barriers*', Discussion Paper No. 71, Kerala Research Programme on Local Level Development Centre for Development Studies Thiruvananthapuram, http://www.cds.ac.in/krpcds/publication/downloads/71.pdf

22. Basant, Rakesh and Sen, Gitanjali (2013), '*Access to Higher Education in India: An Exploration of Its Antecedents*', Working Paper No. 2013-05-011, Indian Institute of Management Ahmedabad-380 015 India.

23. UNESCO (2018), '*Diversity & Social Inclusion in Higher Education*', Produced by: UNESCO Chair in Community Based Research & Social Responsibility in Higher Education, http://unescochair-cbrsr.org/pdf/resource/FICCI%20Doc%20II_ Diversity%20%20Social%20Inclusio n_4Jan.pdf

24. Dr. K. Kamar Jahan, and Dr. D. Christy Selvarani (2015), '*Higher Education in India: Issues and Challenges*', International Conference on Humanities, Literature and Management (ICHLM'15) Jan. 9-10, 2015 Dubai (UAE), http://icehm.org/upload/8262ED0115098.pdf

25. Kockelmans, Joseph J. (1979), '*Interdisciplinarity and Higher Education (ed)*', The Pennsylvania State University Press, University Park and London.

26. Muravska,Tatjana & Zaneta Ozolina, (2011), '*Interdisciplinarity in Social Sciences: Does it Provide Answers to Current Challenges in Higher Education and Research?*'(ed.) Riga, University of Latvia Press.

27. Pramanik, Auditi (2014), '*Role of Interdisciplinary Studies in Higher Education in India*', article published in Journal of Education and Human Development, June 2014, Vol. 3, No. 2, pp. 589-595.

28. Veronica Boix Mansilla, (2010). '*Interdisciplinarity in United States Schools: Past, Present, and Future*' paper published in the journal Issues In Integrative Studies No. 28, pp. 1-27.

29. Elisabeth, J. H. Spelt & Harm, J. A. Biemans & Hilde Tobi & Pieternel A. Luning & Martin Mulder (2010), '*Teaching and Learning in Interdisciplinary Higher Education: A Systematic Review*'. This article is published with open access at Springerlink.com DOI 10.1007/s10648-009-9113-z

30. Elisabete, M. A. Pereira, Ana Maria Carneiro, Mirian Lucia Goncalves (2014), '*Innovation and Evaluation in the Brazilian Higher Education Culture: Interdisciplinary and General Education*', creative education, 2014, 5,1690-1701. http://www.scirp.org/journal/ce

31. William H. Newell (2001), '*A Theory of Interdisciplinary Studies*', Issues in Integrative studies, No. 19, pp. 1-25.

32. Martin Davies and Marcia Devtin (2007), '*Interdisciplinary Higher Education and the Melbourne Model*' Conference Presentation © 2007 Philosophy of Education Society of Australasia.

33. Mary, Adler and Sheila, Flihan (1997), '*The Interdisciplinary continuum: Reconciling theory, Research and Practice*' Report Series 2.36, National Research Center on English Learning & Achievement, University at Albany, State University of New York, Washington Avenue, Albany, New York.

34. Sandra Mathison, Melissa Freeman (1997), *'The Logic of Interdisciplinary Studies'*. the paper Presented at the Annual Meeting of the American Educational Research Association, Chicago.
35. Creso, M. Sa (2007), *'Interdisciplinary strategies' in U.S. research universities'* Paper Published online: 8 June 2007, High Educ (2008) 55:537–552 DOI 10.1007/s10734-007-9073-5.
36. William H. Newell (2001), *'A Theory of Interdisciplinary Studies'* Issues in Integrative Studies, No.19, pp. 1-25.
37. Sharma, Sunita Singh Machiavelli (2015), *'Interdisciplinary research: Transforming Higher Education in India'* International Journal of Interdisciplinary Research and Innovations, Vol. 3, Issue 3, pp: (80-88), Month: July - September 2015.
38. Anne Visholm, Lasse Grosen, Maria Theresa Norn and Rasmus Lund Jensen (2012), '*Interdisciplinary Research is Key to Solving Society's Problem*' publisher DEA Fiolstrade 44, 1171 Kobenhavn K, Denmark
39. Miller, Raymond (1982), '*Varieties of Interdisciplinary Approaches in the Social Sciences: A 1981 Overview*' Published in Issues in Integrative Studies: An Occasional Publication of the Association for Integrative Studies, pp. 1-37.

Chapter - 4

Data Analysis

Introduction

In this chapter, the researcher analyzes primary data of the field. This data was collected through questionnaires from respondents of renowned higher education institutions all over India. Academician, Research students and under-graduation (UG) and post-graduation (PG) students were the respondents for this study. The researcher visited 20 higher education institutions and interacted with minimum two professors, two associate professors and one assistant professor along with five research scholars and five UG/PG students. The institutions were selected through purposive sampling. Interdisciplinary courses or courses with scope for interdisciplinarity was the criteria for selection of various departments of universities, research institutions and national institutes of technology. Post coding and tabulation, the researcher presents the analysis of the primary data as follows:

Personal Details of the Respondents

(i) **Gender:** The research data covered 116 academician responses composed of 62.10% male and 37.90% female. Among research students, 62.50% were male and 33.80% were female respondents. 3.70% research students chose not to fill the gender column. Among 79 UG/PG students there were 49.50% male and 50.60% female respondents.

(ii) **Social Category of the respondents:** The researcher tried to interact with all category respondents for variation in the responses. To gauge inclusiveness in higher education, which is the main objective of this research endeavour, collecting social information of the respondents was necessary. Collection of social and educational information of varied social categories was essential for a comparative understanding of inclusion or exclusion from higher education. The social category-wise breakup of the all respondents is as follows:

Table 4.2: Social Category of the respondents

Sr. No.	Category	Academician	Research Student	Student
1.	General	70(60.30)	59(43.40)	49(62.00)
2.	SC	25(21.60)	30(22.10)	14(17.70)
3.	ST	04(3.40)	08(5.90)	02(2.50)
4.	OBC	15(12.90)	33(24.30)	12(15.20)
5.	NT	01(0.90)	00(00)	02(2.50)
6.	Minority	00(00)	04(2.90)	00(00)
7.	No Response	01(00.90)	02(1.50)	00(00)
	Total	**116(100)**	**136(100)**	**79(100)**

Observation: The above table shows the social-category wise proportion of the respondents. Among 116 academician 60.30% were from general category, 21.60% were from Scheduled Castes (SC), 3.40% from Scheduled Tribes (ST), 12.90% from Other Backward Classes (OBC) and one respondent was from the Nomadic Tribe (NT) category. One academician did not mention his/her social category.

Among 136 research students 43.40% were from general category, 22.10% from SC, 5.90% from ST, 24.30% from OBC and 2.90% from Minorities (Jain, Muslim, Sikh). Two research students did not mention there social category.

Among 79 students of graduation and post-graduation levels 62.00% were from the general category, 17.70% from SC, 2.50% from ST, 15.20% from OBC and 2.50% from NT category.

The variation in social categorisation of all the three respondents is a random output.

Economic profile of the family of Student respondents

The socio-economic conditions of the family affect the educational progress of the students. Availability of adequate financial support from the families opened various educational opportunities for the students. The researcher tried to know the financial background of the students and asked his/her about occupation of his/her father and the responses are as follows:

28.37% students said that their father was in government service, among this 19.53% were research students and 8.84% were students of UG/

PG. 7.44% research students and 5.58% students of UG/PG said their fathers were working in the private sector. 15.35% students replied that their fathers were doing business. 14.88% research students and 8.37% students of UG/PG said their fathers were farmers. 1.86% students said their father were worker and 5.58% students had fathers who worked as labour. And over 6% students did not reply to this query.

The researcher asked the student about their family annual income and the responses are as follows:

The responses show the annual income of the student's family. 10.69% student respondents said their family annual income was less than 30 thousand rupees. 22.32% students said their family annual income was between 30 thousand to 1 lacs rupees in which 13.02% were research students and 9.30% were students of UG/PG. Higher number of the students i.e. 29.76% had family incomes in the range of 1 to 3 lacs rupees. Among them 20.93% were research students and 8.83% were students of UG/PG. 13.95% research students and 9.76% students of UG/PG replied that their annual family income was in the range of 3 to 10 lacs rupees. 5.58% students said their family income was in the range of 10 to 25 lacs and four students said the income was 25 to 50 lacs. 6.50% students did not give any response to this question.

Interpretation: 62.79% students' family annual income was below 3 lacs. The economic condition of most of the students' families was poor or at subsistence levels.

Source of expenditure on higher education and fees - students

Educational expenses being a major factor of exclusion from higher education the researcher asked the students of UG/PG about the source of expenditure on higher education and the responses are as follows:

Observation: As evident from the following graph 69.60% students of undergraduation and post-graduation said their parents were the source for expenditure on higher education. 8.90% students replied that only government scholarship was the source and 10.10% said GOI scholarships along with parental support were the source for expenditure on higher education. Over 3% students replied that besides financial support from the parents he/she has to work part time. 2.50% students did not give any response to this question.

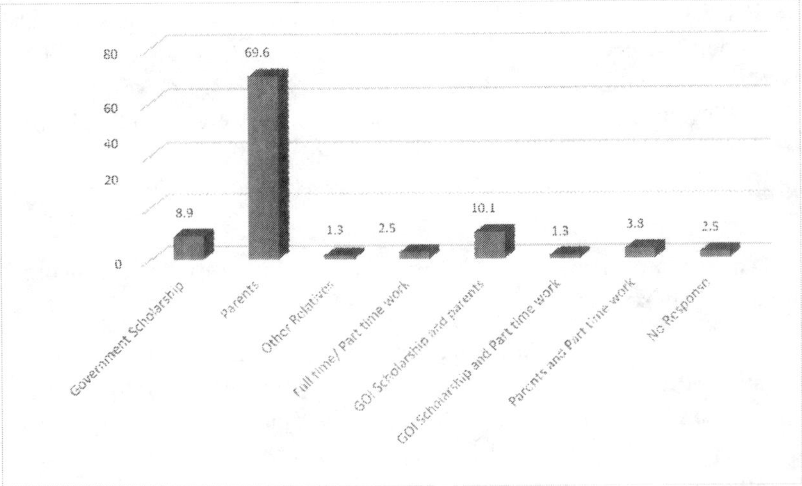

Graph 4.1: Expenditure source for higher education-Students.

Interpretation: As seen in the above table most of the students are dependents on their parents for financial support for higher education. Besides this government scholarships are also important supportive source for the higher education to some students.

- **Capitation fees and other fees for higher education:** Capitation fee is a big hurdle in access to higher education for all sections of the society. The numbers of private colleges are increasing constantly but on the other hand government colleges are decreasing continually. The share of private higher education institutions (77.11%) is far more than government colleges (22.89%) in the year 2014-15. In the private colleges 63.02% colleges are private unaided which implement their own fees structure according to gradation and directed by government fee structure committee.[1] The capitation fees are not affordable to poor and subsistence level students excluding them from higher education. The researcher asked the students about capitation fees for previous admission or for current degree/diploma and the responses are as follows:

Table 4.5: Capitation Fees for previous education by students

Sr. No.	Fees	Previous Education		Current Degree/Diploma
		Research Student	Student	Students (UG/PG)
1.	Yes	11(8.10)	03(3.80)	08(10.10)
2.	No	50(36.70)	27(34.20)	47(59.50)
3.	No Response	75(55.10)	49(62.00)	24(3.40)
	Total	**136(100)**	**79(100)**	**79(100)**

Observation: As evident from the above table 11 (8.10%) research students and 03 (3.80%) students of UG/PG said they had to pay some capitation fees for their previous degree/diploma. Along with this 10.10% students of UG/PG said they paid capitation fees for the current degree/diploma. 36.70% research students and 46.85% students of UG/PG gave a negative response on this query. Surprisingly, 55.10% research students and 62% students of UG/PG did not give any response to this question.

Interpretation: Demanding and paying capitation fees being an illegal act, it is a matter of guessing whether the students felt uneasy about having paid capitation fees for admissions.

Further, the researcher asked about the actual fees for the current degree/diploma. Students indicated variation in amount of fees. For the convenience of tabulation we framed the fees in various ranges with responses as follows:

> 7.60% students said the fees were in the range of 1 to one thousand rupees. 6.30% students replied that the fee was in the range of one thousand to five thousand rupees. 2.50% said it was between five thousand to 10 thousand rupees, 16.50% students said the fee was in the range of 10 thousand to 20 thousand rupees and 50.60% said it was above 20 thousand rupees. 16.50% students of UG/PG did not give any response to this question regarding fees, which is open for interpretation.

Interpretation: As evident from the above two tables, few students said they had to pay capitation fee for the previous as well as current degree/diploma. Moreover, most of the students (50.60%) said they had to pay admission fees above 20 thousand rupees. This data indicates the expensive nature of even public higher education, no less private. This could lead to exclusion of poor and subsistence level students from higher education. Moreover, it is a proven fact that the rate of indigence is higher among the SC and ST students of India. Therefore, this automatically works as a biggest exclusionary obstacle in the pursuit of higher education.

Educational background of the student respondents

The researcher tried to take a review of educational background of the student respondents to gauge the educational progress of the students. Educational background of the family affects the educational progress of the students.

(i) Generational level of Learning:-To know the educational background of the students' family the researcher asked the students about the learning levels of the preceding generations of his/her family and the responses are as follows:

Table 4.7: Generational level of Learning- Students

Sr. No.	Generation	Research Student	Student	Total
1.	First	42(19.53)	18(8.37)	60(27.90)
2.	Second	47(21.86)	29(13.48)	76(35.34)
3.	Third	23(10.69)	18(8.37)	41(19.06)
4.	Fourth	15(6.97)	10(4.65)	25(11.62)
5.	No Response	09(4.18)	04(1.86)	13(6.04)
	Total	**136(63.26)**	**79(36.74)**	**215(100)**

Observation: As evident from the above table 27.90% students were first generation seeking higher education in their family. Among them 19.53% were research students and 8.37% were students of UG/PG. 21.86% research students and 13.48% students of UG/PG said they were second generation who have taken to higher education. 19.06% said they were the third generation and 11.62% said they were the fourth generation of their family who pursued higher education.

Interpretation: The data shows that a significant over 27% research students and students of UG/PG are first generation seeking higher education exposing the very low GER growth pattern of our country. It also means majority of the students have educational family background and an opportunity to pursue higher education. In other words it also means that precedence of higher education is quite a necessity for present generations to enter into the exclusive portals of higher education. This also is another big obstacle to the SC and ST students who generally happen to be first generation learners.

(ii) Discipline of previous education: The researcher asked about the discipline of previous education of the students and the responses are as follows:

Table 4.8: Discipline of previous education of the students

Sr. No.	Discipline	Research Student	Student	Total
1.	Arts	76(35.34)	28(13.02)	104(48.37)
2.	Commerce	02(0.93)	05(2.32)	07(3.25)
3.	Science	41(19.06)	37(17.20)	78(36.26)
4.	Engineering	03(2.20)	00(00)	03(1.39)
5.	No Response	14(6.51)	09(4.18)	23(10.69)
	Total	**136(63.26)**	**79(36.74)**	**215(100)**

Observation: As seen in the above table 48.37% students said that they came from the arts faculty, which included 35.34% research students and 13.02% students of UG/PG. Only 3.25% students were from the commerce background. 36.26% students were from the science faculty, including 19.06% research students and 17.20% students of UG/PG. Only 1.39% were from engineering background. 6.51% research students and 4.18% students from UG/PG did not respond to this question.

Interpretation: As evident from the above table most (48.37%) students were from the arts faculty which is a huge proportion compared to the other discipline. It was huge because all the massive numbers of students who are graded as average of below average are forced to take admission into the arts faculty rendering them with low employment and entrepreneurial opportunities. These masses of students consist of a huge number of SC and ST students leading them to more or less futile higher education.

(iii) Medium of education: English is the dominating medium of learning in higher education. Students from English medium background have greater opportunities for educational progress. The researcher asked the students about the medium of previous and current education and the responses are as follows:

Table 4.9: 1e Student

Sr. No.	Medium	Previous Education			Current Education Students (UG/PG)
		Research Student	Student	Total	
1.	Marathi	05(2.32)	05(2.32)	10(4.65)	00(00)
2.	Hindi	04(1.86)	02(0.93)	06(2.79)	01(1.30)
3.	English	101(46.97)	56(26.04)	157(73.02)	68(86.10)
4.	Kannada	06(2.79)	08(3.72)	14(6.51)	07(8.90)
5.	Bengali	04(1.86)	00(00)	04(1.86)	00(00)
6.	No Response	16(7.44)	08(3.72)	24(11.16)	03(3.80)
	Total	**136(63.26)**	**79(36.74)**	**215(100)**	**79(100)**

Observation: As evident from the above table 46.97% research students and 26.04% students of UG/PG said that English was the medium of previous education as well as 86.10% students of UG/PG said English is the medium of current education. There were insignificant number of students who completed their previous education in regional languages among which 2.32% research students and 2.32% students of UG/PG completed their previous education in Marathi language. 6.51% students completed in Kannada language and four research students completed their previous education in Bengali. 11.16% students did not give any response to this question.

Interpretation: This means a huge number of students were from the English background who had lot of opportunities to learn in the best national higher educational institutions. This also means that higher education is hugely dominated by students who can afford and have access to English medium education. This also is another huge access barrier to higher education for the masses including the SC and ST students.

Shortcomings of Traditional System of Indian Higher Education

(i) **Advantages of rigidly compartmentalised higher education:** Going further into the interdisciplinarity in higher education the researcher queried for the advantages of rigidly compartmentalised higher education with the academicians, research students and UG/PG students.

Table 4.10: Advantages of rigidly compartmentalised higher education

Sr. No.	Rigidly compartmentalised HE-Advantages	Academician	Research Students	Students
1.	Focused in-depth knowledge of the discipline Specialisation or increased skills in particular area	84 (72.40)	75 (55.20)	41 (51.90)
2.	Entrenched structure in particular stream/subject	00 (00)	07 (5.10)	01 (1.30)
3.	Easier for teacher and students to teachand learn unitary stream/subject	09 (7.70)	15 (11.00)	12 (15.20)
4.	Increase possibility of micro level study of any discipline/subject	00 (00)	17 (12.50)	02 (2.50)
5.	All the above	00 (00)	07 (5.10)	11 (13.90)
6.	Increase specialisation, entrenched structure in particular subject	00 (00)	00 (00)	04 (5.10)

(Contd...)

7.	Better Employability	02 (1.70)	00 (00)	00 (00)
8.	None	08 (6.90)	05 (3.70)	04 (5.10)
9.	No Response	13 (11.20)	10 (7.40)	04 (5.10)
	Total	**116** **(100)**	**136** **(100)**	**79** **(100)**

Observation: A majority 72% academician, 55% research student and 41% students of UG/PG thought focused in-depth knowledge of the discipline and specialisation and increased skills in particular areas to be the advantages of rigidly compartmentalised higher education. Over 15% students, 3% academicians and research scholars thought compartmentalisation made teaching and learning unitary stream/subject easier for teachers and students to teach and learn. Over 13% students of UG/PG and 5% research students gave the following advantages - focused in-depth knowledge of the discipline; specialisation or increased skills in particular area; entrenched structure in particular stream/subject; easier for teacher and students to teach and learn unitary stream/subject; increase possibility of micro level study of any discipline/subject. Surprisingly, just about 1% academician thought compartmentalisation of higher education brought better employability.

Interpretation: The miniscule percentage of the last bit of data is interesting and indicates the understanding of limitations of compartmentalisation of higher education among the academicians. This possibly is an indicator of understanding and appreciation of need of interdisciplinarity among social sciences, pure sciences and technology for a holistic creation of knowledge.

(ii) Disadvantages of compartmentalised Higher Education: The researcher further tried to find out the disadvantages of compartmentalised higher education from all three types of respondents and the responses were as follows:

Table 4.11: Disadvantages of compartmentalised Higher Education

Sr. No.	Disadvantages of compartmentalized Higher Education	Academician	Research Students	Students
1.	One refuses to see knowledge holistically	40 (34.40)	49 (36.00)	15 (19.00)
2.	Not permitted to use any perspective or method of other discipline/subject	24 (20.70)	21 (15.40)	11 (13.90)

(*Contd...*)

3.	Compartmentalization leads to one-dimensional employment skills	00 (00)	44 (32.40)	14 (17.70)
4.	All Above	00 (00)	00 (00)	27 (34.20)
5.	Less Job Opportunities, Unemployment	10 (8.60)	01 (0.70)	00 (00)
6.	Certain people can choose better so it creates discrimination, Lack of inclusiveness	12 (10.40)	00 (00)	00 (00)
7.	Lack of team work, less quality	05 (4.30)	00 (00)	00 (00)
8.	None	13 (11.20)	10 (7.40)	01 (1.30)
9.	No Response	12 (10.40)	11 (8.11)	11 (13.90)
	Total	**116 (100)**	**136 (100)**	**79 (100)**

Observation: Over 34% academicians, 36% research students and 19% UG/PG students said that one refuses to see knowledge holistically. Over 20% academicians, 15% research students and 11% students of UG/PG felt that it was not permitted to use any perspective or method of other disciplines /subjects. Over 32% research students and 17% students of UG/PG felt that compartmentalisation leads to one - dimensional employment skills. 34% UG/PG students gave all the above reasoning as disadvantages of compartmentalised higher education. Over 10% academicians felt that certain people can choose better or more employable disciplines that creates discrimination or lack of inclusiveness. Over 4% academicians thought compartmentalised higher education obstructed teamwork leading to loss of quality. Over 11% academicians, 7% research students and 1% UG/PG students did not respond to this query.

Interpretation: Only the academicians have pointed out the situation of access to more employable higher education options for the few, leading to discrimination and exclusion. None of the students have raised this issue. This issue highlights lack of interdisciplinarity because of rigid compartmentalisation. And this compartmentalisation is sourced from the students' senior secondary and higher secondary marks-weightage system. This system of rote learning goes against the socio-economically backward students including the SC and ST due to a number of reasons including lack of educational background, financial instability and irrelevance of curriculum to employment or cultural heritage. So an interweaving interdisciplinary approach among the social sciences, pure sciences and technology application is inevitable. This would understand, co-opt and functionalise the varied strength of students from the social diversity of

India and give impetus to individual and community social mobility leading to true community empowerment in the country.

(iii) Comparative Employability of traditional courses, Science and Technology and Social Sciences Streams: Taking higher education issues further the researcher enquired with the academicians and UG/PG students about the employability of the social sciences, sciences and technology stream.

Table 4.12: Comparative Employability of science and technology and social sciences streams

Sr. No.	Responses	Academicians	Students
1	Yes (Greater than Social Science)	81(69.80)	42(53.20)
2	No (Not greater than Social Science)	34(29.30)	20(25.30)
3	No Response	01(0.90)	17(21.60)
	Total	**116(100)**	**79(100)**

Observation: A huge over 69% academicians and 53% UG/PG students thought that the employability of science and technology streams was greater than the social sciences. But a sizable 29% academicians and 25% UG/PG students felt that the employability of the science and technology streams was not greater than the social sciences.

Interpretation: The positive respondents gave the obvious and realistic answer about science and technology streams having greater employment scope. This is the lopsided reality that this project is trying to reveal. This project hypothesized the relative lower employment and entrepreneurship scope for the social sciences as compared to the science and technology streams. The project has also highlighted, with relevant secondary data, about the SC/ST students being disproportionately being forced into the social sciences streams due to their relatively lower secondary and higher secondary marks. GER of higher education in 2015- All- 24.3, SC-19.1, ST-13.7 and GER at senior secondary level All-54.2, SC -54.3, ST -38.8, (Source- Educational Statistics at a Glance, 2016, MHRD, GOI.) The SC GER at the senior secondary level is the highest at 54.3 but significantly tapers down to 19.1 at the higher education level, much below the higher education GER of all categories which stands at 24.3. Here significantly the all category GER includes the SC and ST data which significantly lowers the all category GER. Were the SC and ST GER deducted from the all category GER the real gap between the SC, ST GER and GER of the others shall be very big.

This, due to school examination systems that favoured memory and oratory skills with presentation in which the SC and ST students traditionally lag behind due to ancient socio-cultural ordination. Interdisciplinarity and interweaving of the social and natural sciences is the only way out to achieve holistic knowledge building and dignity and comparable incentivisation of mental and manual labour.

The research further probed into the reasons for greater employability of the science and technology streams.

Table 4.13: Reasons for Employability of Science and Technology streams

Sr. No.	Reasons for greater employment	Academicians	Students
1.	Company looking for expertise in workforce and natural sciences fulfill this need	07 (6.00)	01 (1.30)
2.	Technology improves analytical and technical ability and employability, helps in development	27 (23.30)	23 (29.10)
3.	Science and technology involve more in real productivity and real knowledge than social science	17 (14.70)	01 (1.30)
4.	Natural sciences have been able to make life easy and comfortable than social sciences.	02 (1.70)	00 (00)
5.	Because there are more openings in the field of higher research	01 (0.90)	03 (3.80)
6.	It is related to societal benefits and development of individual along with social and country development	01 (0.90)	00 (00)
7.	Traditional pattern of syllabus and same pattern is used to teaching and no technology in social sciences, less funding	06 (5.20)	06 (7.60)
8.	Not problem of the discipline but problem inapproach, people have different ideas	02 (1.70)	00 (00)
9.	Social sciences are more aesthetic and useless than pure sciences, Social values are changing	06 (5.20)	01 (1.30)
10.	Not applicable	36 (31.00)	37 (46.80)
11.	No Response	11 (9.50)	07 (8.90)
	Total	**116 (100)**	**79 (100)**

Observation: Over 23% academicians and 29% UG/PG students felt that technology improved analytical and technical ability and employability that help in development. Over 14% academicians and 1% UG/PG students felt that science and technology involved more real productivity and real knowledge than social sciences. Over 6% academicians and 1% UG/PG students felt that the companies looked for expertise in workforce and the natural sciences fulfilled these needs. Over 5% academicians and 1% UG/PG students thought that the social values were changing and even though the social sciences were more aesthetic they were less useful than the pure sciences.

Interpretation: The above data highlights the natural employability strengths of the sciences and technology streams over the social sciences. This is simply because we are following an economic model based on capitalism and consumption where relations between humans and utility objects are highly valued over relationships between individuals and communities. This is a result of the process of competition, instead of cooperation and contributed from the elementary school level itself. The higher the accumulation of the goods of consumption the greater social and financial status. Obviously as stated above the SC and ST are the biggest suffering communities as they are disproportionately lowly represented in the science and technology streams with consequent denial of higher employment opportunities.

The researcher further enquired into the reasons of why the academicians and UG/PG students thought that the sciences and technology streams had lesser employability than the social sciences.

Table 4.14: Reasons for Lower Employability of Social Science Streams compared to Science and Technology

Sr. No.	If no, why	Academicians	Students
1.	Employability depends on the state policy & not necessarily on the knowledge domain of social/ natural sciences	02 (1.70)	00 (00)
2.	All subjects have their own weightage and scope	08 (6.90)	01 (1.30)
3.	Social science is labour intensive where as pure science is laboratory intensive	01 (0.90)	00 (00)
4.	Social science employability is more rather than science and technology, deals with the various aspects of the society	04 (3.40)	04 (5.10)
5.	Both are equal, Employability does not vary much but quality matters	03 (2.60)	00 (00)
6.	Science and technology fields also have unemployment	02 (1.70)	00 (00)
7.	If skills and quality increased then employability will increase automatically in social sciences	02 (1.70)	02 (2.50)
8.	Social science are not linked with science and technology field	00 (00)	04 (5.10)
9.	Employability depends upon level of development in particular society	02 (1.70)	00 (00)
10.	Not applicable	83 (71.60)	62 (78.40)
11.	No Response	09 (7.80)	06 (7.60)
	Total	**116 (100)**	**79 (100)**

Observation: Over 3% academicians and 5% UG/PG students felt that the employability of social sciences is more than science and technology as it deals with the various aspects of the society. Over 6% academicians and 1% UG/PG students thought that all subjects had their own weightage and scope. Less than 1% academicians felt that social sciences was labour intensive whereas the natural sciences were laboratory intensive. Over 2% academicians felt that both were equal and employability did not vary much but quality mattered. Interestingly over 1% academicians thought that employability depended on the state policy and not necessarily on the knowledge domain of social/natural sciences. Over 1% academicians stated that employability depended upon level of development in any particular society.

Interpretation: The above data has sent mix responses and was finding roots of the un-employability of the social sciences in frameworks other than the curriculum and employment utility they possess.

(iv) Measures for Increasing the Employability of Social Sciences: The researcher asked the academicians for measures to increase the employability of social sciences.

Table 4.15: Measures for increasing the employability of social sciences - Academicians

Sr. No.	Responses	Total	Percent
1.	Social sciences should be applied, Introduce interdisciplinary course & their applications in social sciences	35	30.20
2.	Modify the social sciences on the basis of natural sciences, theory to practice	16	13.80
3.	Skills to be provided in the social sciences/ increase employability	13	11.20
4.	Need investment in social sciences and proper policy frame work, develop curricula on the societal needs	18	15.50
5.	Micro planning in all sectors of development, need broad approach in social intervention	01	0.90
6.	Create new knowledge and apply various types of institutions for education branches	02	1.70
7.	By organizing training for effective teaching and learning process	04	3.40
8.	No Response	27	23.30
Total		**116**	**100**

Observation: Over 30% of the academicians stated that the social sciences should be applied and new interdisciplinary courses and their applications in social sciences needed to be introduced. Over 13% of the respondents felt that the social sciences needed to be modified on the basis of the natural sciences where theory was brought to practice. Over 15% of the respondents stated that higher investment were needed in the social sciences with a proper policy framework and development of a curricula based on the societal needs. Over 3% of respondents thought it necessary to organise training for an effective teaching and learning process. Over 11% of respondents stated that skills should be provided in the social sciences to increase the employability.

Interpretation: The above responses highlight the creativity of the academicians for the utilitarian betterment of the social sciences in coalition with the natural sciences.

Interdisciplinarity and its Need

(i) What is Interdisciplinarity in Higher Education?: Going to specifics of interdisciplinarity the researcher queried with all three categories of respondents about what interdisciplinarity in higher education was.

A significant 46% academicians, 64% research student and 38% UG/PG students thought interdisciplinarity was integrating domains of two or more subjects. But even more surprisingly and interestingly over 19% academicians and research students and 44% UG/PG students thought it was integrating domains of the social and natural sciences. Over 26% academicians and 8% research students thought integrating domains of two or more subjects and disciplines was interdisciplinarity in higher education. Over 2% academicians and 1% research students thought the approaches of one field are applied to solve or understand other fields' problem. Over 1% research students and 6% students felt openness of ideas and thoughts for all domains was interdisciplinarity in higher education. And finally over 3% academicians felt that right now we do not have interdisciplinarity in higher education, but it is extremely important to have cross-fertilisation of ideas.

Interpretation: Most significantly justifying the main hypothesis of this research project, a significant numbers of academicians, research students and UG/PG students thought interdisciplinarity was integrating domains of the social and natural sciences and few academicians also thought it extremely important to have cross-fertilisation of ideas. These approaches augur well for the possibility and future of interdisciplinarity between the social and natural sciences making possible an overall change in approach to issue- solving than ego-retaining compartmentalisation of disciplines.

(ii) Scope for the subject to go interdisciplinary with other disciplines: The researcher further probed with all the types of respondents on the scope for their academic subjects to go interdisciplinary with other disciplines.

Table 4.17: Scope for the subject of respondent to go interdisciplinary

Sr. No.	Responses	Academician	Research Students	Students
1.	Yes	110 (94.80)	116 (85.30)	61 (77.20)
2.	No	03 (2.60)	06 (4.40)	14 (17.70)
3.	No Response	03 (2.60)	14 (10.30)	04 (5.10)
Total		**116 (100)**	**136 (100)**	**79 (100)**

Observation: A huge 94% academicians, 85% research students and 77% UG/PG students found scope for their subjects to go interdisciplinary with other disciplines.

Interpretation: This further underlines the necessity of and expectations from interdisciplinarity in higher education for the pursuit of holistic knowledge building.

The researcher enquired in to the reasons, from all types of respondents, as to what scope there subjects had to go interdisciplinary and the responses were as follows:

Table 4.18: Subject domains with scope to go Interdisciplinary

Sr. No.	If yes, with which subject	Academician	Research Students	Students
1.	Science in to science	23 (19.80)	22 (16.20)	05 (6.30)
2.	Science in to social science	12 (10.30)	04 (3.60)	02 (2.50)
3.	Science to science and social science	01 (0.90)	00 (00)	05 (6.30)
4.	Social Science to Social Science	36 (31.00)	56 (41.20)	18 (22.80)

(Contd...)

5.	Social Science to science	12 (10.30)	10 (7.40)	11 (13.90)
6.	All possible discipline	03 (2.60)	00 (00)	00 (00)
7.	Subaltern studies related work	01 (0.90)	00 (00)	00 (00)
8.	Subjects which are similar	02 (1.70)	00 (00)	01 (1.30)
9.	Social science to technology	04 (3.40)	00 (00)	01 (1.30)
10.	Social sciences to science and other social sciences	02 (1.70)	00 (00)	00 (00)
11.	Engineering to Engineering	07 (6.00)	00 (00)	00 (00)
12.	Professional Courses to Social sciences and natural sciences	02 (1.70)	00 (00)	04 (5.10)
13.	Commerce to Social Science	00 (00)	02 (1.50)	01 (1.30)
14.	No Response	05 (4.30)	20 (14.70)	13 (16.50)
15.	Not applicable	06 (5.20)	21 (15.40)	18 (22.80)
Total		**116 (100)**	**136 (100)**	**79 (100)**

Observation: Over 10% academicians, 3% research students and 2% UG/PG students thought that there was scope for interdisciplinarity between science and social sciences. Over 10% academicians, 7% research students and 13% UG/PG students thought that such scope was possible between the social sciences and pure sciences. Over 2% academicians thought there was scope for their subjects to go interdisciplinary as follows – science into science; science into social science; science to science and social science; social science to social science and social sciences to sciences. Over 3% academicians and 1% UG/PG students thought there was scope for interdisciplinarity between social science and technology. All other respondents thought there was scope for interdisciplinarity as is traditionally done among neighbouring subjects in the social sciences and pure sciences.

Interpretation: These perceptions of possibilities of scope for interdisciplinarity among the social sciences, natural sciences and technology are indeed interesting and significant for holistic knowledge outputs and removing the subtle inbuilt untouchability and compartmentalisation in the social and natural sciences.

The researcher further probed all the types of respondents for their reasoning on the lack of possibility for scope of their subjects going interdisciplinary.

Below 1% academicians thought that by nature visibly or invisibly, all subjects are interdisciplinary. Over 1% UG/PG students thought that in their subject they already had to study rural sociology and also psychology of farmers which was an interdisciplinary approach.

Interpretation: The minimal level of reasoning here actually underlines the scope for any subject to go interdisciplinary.

(iii) Scope for the subject to go Interdisciplinary with social/natural sciences: Taking things further, the researcher queried with the academicians, about the scope for their subjects to go interdisciplinary with social/natural sciences.

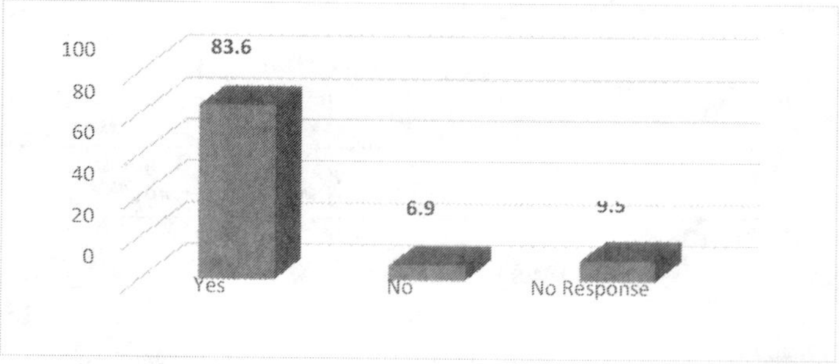

Graph 4.2: Scope for the subject of respondents to go Interdisciplinary with social/natural science – Academician.

Observation: Overwhelming 83% academicians thought there was scope for their subjects to go interdisciplinary with social/natural sciences. This indicates the mature understanding of knowledge building/application with holistic learning outputs and social implications on the part of the academicians.

The researcher asked the academicians on why they thought there was scope for their subjects to go interdisciplinary with the social/natural sciences.

Table 4.20: Reasons for subject to go ID with Social/Natural Sciences- Academician

Sr. No.	If yes, in what way	Academician
1.	As a tool of data collection	02 (1.70)
2.	To understand the subject in holistic manner/ address the problem or issues with the knowledge of both sciences	45 (38.80)
3.	It is already interdisciplinary with science and social science	03 (2.60)
4.	Teaching at international level	01 (0.90)
5.	Limited scope with natural science	02 (1.70)
6.	Appling interdisciplinary approach for their disciplines	18 (15.50)
7.	Not applicable	18 (15.50)
8.	No Response	27 (23.30)
Total		**116 (100)**

Observation: Over 38% said that it was to understand the subject in holistic manner and address the problem or issues with knowledge of both sciences. Over 15% said that they were applying interdisciplinary approach for their disciplines. Over 1% said that interdisciplinarity was a tool of data collection.

Interpretation: These responses underline the positive perceptions and undergoing practice of interdisciplinarity among the social and natural sciences at the higher educational level.

The researcher further queried why, if academicians thought there was no scope for their subjects to go interdisciplinary with social/natural sciences.

Over 1% academicians thought that it was currently difficult and needs sound work. Another 1% thought that the social sciences were governed by different sets of rules.

Interpretation: Such reasoning also underlines the practical difficulties of interdisciplinarity across the social and natural sciences.

(iv) Curriculum of Higher Education:

(a) Academicians' Participation in Curriculum Formation

Committee: The researcher enquired about the academicians' participation in curriculum formation committee.

A huge 69% academician had participated in the important academic task of curriculum formation.

(b) Weightage for the Component in the Curriculum: Further the academicians were queried about the composition of theory or applied in the curricula.

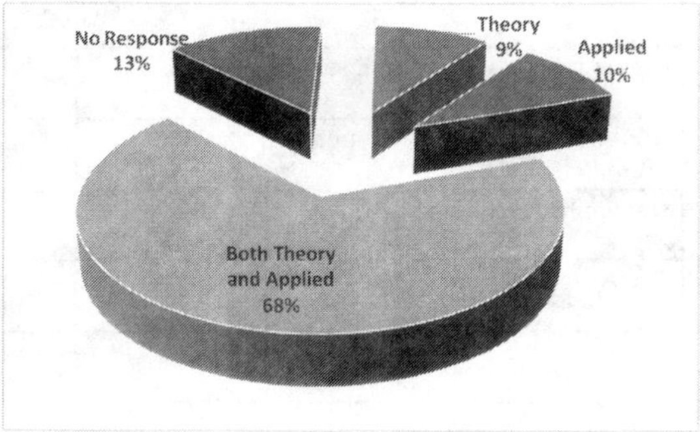

Graph 4.4: Weightage in the Curriculum-Academician.

Observation: A huge 68% academicians responded positively about the composition of both theory and application in curriculum formation. A similar 9.50% of academicians responded with weightage for only theory and only applied as composition of curriculum.

Table 4.22: Reasons behind Theory/Applied weightage in curriculum - Academicians

Sr. No.	Reasons	Total	Percent
1.	Both- Theoretical knowledge combined with practical application is necessary for proper understanding	60	51.70
2.	Theory - Theory teaching of every subject involves fundamental concepts and theory, applied aspect is relatively less	05	4.30
3.	Applied - Application is very important for development of society, empirical can be learnt more easily	09	7.80
4.	It has come as a practice. Now needs to change the system	01	0.90
5.	Not Applicable	15	12.90
6.	No Response	26	22.40
Total		**116**	**100**

The researcher tried to find out the reasoning behind the weightage composition of the curriculum.

Observation: Overwhelming 51% of academicians stated that theory and practical were equally important and theoretical knowledge combined with practical application was necessary for proper understanding.

Interpretation: This approach of the academicians looks balanced for the times but needs to go beyond assignments, project works and laboratory practicals towards real life interventions into socio-economic and technological contexts of life abounding. This was to be coupled with understanding the brick-by-brick construction of social need/products with due respect for manual and mental labour.

(c) Base of the Higher Education Curriculum: The researcher further asked the academicians, research students and students of UG/PG, whether the higher education curriculum be based on demand-supply market rule.

Interestingly 50% academicians, 45% research students and 51% UG/PG students wanted a higher education curriculum to be based on the demand-supply market rule and a shade less 45% academicians, 43% research students and 38% UG/PG students did not want so.

Interpretation: The positive responses probably are for the demand-supply market orientation of curriculum because of inclination towards creation of more employment, which depends on the level of demand in the market. This in a discrete manner, reveals a very practical life approach towards good living based on the principles of the market rather than a holistic view of sustainable social living. This scenario probably is rooted in competition instead of cooperation as the functioning processes from schooling life.

The researcher further asked all three categories of respondents, if they wanted higher education curriculum based on demand-supply marker rule, why it was so.

Table 4.24: Reasons for basis of demand-supply market rule

Sr. No.	If yes, reasons	Academician	Research Students	Students
1.	To increase the employability it should be based on demand supply market rule	26 (22.40)	28 (20.60)	16 (20.30)
2.	Due to development of emerging social status	02 (1.70)	00 (00)	00 (00)

(Contd...)

3.	In professional courses it should depend on demand supply market rule but in social sciences we don't do it	02 (1.70)	01 (0.70)	05 (6.30)
4.	It depends on the political stand and agenda of developed nations	01 (0.90)	00 (00)	00 (00)
5.	For the survival of the subject	02 (1.70)	04 (3.00)	00 (00)
6.	For more acceptability, Increasing demand for higher education	03 (2.60)	00 (00)	02 (2.60)
7.	It should depend on the basic needs, to understand basic human needs	01 (0.90)	05 (3.70)	06 (7.60)
8.	Curriculum should be formulated by taking involvement of industry market people, only then it will be applicable tosociety	02 (1.70)	05 (3.70)	03 (3.80)
9.	Because of higher competition between the student	04 (3.40)	00 (00)	00 (00)
10.	Not Applicable	58 (50.00)	74 (54.40)	38 (48.10)
11.	No Response	15 (12.90)	19 (14.00)	09 (11.40)
Total		**116 (100)**	**136 (100)**	**79 (100)**

Observation: Assessing the reasons given for higher education curriculum to be based on demand supply market rule a significant 22% academicians, 20% research students and 20 % UG/PG students mentioned that higher education curriculum should be based on demand-supply market rule to increase employability. 3% academicians thought of the same because of higher competition between the students. And 1 to 3% academicians, research students and UG/PG students were positive for demand-supply market rule to guide the higher education curriculum for the following reasons- due to development of emerging social status; in professional courses it should depend on demand supply market rule but in social sciences we don't do it; it depends on the political stand and agenda of developed nations; for the survival of the subject; for more acceptability, increasing demand for higher education; it should depend on the basic needs, to understand basic human needs; curriculum should be formulated by taking involvement of industry-market people, only then it will be applicable to society.

Interpretation: The reasoning for demand-supply is contemporary and concentrating on tackling competitive market scenario that is based on demand and supply. But this approach raises issues about who is setting the economic and social agenda of the society for long term interests. This matters for public interest and socio-economic interests of the SC and ST communities.

Assessing the reasons for higher education curriculum to not be based on demand supply market rule the following responses have come up.

Table 4.25: Curriculum not based on demand-supply market rule – reasons

Sr. No.	If no, reasons	Academician	Research Students	Students
1.	Educational institutes have a big role of disseminating knowledge, Higher education is not a commodity	07 (6.00)	00 (00)	08 (10.10)
2.	Because market demand changes dynamically now a days	04 (3.40)	19 (14.00)	06 (7.60)
3.	Social reality, Science and technology can't be effectively handled if it is based on demand supply market rule	02 (1.70)	16 (11.80)	01 (1.30)
4.	It should be knowledge based in holistic nature, we should not produce one dimensional man	24 (20.60)	06 (4.30)	02 (2.50)
5.	Curriculum construction is only based on formalities and subjectivity, It should be based on choice	05 (4.30)	00 (00)	04 (5.10)
6.	Only in terms of employment it should be based on demand supply market rule	00 (00)	04 (2.90)	00 (00)
7.	Curriculum structure is not appropriate for advanced technology	00 (00)	00 (00)	03 (3.80)
8.	Not Applicable	63 (54.30)	77 (56.60)	49 (62.00)
9.	No Response	11 (9.50)	14 (10.30)	06 (7.60)
Total		**116 (100)**	**136 (100)**	**79 (100)**

Observation: Over 20% academicians, 4% research students and 2% students felt that we should not produce a one-dimensional man and it should be knowledge based in holistic nature. 6% academicians felt that higher education was not a commodity and education institutes have a big role in disseminating knowledge. Over 3% academicians 14% research students and 7% students think that the demand supply market rule should apply because the market demand changes dynamically now-a-days. Over 1% academicians 11% research students and 1% UG/PG students think that social reality or science and technology won't be effectively handled if the higher education curriculum was based on demand supply market rule. Between 1 and 5% respondents of all three categories gave the following reasoning for higher education to be based on demand supply-market rule - curriculum construction is only based on formalities and subjectivity, it should be based on choice; only in terms of employment it should be based on demand supply-market rule; curriculum structure is not appropriate for advanced technology.

Interpretation: On a whole the reasoning are holistic and underlined the limitations of demand-supply market rule impact on higher education curriculum and try to understand the dynamics between social reality and science and technology moving towards an interdisciplinary and inclusive approach.

(d) Curriculum Deciding Authority: The researcher further tried to find the most important aspect of higher education i.e. who should decide the curriculum of higher education and why, from all the three categories of respondents and the responses are as follows:

Table 4.26: Curriculum Deciding Authorities and reasons

Sr. No.	Reasons	Academician	Research Students	Students
1.	Government Policy - Because Funding agency, agenda will be beneficial to all society	04 (3.40)	09 (6.60)	05 (6.30)
2.	HEIs – Because they are proficient to do so, They understand the societal needs as they interact with industry, involvement with other stakeholders	29 (25.00)	32 (23.50)	27 (34.17)
3.	Market – It should be comprehensive with community needs, Market gives scope to application, students should get updated knowledge for survival	02 (1.70)	02 (1.50)	01 (1.30)
4.	All - Because all these are the stakeholders, All these are interrelated and creating employment, all these have different perspective	50 (43.10)	50 (36.80)	20 (25.30)
5.	Govt. and HEIs – Because, Universities are not profit making centers in India	03 (2.60)	06 (4.40)	04 (5.10)
6.	No Response	28 (24.10)	37 (27.20)	22 (27.90)
Total		**116 (100)**	**136 (100)**	**79 (100)**

Observation: A significant 43% academicians, 36% research students and 25% UG/PG students responded that all three agencies i.e. government policies, higher education institutions (HEIs) and market should decide the curriculum of higher education because all of them are the stake holders and even when all them have different perspective they are interrelated and creating jobs. Secondly, 25% academicians, 23% research students and a higher 34% UG/PG students feel the HEIs should decide the curriculum of higher education as they are proficient to do so, involved with other stakeholders and understand the societal needs due to interactions with the industry. 3% academicians, 6% research students and UG/PG students thought the government policies should direct the curriculum of higher education as their agenda will be beneficial to the whole society and also because they are the funding agency. Interestingly, over 1% academician, research students and UG/PG students think that the market should decide the curriculum of higher education because students should get updated knowledge for survival as the market underlines the comprehensive community needs with scope for application. Further 2% academicians, 4% research students and 5% UG/PG students felt that the government policies and HEIs should together decide the higher education curriculum because the universities are not profit making centers in India.

Interpretation: The above data shows that a significant number of respondents thought that all the three agencies i.e. government policies, HEIs and market should decide the curriculum shows that a fine balance between the market rule and government agencies working for the welfare of the society at large. Surprisingly, a miniscule 1% of all three categories of respondents were for the market deciding the higher education curriculum. This response shows the huge lack of trust these learned adults have on the market. It reveals their bents towards public initiative and interest of welfare and sustainable development. And also we should not forget that over 80% of the respondents were from publically funded HEIs, components of which generally tend towards government initiative for development and welfare.

(e) Basic principles and features of an Interdisciplinary Curriculum: Taking the issue further the researcher enquired with the academician about the basic principles and features of an interdisciplinary curriculum. And the responses are as follows:

Table 4.27: Basic principles and features of an Interdisciplinary Curriculum - Academician

Sr. No.	Responses	Total	Percent
1.	It should be helpful for solution of problem, Job oriented, society oriented, market oriented	11	9.50
2.	Interaction with different disciplines and working together, Uniformity in social and pure science institutions	19	16.40
3.	New trends must be accommodated in interdisciplinary curriculum, IT must be used	13	11.20
4.	Social sciences need to understand the human value in scientific manner	03	2.60
5.	University have to set the ID course and curriculum and institutional framework	04	3.40

(Contd...)

6.	Theory and practical oriented course	05	4.30
7.	No Idea	02	1.70
8.	Balanced view of both, understanding the differences in nature of reality and knowledge	05	4.30
9.	Inter-related linked between the subjects of pure science	11	9.50
10.	No Idea	06	5.10
11.	No Response	37	31.90
	Total	**116**	**100**

Observation: Over 16% academicians desired uniformity in social and pure sciences in all institutions along with working together and interactions among different disciplines. Over 11% thought information communication technology must be used and new trends must be accommodated for an interdisciplinary curriculum. Over 4% thought that the ID curriculum should be a theory and practical oriented course and another 4% thought that while understanding the differences in nature of reality and knowledge there should be a balanced view of both. Over 9% thought that an interdisciplinary curriculum should be helpful for solutions to problems and jobs that were market and society oriented.

Over 9% thought that interdisciplinary curriculum was interrelated and linked between the subjects of pure science. Between 2 and 3% academicians thought that the university needs the ID course and curriculum with institutional framework and the social sciences need to understand human value in a scientific manner. Surprisingly, a significant 31% did not respond to this query probably because interdisciplinarity is not widespread and well understood in the country.

Interpretation: The reasoning are interesting with a focus on bringing social and pure sciences together to understand the theory and practice of human nature and utility of science and technology. This is actually indicative of an interdisciplinary approach balancing individual and social needs with the efficacy of application of science and technology. In the process, this promotes equality in dignity of mental and manual exertions moving towards social inclusion and sustainable development.

(f) Obstacles of Interdisciplinary Curricular Approach: The researcher further asked the academician to identify the obstacles of interdisciplinary curricular approach and the responses are as follows:

Table Missing

Over 25% academicians felt the lack of institutional framework, proper curriculum or resources to build an interdisciplinary curriculum. Over 25% felt that there was lack of vision, philosophical base, interest, and interdisciplinary knowledge to build such curricular approach. Between 0.9% and 3% academicians mentioned the following obstacles - Lack of interaction between the institutes of higher education, industry/market and society; conflict between students of different fields, mental blacks is one of the biggest obstacles; social sciences needs to understand the human value in scientific manner; team teaching is not involved; poor student will become more poorer than others. A significant 26% did not respond to this query and over 11% had no idea of this issue exposing the overall lack of existing and understanding of curricular interdisciplinarity in higher education.

Interpretation: The above data underlines the overall vacuum of ideas, knowledge, vision institutional framework and team-work in achieving an interdisciplinary curriculum. This also highlights the traditional compartmentalisation and unilinearity of disciplines ranging from the social to pure sciences and application. This is a big obstacle between social realities and applied solutions affecting holistic knowledge building and socio- economic inclusion.

(g) Solution to the obstacles of interdisciplinary curricular approach: The researcher further sought solutions to the obstacles of interdisciplinary curricular approach from the academician and the responses are as follows:

Table 4.29: Solution to the obstacles of Interdisciplinary Curricular approach- Academician

Sr. No.	Responses	Total	Percent
1.	Offer interdisciplinary courses on large scale and encourage students	29	25.00
2.	Need collaboration of industry and education institutions to increase employability	11	9.50
3.	Need of flexibility to design curriculum, integrate subjects which have more employability	12	10.30
4.	Make facilities available	11	9.50
5.	Need new scientific approach, use advanced technology	07	6.00
6.	Arrange sufficient funds for interdisciplinary courses	05	4.30
7.	Permission should not be given to private colleges, Donation system should be banned	01	0.90
8.	No Response	40	34.50
Total		**116**	**100**

Observation: The academicians gave the following solutions on the obstacles of interdisciplinary curricular approach. Over 25% academicians suggested offering interdisciplinary courses on large scale to encourage students. About 15% academicians thought arranging of sufficient funds and making facilities available to be conducive to growth to interdisciplinary curricular approach. And over 9% wanted collaboration of industry and educational institutions to increase the employability and over 10 thought design flexible curriculums and integrated subjects would also increase employability. And 6% academicians sought a new scientific approach and use of advance technology for an interdisciplinary curricular approach.

Interpretation: The solutions offered cover all aspects for creating an interdisciplinary curricular approach but a paradigm shifting step of interweaving the socio-economic context of science and technology leading to holistic knowledge creation and socially inclusive processes is necessary for sustainable development.

(v) Interdisciplinary Research:

(a) Nature of your research topic: The researcher asked the research students about the nature of their research topics.

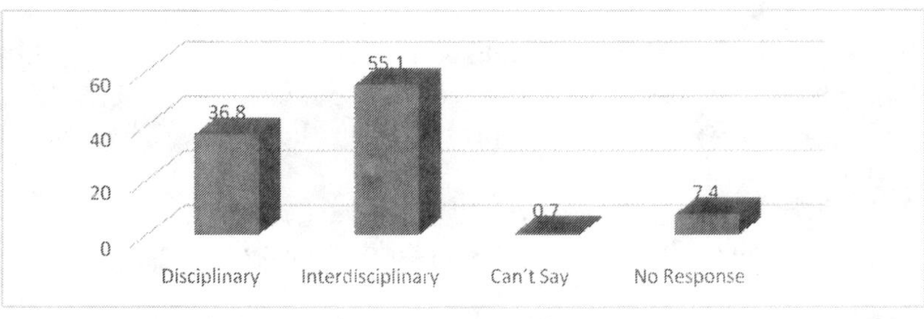

Graph 4.5: Nature of your research topic – Research Students

Observation: Over 36% responded that their research topic was disciplinary but a significantly higher 55% said that their research topic was interdisciplinary in nature.

Interpretation: This reveals the increasing space of interdisciplinary research in higher education but does not clarify about its status across the social and natural sciences.

(b) Strengths of Disciplinary Research: The researcher enquired with the research students about the strengths of disciplinary research and the responses were as follows:

Table 4.30: Strengths of Disciplinary Research– Research Students

Sr. No.	Strengths	Total	Percent
1.	Focused and in-depth study possible	13	9.60
2.	Academic criticism is possible as it is not interdisciplinary	01	0.70
3.	Researcher can explore his particular topic/idea with various angles	08	5.90
4.	We get job opportunities in particular area	02	1.50
5.	Related principles are applied easily, Intensive research work can be carried out	01	0.70
6.	Easy to study, easy to apply the principles and facts	06	4.40
7.	Disciplinary research employs ones knowledge to utilize it fully	01	0.70
8.	Not applicable	87	64.00
9.	No Response	17	12.50
Total		**136**	**100**

Observation: Over 9% research students, said that a focus and in-depth study was possible, underlining the strengths of disciplinary research. Over 5% felt that the researcher can explore his particular topic/idea with various angles. Over 4% felt that disciplinary research was easy to study and easy to apply the principles and facts. Over 1% research students felt that disciplinary research got them job opportunities in particular areas.

Interpretation: The research students underlined the traditional strengths, applications, and employability of disciplinary research.

(c) Weaknesses of Disciplinary Research: The researcher further enquired with the research students about weaknesses of disciplinary research and the responses are as follows:

Over 12% research students felt that due to disciplinary research there was lack of wider knowledge of other subjects and issues related to other subjects could be left out. Over 2% felt that it was not comprehensive and they couldn't get jobs in all domains. Over 1% felt that it creates theoretical knowledge and thinking in only one way. About 1% students felt that there was lack of faculty and material in the interdisciplinary field.

Interpretation: The above reasoning exactly underlines the weaknesses of disciplinary research that is creating the impetus for interdisciplinary research along with the exposure to Western holistic nature of knowledge building and application in higher education.

(d) Strengths of Interdisciplinary Research: The researcher queried with the research students about the strengths of interdisciplinary research and the responses are as follows.

Table 4.32: Strengths of Interdisciplinary Research – Research Students

Sr. No.	Strengths	Total	Percent
1.	Holistic, integrated and inclusive approach, chance to explore interesting outcome using ideas of different subjects	51	37.50
2.	Enable students to build their own interdisciplinary pathway, Able to incorporate social, economic, population science	02	1.50
3.	Greater employability	02	1.50
4.	Increasing skills adapting technology according to needs of our society	01	0.70
5.	It helps to take in account multiple dimensions of a problem	05	3.70
6.	It provides the career options in different fields and endorses the skills and capacity of your strength	02	1.50
7.	Not applicable	61	44.90
8.	No Response	12	8.80
	Total	**136**	**100**

Observation: Over 37% research students felt that interdisciplinary research had a holistic, integrated and inclusive approach, with a chance to explore interesting outcomes using ideas of different subjects. Over 3% thought it helped to take into account multiple dimensions of problems. Over 1% thought interdisciplinary research enabled students to build their own interdisciplinary pathway, provided greater employability in different fields and endorsed the strengths of skills and capacities of research students.

Interpretation: Contemporary times has brought the research students to appreciate the strengths of interdisciplinary research. This is appreciable.

(e) Weaknesses of Interdisciplinary Research: The research further probed, with the research students, about the weaknesses of interdisciplinarity.

Table 4.33: Weaknesses of Interdisciplinary Research – Research Students

Sr. No.	Weaknesses	Total	Percent
1.	In depth study may be not possible, a relative weaker specialisation possibility on a single topic	07	5.10
2.	Integration, confusion and time consuming curriculum preparation	07	5.10
3.	Lack of resource availability, less participation	08	5.90

4.	Some difficulties in understanding other domains, need to put extra efforts	12	8.80
5.	Difficult to seek employment	01	0.70
6.	Cannot focus on a particular issue based on the particular subject	11	8.10
7.	Research facilities not so proper	01	0.70
8.	Increases the cost incurred.	02	1.50
9.	Not applicable	63	46.30
10.	No Response	24	17.60
	Total	**136**	**100**

Observation: Over 8% research students thought there were some difficulties in understanding other domains which required extra efforts. While over 8% students could not focus on a particular issue based on the particular subject. Over 5% research students felt that an in-depth study may not be possible so a relatively weaker specialisation on a single topic; there could be confusion and time consuming curriculum preparation with lack of integration; and also low participation with lack of resource availability. Around 1% thought that interdisciplinary research increased costs along with non-availability of proper research facilities.

Interpretation: The research students had underlined the traditional and continuing difficulties faced by interdisciplinary research which need to be addressed urgently if we are to create holistic knowledge building systems.

(f) Choice of area of research: The researcher enquired with whose help the research students had chosen their area of research.

A huge 65% research students had themselves chosen their area of research. A significant 24% followed their guides' suggestion on an area of research. 2% received suggestions from their peer groups while over 4% articulated their area of research with the help of all the above options.

Interpretation: The huge number of research students choosing their own area of research reflects on their competence and inquisitive mindset for space of research. The self-choice of area of research would probably lead these students to go in-depths of their topics and possibly move into interdisciplinary domains in the quest of quality research outputs.

(g) Language of research: The researcher enquired about the language of research of the research students.

An overwhelming 89% research students conducted their research in English and between 1 and 2% conducted their research in the vernacular medium.

Interpretation: The abundance of students doing research in English is probably related to the researcher visiting elite public educational institutions of the country where English is the medium of instruction. This again is a matter of prejudice and discrimination against the rural, vernacular educated students who incidentally could be comprised heavily with the scheduled castes and scheduled tribes students.

(h) Difficulties in conducting interdisciplinary research: The researcher enquired about the difficulties in conducting interdisciplinary research with the research students.

Table 4.35: Difficulties in conducting interdisciplinary research– Research Students

Sr. No.	Difficulties	Total	Percent
1.	Lack of interdisciplinary study centers	17	12.50
2.	Unavailability of research facilities and literature for interdisciplinary research	14	10.30
3.	Rigid compartmentalisation of disciplines	23	16.90
4.	Unavailability of interdisciplinary faculty guidance	14	10.30
5.	Lack of broader approach towards a system	01	0.70
6.	Lack of interdisciplinary educational facility and funds	33	24.30
7.	All above	06	4.40
8.	None	16	11.80
9.	No Response	12	8.80
	Total	**136**	**100**

Observation: A significant 24% of the research students thought that lack of interdisciplinary education facilities and funds were difficulties in conducting interdisciplinary research. 12% thought lack of interdisciplinary study centers was an obstacle. Over 10% felt unavailability of research facilities and literature for interdisciplinary research were difficulties. Over 6% thought rigid compartmentalisation of disciplines, over 10% unavailability of interdisciplinary faculty guidance and about 1% thought lack of broader approach towards a system were difficulties in conducting interdisciplinary research. Over 4% of research students assigned all the above reasons as difficulties in conducting interdisciplinary research.

Interpretation: A significant 16% have underlined the rigid compartmentalisation of disciplines and a further 24% thought lack of interdisciplinary educational facilities and funds are the difficulties in conducting interdisciplinary research in India highlighting the rigid disciplinary nature of higher education in India and creates necessity for foundational changes, which are recommended in this project, to be undertaken.

(i) Solutions to academic obstacles in conducting Interdisciplinary research: The researcher further asked the research students for solutions to such academic obstacles in conducting interdisciplinary research.

Table 4.36: Solutions to academic obstacles in conducting Interdisciplinary research – Research Students

Sr. No.	Solutions	Total	Percent
1.	Restructure the compartmentalised educational structure, Increase the interactions, need strong interventions	17	12.50
2.	Starting ID study/research centers on large scale, Provision of facilities and literature, New/training faculty in ID	40	29.40
3.	Availability of ID subjects with regular subjects, Preference to interdisciplinary research	32	22.80
4.	All the above	21	15.40
5.	Not applicable	15	11.00
6.	No Response	12	8.80
	Total	**136**	**100**

Observation: Over 12% research students wanted restructuring of the compartmentalised education structure, increased interaction among disciplines with strong interventions as solutions to overcome obstacles in conducting interdisciplinary research. 40% thought starting ID study/ research centers on large scales providing facilities and literature and new faculty with training for expansion of interdisciplinary research. A significant 32% thought preference to be given to interdisciplinary research with availability of interdisciplinary subjects along with regular subjects. And another 21% gave all the above solutions to overcome academic obstacles in conducting interdisciplinary research.

Interpretation: The above data shows research students of the day wanting to find solutions for interdisciplinary research for modern socio-economic and technological issues and initiatives. The main objective of the research project necessitating interdisciplinarity in higher education is being proven.

(vi) Interdisciplinarity in Higher Education and Employability: To take matters further the researcher inquired with the academicians on how they could relate holistic learning, employability and inter-disciplinarity.

Observation: An overwhelming 97% of the academicians thought that they could relate holistic learning, employability and interdisciplinarity.

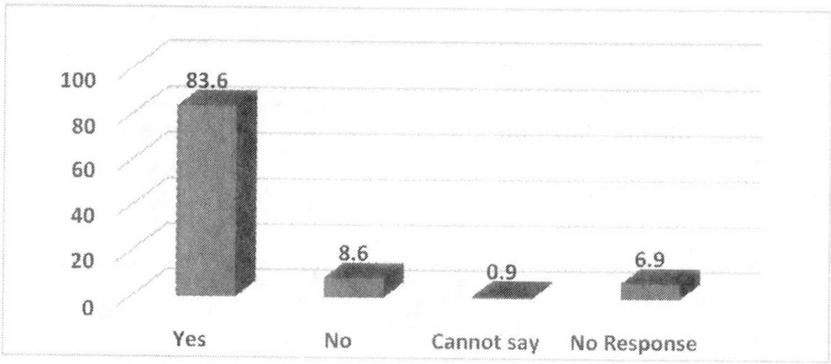

Graph 4.7: Relation between holistic learning, employability and interdisciplinarity- Academician.

Interpretation: This is a huge and positive response to the basic hypothesis of the research project which relates the three processes of holistic learning, employability and interdisciplinarity.

The researcher asked the academicians on how they could relate the above three processes.

Table 4.37: Reasons for relation between Holistic learning, Employability and ID- Academician

Sr. No.	If yes, how	Total	Percent
1.	ID across the discipline will get more employability and knowledge in various areas and develop skills and potential	43	37.10
2.	One has to understand the job market and skill requirements	06	5.20
3.	Design ID curriculum properly without losing depth of both sciences and it will be involved in all sectors	03	2.60
4.	Involve technology in social sciences for holistic knowledge and development	08	6.90
5.	Innovativeness, linking with natural sciences and technological development	04	3.40
6.	Need to spend 6% of GDP on education	01	0.90
7.	To be a professional one needs to be a complete personality, not just good at domain subject	08	6.90
8.	Gross functional knowledge is a requirement for advancement of any field	03	2.60
9.	Improvement in skill oriented sector, encouraging ITI teacher, training etc.	05	4.30
10.	Not applicable	19	16.40
11.	No Response	16	13.80
	Total	**116**	**100**

Observation: Over 37% of the academicians stated that inter-disciplinarity across the disciplines will get more employability, knowledge in various areas and develop skills and potentials. Over 5% felt that one had to understand the job market and skill requirement. Over 6% respondents felt that technology needed to be involved in social sciences for holistic knowledge and development. While another 6% felt that to be a professional one needed to be a complete personality and not just good at domain subject. Over 3% felt that innovativeness and linking with natural sciences and technological development was essential. Over 2% felt the necessity to design interdisciplinary curriculum properly without losing depth of both sciences and to be involved in all sectors. About 1% academicians felt the need to spend 6% of GDP on education.

Interpretation: The above responses highlight the creativity of academicians to relate the processes of holistic learning, employability and interdisciplinarity. Of great interest is the suggestion of spending 6% of GDP on education. India has never spent beyond 4% of GDP on education and within that the social sciences received the least. Here itself the neglect of and prejudices against the social sciences begins. We have never been able to appreciate the foundational significance of the social sciences for peaceful and prosperous community living. We fail to understand that the products of science and technology are just tools for human utility and consumption. Science and technology is an afterthought and development for an enriched social living. Science and technology represent the curiosity and anxiety of human engagement with nature. Social relationships are a priori.

And as stated earlier the SC and ST are disproportionately and unwillingly placed in the social sciences that neither offers much employability nor social status. The only solution to the unilinear leviathan is mouldability and integration with assimilation of the social sciences with the natural sciences in higher education. Only this will create space for holistic knowledge along with dignity of mental and manual labour.

The researcher further enquired into why the three processes could not be related.

Observation: The miniscule negative responses include over 2% academicians stating that holistic learning and employability may not go together in some cases. About 1% felt that the co-relation depended on the particular subject. About 1% thought that there was no relation in employment and social science. And another percent felt that all the three processes were separate and had different forms. Still another percent felt that employability and interdisciplinarity were interlinked but holistic learning was a vague concept.

Table 4.38: Reasons for Non-relation between Holistic learning, Employability and ID - Academician

Sr. No.	If no, why	Total	Percent
1.	It depends on the subject. In management subject these factors are linked	01	0.90
2.	There is no relation in employment and social science	01	0.90
3.	All are separated, they have different forms	01	0.90
4.	Employability and ID is interlinked but holistic learning is a vague concept	01	0.90
5.	Holistic learning and employability may not go together in some cases	03	2.60
6.	No Response	03	2.60
7.	Not applicable	106	91.40
	Total	**116**	**100**

Interpretation: The naysayers expressed their practical difficulties in relating the processes of holistic learning, employability and inter-disciplinarity.

Social and Educational Canvas of Interdisciplinarity

(i) Meaning of Social Inclusion in Higher Education: Coming to the main focus of the research project the researcher enquired with the research and UG/PG students about what they would understand by social inclusion in higher education.

Table 4.39: Understanding of social inclusion in higher education

Sr. No.	Responses	Research Students	Students
1	Equal opportunities of participation for all social sections in higher education	104(76.50)	67(84.80)
2	Providing and giving opportunities to study for all sections and their interdependability	15(15.00)	01(1.30)
3	The aspect of sociology should be appreciated and simultaneously linked with the education	02(1.40)	00(00)
4	No Response	15(11.00)	11(13.90)
	Total	**136(100)**	**79(100)**

Observation: An overwhelming 76% research and 84% UG/PG students underlined the need of equal opportunities of participation for all social sections in higher education. 15% research and 1% UG/PG students thought about providing and giving opportunities of studying for all sections with their interdependability. And over 1% research students felt that the aspect of sociology should be appreciated and simultaneously linked with education.

Interpretation: The overwhelming positive response to social inclusion by all students is incredibly socially progressive. Students realise the variation of contribution from the social diversity of the society as is done, to a large extent, in the United States of America. Proper nurture can take one to places unprecedented, only if cooperation and contribution is given primacy over competition which is an unnatural and anti-social learning process.

(ii) Interdisciplinarity and Human resources: The researcher further asked all the three types of respondents whether an interdisciplinary model of education could give greater justice to the diverse human resources in India.

Table 4.40: Possibility of ID model giving greater justice to the diverse human resources of India

Sr. No.	Responses	Academician	Research Student	Student
1.	Yes	102(87.90)	111(81.60)	66(83.50)
2.	No	06(5.20)	12(8.80)	06(7.60)
3.	No Response	08(6.90)	13(9.60)	07(8.90)
	Total	**116(100)**	**136(100)**	**79(100)**

Observation: A huge 87% academicians, 81% research students and 83% UG/PG students were positive to the idea of an interdisciplinary model giving greater justice to the diverse human resources in India.

Interpretation: This is a huge approval of the basic hypothesis of this project that wanted to relate higher education, interdisciplinarity and social inclusion.

The researcher further asked all the three types of respondents on why they thought such interdisciplinary model shall be giving greater justice to the diverse human resources of India.

Observation: Above 28% academicians, 7% research student and 5% UG/PG students felt that interdisciplinarity enhances skills, potential and increases employability. 6% academicians, 1% research student and 5% UG/PG students felt that innovation by the students with an interdisciplinary mindset will be beneficial for society. 17% academicians, 33% research students and 7% UG/PG students felt that interdisciplinarity provided a complete human resource and will be beneficial for the industry as well as the society. 6% academicians and 29% UG/PG students wanted focus on specific topic problems, exploration using skill and technique to gain complete knowledge. 4% academicians, 7% research students and 3% UG/PG students felt that in interdisciplinarity all sections were included hence it was more inclusive in nature.

Table 4.41: Reasons for ID Model giving greater Justice to human resources of India

Sr. No.	If yes, how	Total	Research Students	Students
1.	Innovation by the students with the ID mindset will be beneficial for society	07 (6.00)	02 (1.50)	04 (5.10)
2.	ID enhances skills, potential and increases employability	28 (24.10)	10 (7.40)	04 (5.10)
3.	ID provides complete human resource, it will be beneficial for industry and society as well	20 (17.20)	45 (33.10)	06 (7.60)
4.	All advanced science and technology needs to spread to the rural areas	02 (1.70)	02 (1.40)	00 (00)
5.	Focus on specific topic problems, Explore using skill and technique, Gain complete knowledge	07 (6.00)	00 (00)	23 (29.10)
6.	In the ID all sections are included hence it is more inclusive in nature	05 (4.30)	11 (7.40)	03 (3.80)
7.	Not Applicable	14 (12.10)	25 (18.40)	13 (16.50)
8.	No Response	33 (28.40)	41 (30.10)	26 (32.90)
	Total	**116 (100)**	**136 (100)**	**79 (100)**

Interpretation: The respondents have given justifiable solutions for an interdisciplinary model to give greater justice to the diverse human resources of India.

The researcher also enquired into why the three types did not feel that an interdisciplinary model will give greater justice to the diverse human resources of India.

Observation: Of the miniscule naysayers among all the types of respondent about 1% academicians and over 1% research students felt that both should have a bit of each other but should not be combined. About 1% academicians, 2% research students and over 3% UG/PG students felt that interdisciplinary education was not practiced in India and it was more confusing. About 1% academicians, research and UG/PG students

Table 4.42: Reasons for ID Model not giving greater Justice to Human Resources of India

Sr. No.	If no, why	Academician	Research Students	Students
1.	Both should have a bit of each other but should not be combined	01 (0.90)	02 (1.50)	00 (00)
2.	Loss of long term objective of education by giving skill development and vocational education	01 (0.90)	02 (1.50)	01 (1.30)
3.	Do not see any interdisciplinarity doing justice	01 (0.90)	02 (1.50)	00 (00)
4.	ID education is not practiced in India, it is more confusing	01 (0.90)	03 (2.20)	03 (3.90)
5.	At some point specialization is the solution	00 (00)	00 (00)	02 (2.50)
6.	Not applicable	110 (94.80)	124 (91.20)	73 (92.40)
7.	No Response	02 (1.70)	03 (2.20)	00 (00)
Total		**116 (100)**	**136 (100)**	**79 (100)**

thought that there was loss of long term objective of education by giving skill development and vocational education. About 1% academicians and research students did not see interdisciplinary model doing any justice to the diverse human resources of India. Over 2% UG/PG students thought that at some point specialisation was the solution.

Interpretation: The naysayers have put up there practical problems of an interdisciplinary model giving greater justice to the diverse human resources of India.

(iii) Reasons for the higher enrolment of underprivileged students in social sciences: The researcher tried to probe the reasons for the higher enrolment of underprivileged students in the social sciences.

Table 4.43: Reasons for the higher enrollment of underprivileged students in social sciences

Sr. No.	Responses	Academician	Research Students	Students
1.	Economic backwardness, cannot afford expensivescience and technology education, social sciences are easier and not expensive	24 (20.70)	23 (16.90)	19 (24.10)
2.	Fear of science and technology, Weak foundation, Natural sciences involve more objective and precise thinking	20 (17.20)	00 (00)	01 (1.30)
3.	Illiterate parents, lack of awareness, lack of guidance	29 (25.00)	08 (5.90)	02 (2.50)

(Contd...)

4.	Accessibility easier for social sciences, lack of science and technology education in rural areas	08 (6.90)	18 (13.20)	17 (21.50)
5.	Restriction on women but trend is changing now bio-tech	02 (1.70)	00 (00)	00 (00)
6.	Social sciences is more concerned with social development and inclusive policy	04 (3.40)	00 (00)	00 (00)
7.	Socio-economic backwardness, lack of guidance and educational institution in rural areas	00 (00)	28 (20.50)	01 (1.30)
8.	Socio-economic backwardness, low access to educational facilities, fall back in memory based education	01 (0.90)	00 (00)	20 (27.90)
9.	Social Backwardness	00 (00)	05 (3.70)	04 (5.10)
10.	All Above	05 (4.30)	36 (26.50)	07 (8.90)
11.	No Response	23 (19.80)	09 (6.60)	06 (7.60)
	Total	**116 (100)**	**136 (100)**	**79 (100)**

Observation: Over 20% academicians, 16% research students and 24% students of UG/PG thought that economic backwardness, unaffordable science and technology education and relative easiness of social sciences are reasons for the higher enrolment of underprivileged students in the social sciences. Over 17% academicians and 1% students thought there was fear of science and technology, weak foundation and the issue of natural sciences involving more objective and precise thinking as the reasons. Over 25% academicians, 5% research students and 2% UG/PG students held that illiterate parents, lack of awareness and lack of guidance to be the reasons. Over 6% academicians, 13% research students and 21% students of UG/PG felt that accessibility was easier to the social sciences and also science and technology education was lacking in the rural areas. Over 3% academicians felt that social science was more concerned with social development and inclusive policy. Over 20% research students and 1% UG/PG students again thought that socio-economic backwardness, lack of guidance and lesser number of education institutions in rural areas were the reason for the same. Nearly 1% academicians and over 23% students interestingly felt that apart from socio-economic backwardness and lack of access the important reason was that the underprivileged students fell back in memory-based examination-education system. Over 4% academicians, 26% research students and over 8% UG/PG students gave all the above reasons for the higher enrolment of underprivileged students in the social sciences.

Interpretation: The above data actually is a reflection of duality between public education and privatisation of education. The socio-economically weaker students are forced to take education from the publically funded schooling system going on to the higher education level with their obvious weaknesses of maths, sciences and languages. The underprivileged students, especially SC and ST, are average or poor in dealing with the rote and memory based examination systems forcing them into the social sciences which have been created uni-dimensionally, lacking in skill-sets and employment opportunities with only abstract and critical thinking abilities. Here in comes the issue of interdisciplinarity bringing together abstract and critical thinking along with skill-sets for holistic knowledge building and social inclusion where the SC and ST students shall get an opportunity to enter interdisciplinary courses with their strengths.

(iv) Inclusivity of Interdisciplinary Model:- The researcher further asked the academicians, research and UG/PG students whether an interdisciplinary model in social and pure sciences could give more opportunities to the underprivileged students.

Table 4.44: ID in social and natural sciences giving more opportunities to underprivileged students

Sr. No.	Responses	Academician	Research Student	Student
1.	Yes	82(70.70)	108(79.40)	64(81.00)
2.	No	18(15.50)	17(12.50)	05(6.30)
3.	Don't know	01(0.90)	00(00)	01(1.30)
4.	No Response	15(12.90)	11(8.10)	09(11.40)
	Total	**116(100)**	**136(100)**	**79(100)**

Observation: An overwhelming 70% academicians, 79% research students and 81% UG/PG students were positive that an interdisciplinary model of higher education in social and pure sciences could give more opportunities to underprivileged students.

Interpretation: This overwhelming response for establishing relationship between higher education, interdisciplinarity and social inclusion is interesting. The main players of the education system are realising the essence of interdisciplinarity and participation and contribution of the social diversity of the country.

The researcher further asked all the three types of respondents on how interdisciplinarity in social and pure sciences could give more opportunities to the underprivileged students.

Table 4.45: Reasons for ID in Social and Natural Sciences giving more Opportunities to underprivileged students

Sr. No.	If yes, How	Academician	Research Students	Students
1.	Offer ID courses across the discipline to underprivileged students which increases their knowledge, employment	37 (31.90)	23 (16.80)	03 (3.80)
2.	Our education needs to be made more effective with interdisciplinary courses	03 (2.60)	04 (3.00)	00 (00)
3.	Student may have to choose the subjects which are more in demand in the market	07 (6.00)	00 (00)	05 (6.30)
4.	Providing technological skills to students from rural and disadvantaged groups gives more opportunities	04 (3.40)	12 (8.90)	24 (30.40)
5.	ID generates more opportunities but might not be more inclusive	01 (0.90)	38 (27.90)	01 (1.30)
6.	There are quota system in all part of the education so it is helpful to inclusion	02 (1.80)	00 (00)	00 (00)
7.	ID explores the domains of science and technologyIt will be useful to all members of society	06 (5.20)	08 (5.90)	03 (3.80)
8.	Language and computer skill is to be improved	02 (1.70)	00 (00)	03 (3.80)
9.	Not Applicable	34 (29.30)	28 (20.60)	15 (19.00)
10.	No Response	20 (17.20)	25 (18.40)	25 (31.60)
	Total	**116 (100)**	**136 (100)**	**79 (100)**

Observation: Over 31% academicians, 16% research students and 3% UG/PG students responded that offering interdisciplinary courses across the disciplines to underprivileged students shall increase their knowledge and employment levels. Over 2% academicians and 3% research students felt that our education system has to be made more effective with interdisciplinary courses. Over 3% academicians, 8% research students and over 13% UG/PG students thought that by providing technological skills to students from rural and disadvantaged groups creates more opportunities. About 1% academicians, 27% research and over 1% students of UG/PG felt that interdisciplinarity generates more opportunities but might not be more inclusive. Over 5% academicians and research students along with 3% UG/PG students thought that interdisciplinarity explored the domains of science and technology which shall be useful to all members of the society.

Interpretation: The above data proves the overwhelming response of the academicians, research students and UG/PG students for the positive and practical implications in favour of the underprivileged students including SC and ST, if an interdisciplinary model of higher education in social and pure sciences in implemented.

The researcher further enquired with the miniscule naysayers among the academicians, research students and UG/PG students why they thought an interdisciplinary model of higher education in social and natural sciences shall not give more opportunities to the underprivileged students.

Table 4.46: Reasons for ID Model in Social and Natural Sciences not giving more opportunities to underprivileged students

Sr. No.	If no, why	Academician	Research Students	Students
1.	Employment and employability cannot be combined	03 (2.60)	00 (00)	00 (00)
2.	The teaching and learning of sciences should not be manipulated with other objectives	01 (0.90)	00 (00)	00 (00)
3.	Inclusion does not depend on ID of different disciplines, Inclusive policy should be strengthened at higher level	03 (2.60)	00 (00)	00 (00)
4.	Exclusion does not emerge by compartmentalization of subject, it is social, geographical and financial problem	01 (0.90)	00 (00)	00 (00)
5.	Relation of interdisciplinary study with the underprivileged, any other special case students need to be justified	00 (00)	03 (2.20)	00 (00)
6.	Science and technology education is expensive underprivileged students need financial assistance	01 (0.90)	03 (2.20)	00 (00)
7.	Lack of institution to give quality education, lack of resources	04 (3.50)	00 (00)	00 (00)
8.	Need to give education of their interest to all	03 (2.60)	00 (00)	01 (1.30)
9.	Conditions of unemployment in India was not because of Inter disciplinarity	00 (00)	03 (2.20)	00 (00)
10.	It will be helpful to privileged students to monopolize the mainstream academics	00 (00)	04 (2.90)	00 (00)
11.	Students will be confused to get job in a particular field	00 (00)	00 (00)	02 (2.60)
12.	Not applicable	98 (84.50)	119 (87.50)	74 (93.70)
13.	No Response	02 (1.70)	04 (2.90)	02 (2.50)
	Total	**116 (100)**	**136 (100)**	**79 (100)**

Observation: The miniscule naysayers include 2% academicians who said employment and employability cannot be combined. Over 2% academicians felt that inclusion did not depend on interdisciplinarity of different disciplines and the inclusion policy should be strengthened at higher levels. About 1% academicians feel that exclusion did not emerge by compartmentalisation of subjects, it is social, geographical and financial problem. Over 2% research students felt that relation of interdisciplinary study with the underprivileged or any other special case students' needs to be justified. Over 2% research students said that conditions of unemployment in India were not due to interdisciplinarity. Over 2% UG/PG students felt that higher education students will be confused to get job in a particular field.

Interpretation: The above data expresses the difficult path in achieving an interdisciplinary social and natural sciences model of higher education with positive implications for the underprivileged students.

(v) Social Category-wise responses on Interdisciplinarity: The researcher asked all respondents about the necessity of interdisciplinarity, how interdisciplinarity helps all in general and the underprivileged students in particular. The category-wise perceptions of the respondents are as follows:

Table 4.47: Perceive Necessity of Interdisciplinarity across the Social and Natural Sciences: Social Category-wise Perception of research students

Social Categoryof Research Students	Perceive Necessity of Interdisciplinarity across the Social and Natural Sciences						Total	
	Yes		No		No Response			
	Research Students	Students UG&PG	Research Students	Students UG&PG	Research Students	Students UG&PG	Research Students	Students UG&PG
Open	52 (88.13)	45 (91.84)	03 (5.08)	02 (4.08)	04 (6.78)	02 (4.08)	**59 (100)**	**49 (100)**
SC	26 (86.67)	11 (78.57)	02 (6.67)	01 (7.14)	02 (6.66)	02 (14.29)	**30 (100)**	**14 (100)**
ST	06 (75)	01 (50)	00 (00)	00 (00)	02 (25)	01 (50)	**08 (100)**	**02 (100)**
OBC	33 (100)	10 (83.33)	00 (00)	02 (16.67)	00 (00)	00 (00)	**33 (100)**	**12 (100)**
Minority	04 (100)	--	00 (00)	--	00 (00)	--	**04 (100)**	--
No Response	02 (100)	01 (50)	00 (00)	00 (00)	00 (00)	01 (50)	**02 (100)**	**02 (100)**

Social category-wise perception of research students and UG/PG students about necessity of interdisciplinarity across the social and natural sciences is given in the above table. The table reveals that a huge numbers of respondents from various category perceive necessity of interdisciplinarity across the social and natural science. Over 88% research students from open category, over 86% research students of SC category, 75% from ST and 100% of OBC and Minority research students perceived the necessity of interdisciplinarity between the social and natural sciences. Only 5% of open and over 6% from SC category research students did not perceive the necessity interdisciplinarity in social and natural sciences.

As per above table all UG and PG students gave a positive response to this question. A huge number of over 91% students from open category, over 78% from SC, over 83 from OBC and 50% from ST and NT category perceived the necessity of interdisciplinarity across the Social and Natural sciences. Only 16% from OBC category, over 4% from open and 7% from SC category UG and PG students did not perceive necessity of interdisciplinarity across the science and social sciences. 6 students from all the category did not respond to this question.

The above table clearly shows that an overwhelming percentage of research, UG and PG students perceived the necessity of interdisciplinarity across the social and natural sciences this reveals their awareness of the strengths and weakness of the social and natural sciences in independent perspectives. They show the awareness of the needs of diverse job portfolio that required an interdisciplinary knowledge perspective for enhanced productivity and sustenance.

The researcher asked the research students and UG and PG about the helpfulness of interdisciplinary model for the diverse human resources of India and the responses are as follows:

Table 4.48: Shall ID model give greater Justice to the Diverse Human Resources in India Category-wise perception of Research Students

<table>
<tr><th rowspan="3">Social Categoryof Research Students</th><th colspan="6">Shall ID model give greater justice to the diverse human resources in India</th><th colspan="2" rowspan="2">Total</th></tr>
<tr><th colspan="2">Yes</th><th colspan="2">No</th><th colspan="2">No Response</th></tr>
<tr><th>Research Students</th><th>Students UG&PG</th><th>Research Students</th><th>Students UG&PG</th><th>Research Students</th><th>Students UG&PG</th><th>Research Students</th><th>Students UG&PG</th></tr>
<tr><td>Open</td><td>49 (83.05)</td><td>43 (87.75)</td><td>03 (5.08)</td><td>03 (6.12)</td><td>07 (11.86)</td><td>03 (6.12)</td><td>**59 (100)**</td><td>**49 (100)**</td></tr>
<tr><td>SC</td><td>25 (83.33)</td><td>11 (78.57)</td><td>02 (6.67)</td><td>01 (7.14)</td><td>03 (10)</td><td>02 (14.28)</td><td>**30 (100)**</td><td>**14 (100)**</td></tr>
<tr><td>ST</td><td>06 (75)</td><td>01 (50)</td><td>00 (00)</td><td>00 (00)</td><td>02 (25)</td><td>01 (50)</td><td>**08 (100)**</td><td>**02 (100)**</td></tr>
<tr><td>OBC</td><td>27 (81.82)</td><td>10 (83.33)</td><td>06 (18.18)</td><td>02 (16.67)</td><td>00 (00)</td><td>00 (00)</td><td>**33 (100)**</td><td>**12 (100)**</td></tr>
<tr><td>Minority</td><td>03 (75)</td><td>--</td><td>00 (00)</td><td>--</td><td>01 (25)</td><td>--</td><td>**04 (100)**</td><td>--</td></tr>
<tr><td>NT</td><td>--</td><td>01 (50)</td><td></td><td>00 (00)</td><td>--</td><td>01 (50)</td><td>--</td><td>**02 (100)**</td></tr>
<tr><td>No Response</td><td>01 (50)</td><td>--</td><td>01 (50)</td><td>--</td><td>00 (00)</td><td>--</td><td>**02 (100)**</td><td>--</td></tr>
</table>

A huge over 83% of research students from open category, 83.33% from SC, 75% from ST, over 81% from OBC and 75% of Muslim minority gave positive response that the Interdisciplinary model can give greater justice to the diverse human resources in India. Only 5% research students from open category, over 6% from SC and above 18% from OBC category gave negative response.

A huge 87.75% UG/PG students from open category, above 78% from SC, above 83% from OBC, 1 students from ST and 1 from NT gave positive response to this query. 16.67% students from OBC category, 7% from SC and only 6% from open category gave a negative response and 7 students did not respond to this question.

The above table reveals in a huge manner the perceptions of research, UG and PG students that an interdisciplinary model shall give greater justice to diverse human resources of India. This positive response acknowledges that students with particular social background find the necessity of acquiring diverse knowledge and skill sets for improved outcomes.

Further the researcher asked the research students and UG&PG students whether interdisciplinary model across the Social and Natural sciences gave more justice to the underprivileged students and the responses are given below-

Table 4.49: ID in Social and Natural Sciences could give more opportunities to Underprivileged student's-perception of Research Students

Social Category ofResearch Students	ID in social and pure sciences could give more opportunities to underprivileged students							Total	
	Yes		No		Don't Know	No Response			
	Research Students	Students UG&PG	Research Students	Students UG&PG	Students UG&PG	Research Students	Students UG&PG	Research Students	Students UG&PG
Open	43 (72.88)	42 (85.71)	10 (16.95)	01 (2.04)	01 (2.04)	06 (10.17)	05 (10.20)	**59 (100)**	**49 (100)**
SC	26 (86.66)	10 (71.42)	02 (6.67)	02 (14.29)	00 (00)	02 (6.67)	02 (14.29)	**30 (100)**	**14 (100)**
ST	05 (62.50)	01 (50)	01 (12.50)	00 (00)	00 (00)	02 (25)	01 (50)	**08 (100)**	**02 (100)**
OBC	28 (84.85)	10 (83.33)	04 (12.12)	02 (16.67)	00 (00)	01 (3.03)	00 (00)	**33 (100)**	**12 (100)**
Minority	04 (100)	--	00 (00)	--	--	00 (00)	--	**04 (100)**	**--**
No Response	02 (100)	01 (50)	00 (00)	00 (00)	00 (00)	00 (00)	01 (50)	**02 (100)**	**02 (100)**

All the research students from different categories gave positive reply to this question. In that over 72% research students from open category, over 86% from SC, over 62% from ST, over 84% from OBC and all students from Muslim minority students agreed about the importance of the interdisciplinary model for availability of greater opportunities to the underprivileged students. On the other hand only 16% research students from open category, about 12% from ST and OBC and only over 6% research students from SC category deny the importance of ID model to get the opportunities to underprivileged students. 10% from open, 2 from SC, ST and 1 research student from OBC category did not give any response to this query.

An overwhelming 85% students from open category, 83% from OBC, 71% from SC category and 50% students from ST and NT category gave a positive response to this question. Only over 16% students from OBC, 14% from SC and 2% from open category gave a negative response. 10% from open category, 14% from SC and 1 from ST and 1 students from NT category did not give any response to this query.

The above table hugely acknowledges the hypothesis of poor opportunity space for the underprivileged student ranging from the social to the natural sciences and technical professions. This acknowledgement validates this book basic hypothesis of the interrelationship between higher education, interdisciplinarity and inclusiveness. This outcome of the table also throws lights upon the schooling evaluation system largely based on memorisation and presentation with little understanding leading to underperformance, especially of the socio-economically underprivileged students who lack in background, grooming, provisions and thus confidence.

Acceptability of new Interdisciplinary Approach

(i) Do you perceive necessity of Interdisciplinarity across the Social and Natural Sciences: To take matters further the researcher probed – do you perceive necessity of interdisciplinarity across the social and pure sciences with all the three categories of respondents.

Table 4.50: Necessity of Interdisciplinarity Across the Social and Natural Sciences

Sr.No.	Responses	Academician	Research Scholar	Students
1.	Yes	101(87.10)	123(90.40)	68(86.10)
2.	No	15(12.90)	05(3.70)	05(6.30)
3.	No Response	—	08(5.90)	06(7.60)
	Total	**116(100)**	**136(100)**	**79(100)**

Observation - A huge 87% academicians, over 90% research students and 86% UG/PG students perceived the necessity of interdisciplinarity across the natural and social sciences. While 12% academicians 3% research students and 6% students of UG/PG did not perceive any such necessity.

Interpretation: This huge positive response underlines the academicians and students realisation of limitations of compartmentalised higher education and yearning for interdisciplinary approach in the same.

The researcher further probed with all the three types of respondents on why they perceived the necessity of interdisciplinarity across the social and the pure sciences.

Table 4.51: Positive Necessity of ID across social and natural sciences - reasons

Sr. No.	Reasons	Academician	Research Scholar	Students
1.	Essential for holistic knowledge	17 (14.70)	26 (19.20)	13 (16.50)
2.	It helps to expand learning and employability in social sciences	02 (1.70)	14 (10.20)	04 (5.10)
3.	Better understanding of social issues refining output of natural sciences and technology	23 (19.80)	26 (19.10)	32 (40.50)
4.	For holistic knowledge and better employability	23 (19.80)	26 (19.20)	07 (8.80)
5.	Exploration for needs of society and country is necessary	02 (1.70)	03 (2.20)	00 (00)
6.	All above	22 (19.00)	00 (00)	07 (8.80)
7.	For holistic knowledge and understand the social utility and refinement of technology	00 (00)	27 (19.80)	04 (5.10)
8.	Not Applicable	15 (12.90)	13 (9.60)	08 (10.10)
9.	No Response	12 (10.30)	01 (0.70)	04 (5.10)
Total		**116 (100)**	**136 (100)**	**79 (100)**

Observation: Over 14% academicians, 19% research students and 16% students of UG/PG thought interdisciplinarity across the social and pure sciences was essential for creation of holistic knowledge. 19% of academicians and research scholars along with 40% students of UG/PG thought better understanding of social issues would be refining output of natural sciences and technology. 19% academicians and research scholars with 8% UG/PG students thought this interdisciplinarity brought holistic knowledge and better employability. 1% academicians, 10% research scholars and 5% students thought this interdisciplinarity would expand learning and employability in social sciences. 1% academicians and 2% research students thought such interdisciplinarity was essential for exploration to fulfill needs of society and the country. 19% academicians and 8% UG/PG students gave all the above reasoning for their perceived necessity of interdisciplinarity across the pure and social sciences.

Interpretation: All the above reasoning underlines the understanding and appreciation of interdisciplinarity across social and natural sciences as understood by all the three types of respondents. This bodes well for the upcoming dynamics of knowledge creation and assimilation to be formed on the all-round issue based approach and socially inclusive pursuit of solutions.

The researcher further asked about the reasons of why a few respondents did not perceive the necessity of interdisciplinarity across the social and pure sciences.

Over 3% academicians, below 1% research students and 1% UG/PG students thought that the sciences had different approaches than social sciences and interdisciplinarity was possible within the social sciences only. Over 1% academicians and research students and 2% UG/PG students thought that one could get mastery in one subject only, there was no time to spend on other subjects to go interdisciplinary and also in-depth knowledge was not possible. Over 1% academicians thought there was little scope for social sciences to go interdisciplinary like medical sociology.

Interpretation: These miniscule naysayers have underlined the practical problems obstructing interdisciplinarity across the social and natural sciences. But there sheer minimal numbers against the huge positive approach of the earlier table underlines the feasibility and future of interdisciplinarity across social and natural sciences in higher education of India.

(ii) Current Degree/Diploma of Students: Further, the researcher asked the students about his/her current degree/diploma and the responses are as follows:

Table 4.11: Current Degree/ Diploma – Students

Sr. No.	Current Degree	Total	Percent
1.	M.A.	10	12.70
2.	M. Sc	05	6.30
3.	M. Ed	08	10.10
4.	B. Ed	08	10.10
5.	B. Sc	14	17.70
6.	MSW	10	12.70
7.	MBA	05	6.30
8.	B. Tech	06	7.60
9.	LLB	10	12.70
10.	No Response	03	3.80
Total		**79**	**100.0**

As evident from the above graph 12.70% students of the UG/PG were pursing M.A., 6.30% M.Sc., 10.10% M.Ed., 10.10% B.Ed., 17.70% B.Sc.,

12.70% MSW, 6.30% MBA, 7.60% B. Tech and 12.70% LLB. Moreover, 3.80% students did not give any response to this question.

In all, among the UG/PG students, 48.10% were pursuing post-graduation degree and 48.10% students pursing graduation degree.

(iii) Reasons for undertaking the current degree/diploma: The researcher tried to find the logic of pursuit of particular degree/diploma by the students and the responses are as follows:

Table 4.53: Reasons for undertaking the current degree/diploma- Students

Sr. No.	Reasons for undertaking the current degree/diploma	Total	Percent
1.	High employability of the Degree/ Diploma	13	16.50
2.	Didn't get admission in Degree/ Diploma of first choice	05	6.30
3.	On the suggestion of parents and relatives	02	2.60
4.	Peer group choice	03	3.80
5.	My own choice	54	68.30
6.	No Response	02	2.50
	Total	**79**	**100**

Observation: From the above table it is to be noted that a huge 68% students made their own choices of higher education degree/diploma pursuits. This shows the empowered decision-making of the youth of the day. Over 16% students considered the employability prospect of the degree/ diploma they pursued.

(iv) Want to change the current degree/ diploma: The researcher asked the students whether they wanted to change their current degree/ diploma.

Table 4.54: Want to change the current degree/ diploma – Students

Sr. No.	Change the current degree	Total	Percent
1.	Yes	08	10.10
2.	No	70	88.60
3.	No Response	01	1.30
	Total	**79**	**100**

Observation: A huge over 88% students declined to change from their current degree/diploma pursuits expressing well informed confidence levels. The researcher went into the reasons of the 10% students that wanted to change their current degree/diploma.

Table 4.55: Reasons for change in current degree/diploma - Students

Sr. No.	If yes, specify reasons	Total	Percent
1.	Not enough scope this course	02	2.50
2.	Because of competition and employment opportunity	01	1.30
3.	Due to high interest in subject of physics	01	1.30
4.	Paper study structure and syllabus not updated	01	1.30
5.	I feel the practical exposure which we get could be enhanced as the course has a lot application in field	01	1.30
6.	Different area of interest	02	2.50
7.	Not applicable	70	88.60
8.	No Response	01	1.30
	Total	**79**	**100**

Observation: The above table explains various reasons of the students wanting to change from their current degree/diploma. These include 2.50% who said that there was not enough scope in this course, 1.30% said less employment opportunity, 1.30% said he/she had high interest in subject of physics, 1.30% said paper study structure and syllabus not updated, 1.30% feel the practical exposure which we get could be enhanced as the course has a lot of application in the field, 2.50% students were interested in the other subjects and 1.30% did not give any response to this question.

(v) Nature of Subject/ Degree/ Diploma of the Students: The researcher enquired about the theory and practical contents of the degree/ diploma with the students and the responses are as follows:

Table 4.56: Nature of Subject/ Degree/ Diploma- Students

Sr. No.	Nature of Subject	Course/Programme of the Students							
		M.A	M.Ed.	LLB	MSW	MBA	B.Sc.	M.Sc.	B.Tech
1.	Heavily theory oriented	02 (2.53)	01 (1.26)	02 (2.53)	00 (00)	01 (1.26)	05 (6.32)	00 (00)	00 (00)
2.	Practical oriented	01 (1.26)	00 (00)	00 (00)	01 (1.26)	01 (1.26)	00 (00)	05 (6.32)	01 (1.26)
3.	Mixture of Both	06 (7.59)	18 (22.78)	07 (8.86)	09 (11.39)	03 (3.79)	09 (11.39)	00 (00)	06 (7.59)
4.	No Response	00 (00)	00 (00)	01 (1.26)	00 (00)	00 (00)	00 (00)	00 (00)	00 (00)
	Total	**09 (11.39)**	**19 (24.05)**	**10 (12.65)**	**10 (12.65)**	**05 (6.32)**	**14 (17.72)**	**05 (6.32)**	**07 (8.86)**

Observation: From the above table it is interesting to note that over 7% students from the general M.A. course opined that their curriculum was a mixture of both theory and practice. Here they probably considered assignments and such project work including fieldwork as practical content which is fair enough. Students of the professional courses like M.Ed., LLB and MBA also significantly opined to have a curriculum composed of both theory and practicals. Even the students of professional degree of B. Tech. said that their curriculum was a mixture of both. And interestingly, all the students of M.SC opined that their course was practical oriented.

Interpretation: The above data is heavily in favour of mixture of theory and practical but in actuality the marks-wise theory weightage is much more than practicals. This peculiar mixture represents the domination of the mental and presentation exertions of the students on the learning process based on doing and learning represented by physical or manual actions. As explained earlier this equation also represents the ancient model of dominance by the head over the hands leaving members of the lower strata at a loss without comparative skills of reading, reciting and presentation.

(vi) Percentage of practical content in Subject/ Degree/ Diploma: The researcher further queried about the percentage composition of the practicals with the students.

Table 4.57: Percentage of practical component in Curriculum- Students

Sr. No.	Percent of the practical	Total	Percent
1.	10% to 20%	04	5.10
2.	21% to 30%	10	12.70
3.	31% to 40%	11	13.90
4.	41% to 50%	13	16.50
5.	Above 51%	11	13.90
6.	No Response	30	38.00
	Total	**79**	**100**

Observation: The above table represents the practical component of curricula as a rising graph with over 5% claiming their practical content to be between 10 and 20% to over 13% students claiming it to be above 50 percent. This pattern probably reflects the rising curricular components of practicals from social sciences to the natural sciences and technology.

(vii) Need of practical content to improve learning: The researcher further queried, with the students, about the need of practical content to improve the employability prospects and the responses are as follows:

Table 4.58: Need of practical content to improve learning and employability prospects-Students

Sr. No.	Responses	Total	Percent
1.	Yes	45	57.00
2.	No	30	38.00
3.	No Response	04	5.10
	Total	**79**	**100**

Observation: A significant 57% wanted increase in practical content for improved learning and employability prospects. But surprisingly a significant 38% did not find necessary any increase in the practical contents.

Interpretation: Probably these students were from the social sciences background that did not require any practical component. This also exposes the uni-dimensionality and irreverence to the relationship between learning, skills and employability or entrepreneurship. This is another major reason and objective of this project to understand mutual exclusion of higher education, interdisciplinarity and inclusion.

On further query of how the practical content could be incorporated, the students gave the following responses.

Table 4.59: Ways of incorporation of practical content - Students

Sr. No.	If yes, in what way	Total	Percent
1.	Practically engagement helps to understand the subject easily, field work oriented content to be include	25	31.60
2.	Apply the statistical tools to understand the real life	03	3.80
3.	More field work and internship opportunities	06	7.60
4.	By providing practical equipment's and facilities to each student	03	3.80
5.	Communication skill development, use of technology	01	1.30
6.	It improve the knowledge and quality of education	03	3.80
7.	Not applicable	30	38.00
8.	No Response	08	10.10
	Total	**79**	**100**

Observation: Over 31% students wanted fieldwork oriented content to be included and thought that practical engagement helped to understand the subject easily. Over 3% students wanted to apply statistical tools to understand real life. Over 7% students wanted more fieldwork and internship opportunities. Over 3% students wanted practical equipment and facilities to increase practical content and similar over 3% students thought that practicals improved the knowledge and quality of education. While as practical content, over 1% students wanted the use of technology and communication skills development. Over 10 % students did not respond to this query.

Interpretation: All these responses express a healthy understanding and desire of the students for practical composition of knowledge building. This also reveals an unstated inclination towards a combination of mental and manual exertions in pursuit of holistic learning. It is a historical social fact that mental/intellectual labour was a privilege of the few as against the socially ordained manual/labour exposition of the many, including the scheduled castes and scheduled tribes students.

Chapter - 5

Conclusion and Suggestions

The researcher here presents major findings of the study and gives some suggestions, along with an indicative interdisciplinary curricular model, to integrate the social and pure sciences in an interdisciplinary manner for holistic knowledge building and socially inclusive approach. Our higher education system is rigidly compartmentalised and exclusionary in nature. As a solution interdisciplinarity in higher education can be a more inclusive model with integration of social and natural sciences. Exploration requires perspective of more than a discipline but compartmentalisation of every discipline keeps it in a limited area of knowledge. So in order to give justice to the objective undertaken an interdisciplinary approach is feasible and appropriate.

The fieldwork data shows that most respondents are for the interdisciplinary system of approach. The overall benefits of interdisciplinary creation of knowledge will break the barriers of established knowledge. And hence the overall implications of knowledge will have a comprehensive and elevated impact.

5.1 Major Findings

5.1.1 Economic status of the student respondents

1. The economic condition of 62.79% of the students' families was poor or at subsistence levels.
2. Most (69.50%) of the students are dependents on their parents for financial support for higher education. Besides this government scholarships are also important supportive source for the higher education to some students.
3. Few students said they had to pay capitation fees for the previous as well as current degree/diploma. Moreover, majority of the

students (50.60%) said they had to pay admission fees above 20 thousand rupees per annum.

This data indicates the expensive nature of even public higher education, no less private. This could lead to exclusion of poor and subsistence level students from higher education. Moreover, it is a proven fact that the rate of indigence is higher among the SC and ST students of India. Therefore, this automatically works as the biggest exclusionary obstacle in the pursuit of higher education. This situation is directly related to the below par expenditure on education (4.23% of GDP). And in this the general social sciences higher education receives much less. The social sciences are considered to be of low employability potential and so given secondary status. And the fact that a disproportionately high number of SC and ST students are forced into joining the social science courses leads us to try and develop a relationship between higher education, interdisciplinarity and social inclusion.

5.1.2 Educational Profile of the Student Respondents

1. **Generational level of Learning-** Significant numbers of (27.90%) research students and students of UG/PG are first generation seeking higher education exposing the low growth GER pattern of our country. It also means that majority of the students, with elite socio-economic background, have educational family background and an easier opportunity to pursue higher education.

    In other words it also means that antecedence of higher education is quite a necessity for present generations to enter into the exclusive portals of higher education. This also is another big obstacle to the SC and ST students who generally happen to be first generation learners.

2. **Discipline of previous education of the students-** 48.37% students were from the arts faculty which is a huge proportion compared to other disciplines. It was huge because all the massive numbers of students who are graded as average or below average are forced to take admission into the arts faculty rendering them with low employment and entrepreneurial opportunities. These masses of students consist of a huge number of SC and ST students leading them to more or less futile higher education and educational exclusion.

3. **Medium of education of Students-** A huge number (73.02%) of students were from the English medium background who had lot

of opportunities to learn in the best national higher educational institutions. This also means that higher education is hugely dominated by students who can afford and have access to English medium education. This also is another huge access barrier to higher education of the masses including the SC and ST students who generally come from the vernacular medium.

5.1.3 Shortcomings of traditional system of Indian higher education

1. **Advantages of compartmentalised higher education** – Over 60% of the respondents thought focused in-depth knowledge of the discipline and specialisation increased skills in particular areas to be the advantages of rigidly compartmentalised higher education. The miniscule percentage (1.70%) saying that rigid compartmentalisation improves employability is interesting and indicates the understanding of limitations of compartmentalisation of higher education among the other academicians. This possibly is an indicator of understanding and appreciation of the need of interdisciplinarity among social sciences, pure sciences and technology for a holistic creation of knowledge.
2. **Disadvantages of compartmentalised higher education-** 31% respondents said that in compartmentalised higher education, one refuses to see knowledge holistically and 16% felt that it did not permit use of any perspective or method of other disciplines / subjects.

   Only the academicians have pointed out the situation of access to more employable higher education options, for the few, leading to discrimination and exclusion. None of the students have raised this issue. This issue highlights lack of interdisciplinarity because of rigid compartmentalisation. And this compartmentalisation is sourced from the students' senior secondary and higher secondary marks-weightage system. This system of rote learning goes against the socio-economically backward students including the SC and ST due to a number of reasons including lack of educational background, financial instability and irrelevance of curriculum to employment or cultural heritage. So an interweaving interdisciplinary approach among the social sciences, pure sciences and technology application is inevitable. This would understand, co-opt and functionalise the varied strength of students from the social diversity of India and give impetus to individual and community social mobility leading to true community empowerment in the country.

3. **Comparative employability of science and technology and social sciences streams** – A huge over 69% academicians and 53% UG/PG students thought that the employability of science and technology streams was greater than the social sciences.

   The positive responses gave the obvious and realistic answer about science and technology streams having greater employment scope. This is the lopsided reality that this project is trying to reveal. This project hypothesized the relative lower employment and entrepreneurship scope for the social sciences as compared to the science and technology streams. The project has also highlighted, with relevant secondary data, about the SC/ST students being disproportionately being forced into the social sciences streams due to their relatively lower secondary and higher secondary marks. (GER of higher education in 2015- All- 24.3, SC-19.1, ST-13.7 and GER at senior secondary level All-54.2, SC -54.3, ST -38.8, Source- Educational Statistics at a Glance, 2016, MHRD, GOI.) The SC GER at the senior secondary level is the highest at 54.3 but significantly tapers down to 19.1 at the higher education level, much below the higher education GER of all categories which stands at 24.3. Here significantly the all category GER includes the SC and ST data which significantly lowers the all category GER. Were the SC and ST GER deducted from the all category GER the real gap between the SC, ST GER and GER of the others shall stand exposed. Then again the GER of the SC and ST comprises of majority of the students in the social sciences as compared to the natural sciences and technology, exposing the misleading 'higher' GER of SC and ST students.

   This, due to a school examination system that favoured memory and oratory skills with presentation in which the SC and ST students traditionally lag behind due to ancient socio-cultural ordination. Interdisciplinarity and interweaving of the social and natural sciences is the only way out to achieve holistic knowledge building and dignity and comparable incentivisation of mental and manual labour.

4. **Reasoning for the better employability of science and technology** - The responses highlight the natural employability strengths of the sciences and technology streams over the social sciences. This is simply because we are following an economic

model based on capitalism and consumption were relations between humans and utility objects are highly valued over relationship between individuals and communities. This is a result of the process of competition instead of cooperation and contribution from the elementary school level itself. The higher the accumulation of the goods of consumption the greater social and financial status. Obviously as stated above the SC and ST are the biggest suffering communities as they are lowly represented in the science and technology streams with consequent denial of higher employment opportunities.

5. **Measures for increasing the employability of social sciences -** Over 30% of the academicians stated that the social sciences should be applied and new interdisciplinary courses and their applications in social sciences needed to be introduced. Over 13% of the respondents felt that the social sciences needed to be modified on the basis of the natural sciences where theory was brought to practice. Over 15% of the respondents stated that higher investment were needed in the social sciences with a proper policy framework and development of a curricula based on the societal needs.

The above responses highlight the creativity of the academicians for the utilitarian betterment of the social sciences in coalition with the natural sciences.

5.1.4 Interdisciplinarity and its need

1. **What is Interdisciplinarity -** A significant 46% academicians, 64% research students and 38% UG/PG students thought interdisciplinarity was integrating domains of two or more subjects. But even more surprisingly and interestingly over 19% academicians and research students and 44% UG/PG students thought it was integrating domains of the social and natural sciences.

Most significantly, justifying the main hypothesis of this research project, a significant numbers of academicians, research students and UG/PG students thought interdisciplinarity was integrating domains of the social and natural sciences and few academicians also thought it extremely important to have cross-fertilisation of ideas. These approaches augur well for the possibility and future of interdisciplinarity between the social and natural sciences making possible an overall change in approach to issue-solving than ego-retaining compartmentalisation of disciplines.

2. **Subject for Interdisciplinarity** - The perceptions of responses to go interdisciplinary highlights the possibilities of scope for interdisciplinarity among the social sciences, natural sciences and technology are indeed interesting and significant for holistic knowledge outputs and removing the subtle untouchability and compartmentalisation in the social and natural sciences.

   An overwhelming 83% academicians thought there was scope for their subjects to go interdisciplinary with social/natural sciences. This indicates the mature understanding of knowledge building/application with holistic learning outputs and social implications on the part of the academician.

3. **Participation of academician in curriculum formation committees** – A huge 69% academicians had participated in the important academic task of curriculum formation.

4. **Weightage in the curriculum-** A huge 68% academicians gave weightage to both theory and application in curriculum formation. Most academician stated that theory and practical were equally important and theoretical knowledge combined with practical application was necessary for proper understanding.

   This approach of the academicians looks balanced for the times but needs to be go beyond assignments, project works and laboratory practicals towards real life interventions into socio-economic and technological contexts of life abounding. This to be coupled with understanding the brick-by-brick construction of social need/ products with due respect for manual and mental labour.

5. **Should the higher education curriculum be based on demand-supply market rule** - Interestingly around fifty percent of the respondents wanted a higher education curriculum to be based on the demand-supply market rule. The positive responses probably are for the demand-supply market orientation of curriculum because of inclination towards creation of more employment, which depends on the level of demand in the market. This in a discrete manner reveals a very practical life approach towards good-living based on the principles of the market rather than a holistic view of sustainable social living. This scenario probably is rooted in competition instead of cooperation and contribution as the functioning processes from schooling life.

The reasoning for demand-supply is contemporary and concentrating on tackling competitive market scenario that is based on demand and supply. But this approach raises issues about who is setting the economic and social agenda of the society for long term interests. That matters for public interest and socio-economic interests of the SC and ST communities.

6. Around fifty percent of the respondents did not want a higher education curriculum to be based on the demand-supply market rule. The reasoning for the same are underlined by the limitations of demand-supply market rules impact on higher education curriculum. This fifty percent is probably trying to understand the dynamics between social reality and science and technology moving towards an interdisciplinary and inclusive approach.

7. **Who should decide the curriculum of higher education** - A significant number (36.25%) of respondents thought government policies, higher education institutions and market should decide the curriculum. It shows a fine balance between the market rule and government agencies working for the welfare of the society at large. Surprisingly a miniscule 1% of all three categories of respondents were for the market deciding the higher education curriculum.

   This response shows the huge lack of trust these learned adults have on the market. It reveals their bent towards public initiative and interest of welfare and sustainable development. As also we should not forget that over 80% of the respondents were from publically funded HEIs, components of which generally tend towards government initiative for development and welfare.

8. **Basic principles and features of an Interdisciplinary Curriculum** – A majority trend of the academicians indicated for an interdisciplinary approach in principle, with a focus on bringing social and pure sciences together to understand the theory and practice of human nature and utility of science and technology.

   This is actually indicative of an interdisciplinary approach balancing individual and social needs with the efficacy of application of science and technology. In the process, this promotes equality in dignity of mental and manual exertions moving towards social inclusion and sustainable development.

9. **Obstacles of interdisciplinary curricular approach** - The academicians specify the obstacles in interdisciplinary curricular

approach as the overall vacuum of ideas, knowledge, vision, institutional framework and team-work in achieving an inter-disciplinary curriculum.

This also highlights the traditional compartmentalisation and unilinearity of disciplines ranging from the social to pure sciences and application. This is a big obstacle between social realities and applied solutions affecting holistic knowledge building and socio-economic inclusion.

10. **Solution to the obstacles of interdisciplinary curricular approach-** The academicians gave the following solutions on the obstacles of interdisciplinary curricular approach. 25% suggested offering interdisciplinary courses on large scale to encourage students. 15% academicians thought of arranging sufficient funds and making facilities available to be conducive to growth for interdisciplinary curricular approach. And over 9% wanted collaboration of industry and educational institutions to increase the employability.

    The solutions offered cover all aspects for creating an interdisciplinary curricular approach but a paradigm shifting step of interweaving the socio- economic context of science and technology leading to holistic knowledge creation and socially inclusive processes is necessary for sustainable development.

11. **Nature of research topic of research students** – Over 36% responded that their research topic was disciplinary but a significantly higher 55% said that their research topic was interdisciplinary in nature.

    This reveals the increasing space of interdisciplinary research in higher education but does not clarify about it status across the social and natural sciences.

12. **Strengths of Disciplinary Research-** Only research students underlined the traditional strengths, applications, and employability of disciplinary research.

13. **Weaknesses of Disciplinary Research-** 64% research students mentioned the weaknesses of the disciplinary research that is creating the impetus for interdisciplinary research along with the exposure to western holistic nature of knowledge building and application in higher education.

14. **Strengths of Interdisciplinary Research-** Over 37% research students felt that interdisciplinary research had a holistic, integrated

and inclusive approach, with a chance to explore interesting outcomes using ideas of different subjects. Contemporary times has brought the research students to appreciate the strengths of interdisciplinary research. This is appreciable.

15. **Weaknesses of Interdisciplinary Research** – 36% research students had underlined the traditional and continuing difficulties faced by interdisciplinary research which need to be addressed urgently if we are to create holistic knowledge building systems.
16. **Choice of the area of research** – The huge number of research students choosing their own area of research reflects on their competence and inquisitive mindset for space of research. The self-choice of area of research would probably lead these students to go in-depths of their topics and possibly move into interdisciplinary domains in the quest of quality research outputs.
17. **Language of research** – An overwhelming 89% research students conducted their research in English. The abundance of students doing research in English is probably related to the researcher visiting elite public educational institutions of the country where English is the medium of instruction. This again is a matter of prejudice and discrimination against the rural, vernacular educated students who incidentally could be comprised heavily with the scheduled castes and tribes students'.
18. **Difficulties in conducting interdisciplinary research**– A significant 16% have underlined the rigid compartmentalisation of disciplines and a further 24% thought lack of interdisciplinary educational facilities and funds are the difficulties in conducting interdisciplinary research in India highlighting the rigid disciplinary nature of higher education in India and indicates for foundational changes, which are recommended in this project, to be undertaken.
19. **Solutions to such academic obstacles in conducting interdisciplinary research**– Over 12% research students wanted restructuring of the compartmentalised education structure, increased interaction among disciplines, 40% thought starting ID study/research centers on large scales providing facilities and literature and new faculty with training for expansion of interdisciplinary research. 32% thought preference to be given to interdisciplinary research with availability of interdisciplinary subjects along with regular subjects and 21% gave all the above

solutions to overcome academic obstacles in conducting interdisciplinary research.

It shows research students of today wanting to find solutions for interdisciplinary research for modern socio-economic and technological issues and initiatives. The main objective of the research project necessitating interdisciplinarity in higher education is being proven.

5.1.5 Nature and Status of Interdisciplinarity in Western Countries

1. Secondary data concerning interdisciplinarity in higher education among the Western countries shows an advanced relationships between higher education and interdisciplinarity with its holistic implications and also revealing the contextual relationship between science and technology and social and environmental concerns in the framework of sustainable development.

5.1.6 Social and Educational Canvas of Interdisciplinarity

1. **What would you understand by social inclusion in higher education** - An overwhelming 76% research and 84% UG/PG students underlined the need of equal opportunities of participation for all social sections in higher education.

   The overwhelming positive response to social inclusion by all students is incredibly socially progressive. Students realise the variation of contribution from the social diversity of the society as is done, to an extent, in the United States of America. Proper nurture can take one to places unprecedented only if cooperation and contribution is given primacy over competition which is an unnatural and anti-social learning process.

2. **Shall ID model give greater justice to the diverse human resources of India?**- A huge 87% academicians, 81% research students and 83% UG/PG students were positive to the idea of an interdisciplinary model giving greater justice to the diverse human resources in India.

   This is a huge approval of the basic hypothesis of this project that wanted to relate higher education, interdisciplinarity and social inclusion.

3. **If yes, how?** - Above 28% academicians, 7% research students and 5% UG/PG students felt that interdisciplinarity enhances skills, potential and increases employability. 6% academicians,

1% research student and 5% UG/PG students felt that innovation by the students with an interdisciplinary mindset will be beneficial for society.

The respondents have given justifiable solutions for an interdisciplinary model to give greater justice to the diverse human resources of India.

4. **If no, why?** – Among the miniscule naysayers of all the types of respondents about 1% academicians and over 1% research students felt that both should have a bit of each other but should not be combined.

   The naysayers have put up there practical problems of an interdisciplinary model giving greater justice to the diverse human resources of India.

5. **Reasons for the higher enrolment of underprivileged Students in social sciences-** Over 20% academicians, 16% research students and 24% students of UG/PG thought that economic backwardness, unaffordable science and technology education and relative easiness of social sciences are reasons for the higher enrolment of underprivileged students in the social sciences.

   The above data actually is a reflection of duality between public education and privatisation of education. The socio-economically weaker students are forced to take education from the publically funded schooling system going on to the higher education level with their obvious weaknesses of maths, sciences and languages. The underprivileged students, especially SC and ST are average or poor in dealing with the rote and memory-based examination systems forcing them into the social sciences which have been created uni-dimensionally, lacking in skill-sets and employment opportunities with only abstract and critical thinking abilities. Here in comes the issue of interdisciplinarity bringing together abstract and critical thinking along with skill-sets for holistic knowledge building and social inclusion where the SC and ST students shall get an opportunity to enter interdisciplinary courses with their strengths.

6. **Interdisciplinarity in social and natural sciences could give more opportunities to underprivileged students** - An overwhelming 70% academicians, 79% research students and 81% UG/PG students were positive that an interdisciplinary model of higher education in social and pure sciences could give more opportunities to underprivileged students.

This overwhelming response for establishing relationship between higher education, interdisciplinarity and social inclusion is interesting. The main players of the education system are realising the essence of interdisciplinarity and participation and contribution of the social diversity of the country.

7. **If yes, how?** - Over 31% academicians, 16% research students and 3% UG/PG students responded that offering interdisciplinary courses across the disciplines to underprivileged students shall increase their knowledge and employment levels.

   The above data proves the overwhelming response of the academicians, research students and UG/PG students to the positive and practical implications for the underprivileged students including SC and ST, if an interdisciplinary model of higher education in social and natural sciences is implemented.

8. **If no, why?** - The miniscule naysayers include 2% academicians who said employment and employability cannot be combined. Over 2% academicians felt that inclusion did not depend on interdisciplinarity of different disciplines and the inclusion policy should be strengthened at higher levels.

   The above data expresses the difficult path in achieving an interdisciplinary social and natural sciences model of higher education with positive implications for the underprivileged students.

9. **Can we relate holistic learning, employability and interdisciplinarity?** - An overwhelming 97% of the academicians thought that they could relate holistic learning, employability and interdisciplinarity.

   This is a huge and positive response to the basic hypothesis of the research project which relates the three processes of holistic learning, employability and interdisciplinarity.

10. **If yes, how?** - Over 37% of the academicians stated that interdisciplinarity across the disciplines will get more employability, knowledge in various areas and develop skills and potentials. Over 5% felt that one had to understand the job market and skill requirement. Over 6% respondents felt that technology needed to be involved in social sciences for holistic knowledge and development. While another 6% felt that to be a professional one needed to be a complete personality and not just good at domain subject.

The responses highlights the creativity of academicians to relate the processes of holistic learning, employability and interdisciplinarity. Of great interest is the suggestion of spending 6% of GDP on education. India has never spent beyond 4% of GDP on education and within that the social sciences received the least. Here it self the neglect of and prejudices against the social sciences begin. We have never been able to appreciate the foundational significance of the social sciences for peaceful and prosperous community living. We fail to understand that the products of science and technology are just tools for human utility and consumption. Science and technology is an afterthought and development for an enriched social living. Science and technology represent the curiosity and anxiety of human engagement with nature. Social relationships are a priori.

11. **If no, why?** – The miniscule negative responses include over 2% academicians stating that holistic learning and employability may not go together in some cases. About 1% felt that the co-relation depended on the particular subject. About 1% thought that there was no relation in employment and social science. And another percent felt that all the three processes were separate and had different forms. Still another percent felt that employability and interdisciplinarity were interlinked but holistic learning was a vague concept.
12. A huge numbers of Research students and UG and PG students from various social categories perceive necessity of interdisciplinarity across the social and natural science. This is reveling of the awareness of the modern students of their knowledge and skill requirements that supplement the market job and entrepreneurial.

5.1.7 Acceptability of new Interdisciplinary Approach

1. **Necessity of interdisciplinarity across the natural and social sciences** - A huge 87% academicians, over 90% research students and 86% UG/PG students perceived the necessity of interdisciplinarity across the natural and social sciences. This huge positive response underlines the academicians and students realisation of limitations of compartmentalised higher education and yearning for interdisciplinary approach in the same.

   The reasoning for the same underlines the understanding and appreciation of interdisciplinarity across social and natural science as understood by all the three types of respondents. This bodes well for the upcoming dynamics of knowledge creation and assimilation to be formed on the all-round issue based approach and socially inclusive pursuit of solutions.

2. Only 7% refuse the necessity of interdisciplinarity across the social and natural sciences. These miniscule naysayers have underlined the practical problems obstructing interdisciplinarity across the social and natural sciences. But there sheer minimal numbers against the huge positive approach underlines the feasibility and future of interdisciplinarity across social and natural sciences in higher education of India.
3. **Scope of the subject of respondents to go interdisciplinary-** An overwhelming 94% academicians, 85% research students and 77% UG/PG students believed that there was scope for their subjects to go interdisciplinary with other disciplines.
4. A significant 57% wanted increase in practical content for improving learning and employability prospects. But surprisingly, a significant 38% did not find necessary any increase in the practical contents. Probably these students were from the social sciences background that did not require any practical component. This also exposes the uni-dimensionality and irreverence to the relationship between learning, skills and employability or entrepreneurship. This is another major reason and objective of this project to understand mutual exclusion of higher education, interdisciplinarity and inclusion in India.

All the above have been conclusions arrived from responses of the academicians, research students and UG, PG students establishing a relationship between higher education, inter-disciplinarity and social inclusion. As a suggestion and an objective of this research project an indicative interdisciplinary curricular model of a science rooted in the socio-economic contexts is presented in the next and final chapter.

Chapter - 6

Indicative Interdisciplinary Model Curriculum

Interdisciplinary Degree for Graduation: 'Agriculture and Development'

6.1 Philosophy of the Interdisciplinary Model

Human interaction with nature is as old as the human history. The human species, that has existed for about 2,50,000 years, survived as foragers or hunter-gatherers, gathering wild plants and hunting animals in their natural environment. Around 10,000 years ago human engagement with nature shifted from foraging to farming. This development of agriculture formed the basis of advanced civilisation in both the western and eastern worlds. Over the centuries, agriculture societies spread into those environments that could be easily adapted to agriculture and foragers gradually became restricted ot marginal areas. Since 1960s archeologists suggested that origin of agriculture was not a revolution but the result of a gradual cultural evolution. They reasoned that hunter gatherers knew the wild plants, knew how they grew and would incorporate faming along with foraging as part of an overall food collection strategy, when necessary.

Many archeologists believe that there was a transitional stage between simple foraging, in which small nomadic bands followed the wild plants and animals and agricultural societies with their sedentary life style. During this transitional stage, foraging groups formed settlements but sent out members to hunt and gather. This more complex strategy resulted in changes in the social organisation of the groups and permitted population to increase. This transitional stage lasted for several thousands of years in some location until resource stress or environmental change led to the switch to agriculture[1].

The evolution of agriculture underlines the instinctive relationship between man and nature and between man and man on being settled for agricultural purposes. This underlines the umbilical relationships between nature and social approach. This further underlines the relationship between agriculture that later developed as a science and social organisation. This mandates handling of agriculture and its education in an interdisciplinary manner with social sciences. Further the Indian contextual relevance is also underlined by the allocation of duties and functions to specified social communities, wherein agriculture was the function of the Balutedars and Shudras, who comprise the lower end of the socially stratified structure of the Indian society.

Traditional agriculture co-evolved with people in different eco-system, contributing to human health in terms of food and diets. Food and the ceremonies surrounding food are an important part of traditional agriculture and the well-being of the groups that practice it. Rituals and ceremonies performed by agricultural communities honoured the earth and human mindfulness of it. But settled societies and colonisation separated cultural capital and agriculture, separating people from the land and from each other. Hegemony of the ability of the one group to impose its culture- the beliefs about what should be and what is possible to change- on others. Settled life permitted the division of labour and the gradual appearance between rich and poor. Thus, for dominant culture, with privatisation and mechanisation of farming, there values re-enforce the primacy of increasing production to generate money, and other values are viewed as sentimentality and blocking progress. These hegemonic values are then translated into laws that often deprived indigenous people of their land.[2] The major revolution in agriculture of these early days, however, came with irrigation, which then gave rise to an important social change, consisting of strict division of labour and the accumulation of wealth for a few. This social change underlined the potential of social dynamics of agriculture impacting social organisation.

In the Indian context agriculture has followed the tenets of social organisation with preordained scriptural values and believes, and socio-economic domination of the market middleman and the consumer over the producer.

Agriculture is a culture activity underlined by three important cultural aspects of the Andean of farms fields of Latin America:

4. The relation between cultivators and their crops is personal,

5. Agricultural practices are performed as rituals, and
6. A fine and detailed conversation with nature is necessary to undertake agricultural work at a proper time, in a proper place and in a proper way.

This also is underlined in the traditional Indian way of family farming done in the framework of piety, respect for nature, community activity and natural living. The whole effect is most important than rationality, communal sentiment pre-dominates over individualism, and humans continue to be part of nature rather than seeking to control it. This underlines socially inclusive nature of agriculture that mandates agricultural education to be taught in an interdisciplinary manner with the social sciences and to make it socially inclusive especially in the Indian context.

The normative principles of pre-colonial agriculture was not the maximisation of production but the management, conservation and improvement of the fertility of soils over the long term, with social relations formed to meet the collective needs of the society within the limits of each vernacular eco-system. Further evolution of agriculture in modern times in pursuit of massification has seen overt attempts of destroying indigenous cultures, by separating people from their land that had serious impact on people, place and bio-diversity leading to socio-economic problems like tribal unrest in India.[3]

This changed canvas of agriculture and social living allowed some members of the society to produce food and other members to concentrate on other things. Perhaps more importantly, it required changes in our ways of thinking about the world around us, and those changes affected how we arranged ourselves. It facilitated and promoted many revolutionary social changes: urbanism and urbanisation, writing and accounting, division of labour, concentration of population, and the formation of social classes based upon allocation of the food surplus. In the Indian social context the agricultural communities or the Balutedars and Shudras were pre-ordained to the duties of farming and providing for the superior social categories.

Modernisation in pursuit of agricultural productivity is disconnecting us from nature and does not allow us to notice the damage it inflicts on nature and its settings. For all our human history, we have been shaped by nature, while shaping it in return. But in our industrial age, we are losing the stories, memories and language about land and nature. This affects cultural capital and thus social relationships.[4] If agriculture is to be developed in a holistic manner inequalities in the social and thus political structures must be demolished and agro-economic targets must be oriented towards the existing, regionally varied structural and cultural living conditions of the farming community. This presupposes confidence in the capacity for change and readiness to integrate on the part of the farming community. But it also requires restricting the demands for modernisation on the part of different scientific and political agrarian institutions.[5]

Considering the above analytical relationship between nature and man, between agriculture and community living it is essential that agricultural education is handled in a special manner. Since this relationships is an evolution from instinctive biological needs to a bond between nature and culture underlined by social dynamics and essence of human community living. So the agriculture curriculum at the undergraduate level needs to be interdisciplinary in approach, placing agriculture in the realms of social equilibrium and accommodating the scientific and technological tools in social interest.

A significant ground reality data was received when we queried with senior agriculture academicians on what their graduates pursue as a career or avocation on completion of their agriculture studies. The response was that many of them pursued the state or central civil services careers, quite a few entered the banking sector in agriculture positions, some pursued the agro or pharma industries and some others pursued middle or low level careers which had nothing to do with agriculture. Amazingly very few agriculture graduates pursued proper farming activities. The whole or at least the major objective of agriculture education at higher level has been to produce modern farmers. India still primarily being an agricultural country, it was accepted that we create modern, well-trained and indigenous farmers to raise the quality and quantity of agricultural outputs including paradigm of the white and blue revolutions. We have never wondered why only a very small number of our agriculture graduates enter into farming as proper vocation. Is it the lack of good agriculture output, is it the low agriculture produce prices or is it the lack of proper storage facilities or lack of proper market system that creates alienation from agriculture. Or is it also something to do with the social status give into agriculture from ancient times or with working manually in the muds per se. From ancient times agriculture activity has been scripturally pre-ordained to the 'Balutedari' caste categories. The balutedar castes were to engage in farming activities and perform duties as suppliers of food to the higher social castes. The balutedars who today comprise the other backward classes actually come under the category of shudras i.e. the then untouchables. Is it then that we carry vestiges of ancient prejudices against those working in the muds even when they were engaged in the most important activity of supplying food for life. All the above mentioned weaknesses regarding our tackling agriculture in modern times indicates lack of proper and modern professional perspective of agriculture as a vocation, most important for the sheer survival of humanity.

The rural based youngsters coming to agriculture colleges get frustrated if they do not get white or blue collar jobs in the cities or in the district headquarters. They hate to go back to their native places to engage in modern farming. This is simply because we have not made farming a lucrative career and we have simply not given it the social status as is given to the other most important paradigm of social living i.e. education. So there is great need to build higher education structures and systems with an interdisciplinary approach among domains of the social sciences, natural sciences and technological applications giving equal dignity and financial incentive to both mental and manual labour.

We have come to the conclusion that any knowledge building or application is incomplete without being rooted in the social reality or organisation. Agriculture is a field of knowledge that has non-paralleled paradigms ranging from the sciences to the social sciences and application. It actually has the domain to be roots of a whole economic model that could represent the strength, especially of a country like India, which still primarily is an agricultural country. So in order to turn around the education system and ultimately the country we need to access and adopt the interdisciplinary approach of evolution.

To exemplify an interdisciplinary curricular approach we attempt to present the first year undergraduate programme for agriculture. It is to be understood that this model is indicative in nature and underlines the ground level socio-economic, scientific and technology dynamics being reflected in an interdisciplinary curricular guideline. The success of this new approach also depends on making interdisciplinarity the soul of all curricula starting from the primary education to the tertiary levels. For example, to get good results of an interdisciplinary approach in the undergraduate agriculture curriculum we need to introduce agriculture and more, right at the primary schooling level. This gradual introduction and evolution needs to be carried on at the secondary level making the students competent enough to engage with agriculture education on a vast social canvas. This experiment shall be confronted with structural and systemic obstacles. For example, the present undergraduation agriculture teachers shall not be able to handle the socio-economic canvas of agriculture. As a solution, social science teachers from other colleges and universities could be invited for credits to cover these paradigms. Eventually with these agricultural graduates and post graduates, we shall have teachers interdisciplinarily competent to teach the agriculture students in the interdisciplinary mode.

Even if the prime pursuit of agriculture is scientific probe and application it shall be highly productive in a holistic manner only when rooted in the socio-economic ground realities. After understanding and studying agriculture on the larger socio-economic canvas there should be rigours of science with its objectivity and application but which should also be framed in indigeneity and native socio-economic utility. This should also be a model of agriculture based on sustainable development taught to the students in the second, third and fourth years. This pursuit of knowledge of agriculture in the scientific sense shall be more fruitful and holistic because of the overall social framework that we have initially inculcated in the young students. In the last year and to the stage of a paradigm of specialisation in agriculture the students should again be made to understand the socio-economic canvas of their particular specialisation in agriculture. This whole exercise shall lead to a satisfying, fruitful and financially fulfilling knowledge pursuit.

A product model as a manifestation of this exploratory survey based research project is arrived at. As a product model an effort has been made to prepare a proposed indicative interdisciplinary syllabus initially for first 2 semesters.

The draft syllabus has been prepared on an exploratory research methodology with the basis of fieldwork data inputs and after consulting national and international, central and state universities agriculture and interdisciplinary syllabi along with private agriculture universities/ institutions. The project fieldwork included questionnaires for Professors, Associate Professors, Assistant Professor, Research Students and UG and PG students that helped articulate the proposed indicative syllabus on agriculture titled 'Agriculture and Development'. Besides the latest syllabus of the first year agriculture under graduation course was considered along with consultation of senior professors of the local government agriculture college. Along with this a detailed assessment of agriculture and interdisciplinary syllabi was conducted online to construct the proposed indicative interdisciplinary syllabus titled 'Agriculture and Development'.

6.2 Curriculum:- I[st] Semester

Topic (I) Agriculture –

Objectives - To understand and learn a domain of knowledge one needs to go into and unearth the historical and philosophical roots. Here with history and philosophy of agriculture we shall understand the when, why and how, placing it in the right perspective, theoretical and applied, to be taken ahead in the best interests of humanity. The indegeneity and modern context of agriculture needs to be understood with the help of literary expanse on agriculture worldwide. The indigenous and international exposure shall put agriculture in the best interdisciplinary framework.

Contents –

(e) Evolution of Agriculture

(f) Philosophy of Agriculture

(g) Modernity, Indigeneity and Agriculture

(h) Literature on Agriculture- National and International

Practical – Field visit to local village for socio-economic and agriculture data –For practicals the students could visit local villages for socio-economic and agriculture data to get the overall picture of village life.

Topic (II) Fundamentals of Agriculture –

Objectives -From the larger social canvas going to proper agriculture as a science we need to understand the fundamentals of various paradigms such as horticulture, floriculture and veterinary science that helped achieve the green, white and blue revolutions in India. As a practical content the students need to visit and evaluate agro-establishments concern with the various paradigms of agriculture.

Contents –

(h) Agriculture

(i) Horticulture

(j) Floriculture

(k) Animal Husbandry

(l) Veterinary Science

(m) Revolution- Green, White and Blue

(n) Medicinal Agriculture

(o) Visit to above agro establishments

Topic (III) Agriculture and Rural Life –

Objectives - To understand agriculture as a system it needs to be contextualised with the whole i.e. the rural life. The social and economic relationships between rural life or tribal life and agriculture to understand the grave issues arising out of politico-social lacunae governing the rural hinterland.

Contents –

(f) Family Farming, Community Farming and Corporate Farming

(g) Rural Life and Agriculture

(h) Forestry and Livelihood

(i) Tribal Life and Agriculture

(j) Agriculture and Socio-economic issues –

(i) Poverty (ii) Agriculture and Gender

(iii) Social Forestry (iv) Regional Agro History

Practical

For practical experience students need to visit variation of farming, forestry and tribal life with understanding of socio-economic particularities.

Topic (IV) Indian Economy and Agriculture-

Objectives - India being an agricultural country, agriculture plays a huge socio-economic role in the Indian economic system. The basis of the country including food security, labour welfare and surplus incentive needs to be underlined in the overall strengthening of the country.

Contents -

(f) Agriculture as basis of Indian Economic Model

(g) Planning and NITI Ayog on Agriculture

(h) Agriculture and Food Security

(i) Role of Agriculture in Indian Economy

(j) Economy of Labour and capital Incentive Agriculture in India

Practical

As a project work the students need to be assigned a project largely comprising the planning and economy, with data bank, of agriculture, to be taken up as case studies of regional/state level agriculture variations representing different agro systems.

- **NSS/Native + Modern Sports Activities-**

National service scheme shall help identify and familiarise students with rural life and help understand the cultural and occupational system of the village. For cultural activities the students need to learn and perform the cultural activities and dances that are home to the village life. Native sports activities along with the modern, shall keep the students healthy, sporting and grounded to the native sports culture.

6.3 Curriculum: IInd Semester

Topic (I) Agriculture and Interdisciplinarity

Objectives - The soul of this exercise is the interweaving of different disciplines from social sciences to sciences and application, in to production of a holistic knowledge stream, in this case agriculture. Basically being considered a science, agriculture needs to understand the biology, chemistry and physics along with technology and putting the whole in the socio-economic context for suitability and relevance for maximum utility. Avocation from agriculture needs to be a natural extension.

Contents

(d) Agriculture- Science and Social sciences

(e) Introductory Agri - Biology, Chemistry, Physics and Technology with socio-economic contexts

(f) Vocational Education based on Agriculture

Practical

For literary review or extension, students need to study and understand the national and international advances and applicability of interdisciplinary approach and practice in agriculture with the sciences and the social sciences.

Topic (II) Sociology of Agriculture

Objectives – 'Socious' that is community living is the basic characteristic of mankind. Agriculture is the means of subsistence and community living. We need to understand the traditional and modern socio-economic issues covering labour, suicide, social system with all its dynamics along with western models for suitable reference.

Contents -

(h) Agriculture and Culture

(i) Water Management – Agriculture, Conservation and Inclusion

(j) Farmer Suicide – Agri Socio-economic Context

(k) Perspective on Agricultural Labour

(l) Stratified Indian social system and status of Agriculture- Mental and Manual Labour – as social processes

(m) Western Social System and status of Agriculture

(n) Agriculture and Land Reform

Practical

Through a literary review students need to study and understand with on-field interaction about the dynamics between the social, economic and agricultural system along with the western counterparts.

Topic (III) Agro Economics-

Objectives - Advanced human interaction required a medium of transition understood through economics. Agriculture subsistence has evolved into barter and later trade even at the international level, in the era of globalisation. The socio-economic and political dynamics needs to be understood for a balance between agriculture output food security, international trade and social inclusion.

Contents –

(k) Socio-economic contextuality of Traditional and Commercial Crops

(l) Globalisation, Liberalisation, the WTO and Agriculture

(m) Agriculture, Cooperation and rural politics

(n) Agricultural Finance and Inclusion

(o) Rural Money Lending – Socio-economic Context

(p) Agriculture and Trade

(q) Agricultural Business Management

(r) Agriculture – Taxation and Socio-Political Context

(s) Agri Pricing and Socio-economic context

(t) Agro based Industries- India and world

Practical

Modern agriculture dynamics has to be understood through on field visits to agro finance, business, industries and market committees. Understanding the commerce of agriculture with financial and social inclusion is a fine objective to be achieved.

Topic (IV) Agro Ecology -

Objectives - Advanced community living has sensitised humanity to a balance between need and greed, moving towards the principles of sustainable development for a secure future of the planet. Agro-ecology with all its social, ecological, biological and technical paradigms with international experience, needs to understood pursuit of agriculture with a balance between nature and modernisation.

Contents

(f) Agriculture as a part of Environment

(g) Ecology Concepts and Principles of Farming Systems

(h) Agro Eco System – Social Perspective, Ecological Perspective, Biological Perspective, Technical Perspective

(i) Sustainable Development and Agriculture

(j) Contemporary Agriculture

Practical

Agriculture and sustainable development for the future of the planet needs to be understood and sensitised to the students by arranging on field activities in modern agro eco systems.

Topic (V) Rural Communication -

Objectives - Lastly, especially in the era of globalisation, we need to strike a balance between the local and the global. Local dialects and international inputs have to be converged to understand the latest local and global research and development in agriculture.

Contents –

(c) Various local Dialects, ICT for Agriculture

(d) Research and Development

Practical

Communication versatility requires students to learn local and international languages and be trained with basic to advanced level computing for research and development.

References

1. http://www.life.illinois.edu/ib/102/Levetin/11.%20Origins%20of%20 Agriculture.pdf
2. C Butler Flora (2014), '*Social Justice: Preservation of Culture in Traditional Agriculture*' Encyclopedia of Agriculture and Food Systems, Vol. 5, p. 133.
3. *Ibid*, p. 134.
4. Jules, Pretty (2002), '*Agriculture Reconnecting People, Land and Nature*' London: Earth scan Publications Limited.
5. Pongratz, Hans (1990), '*Cultural Tradition and Social Change in Agriculture*' Sociologia Ruralis, Vol. XXX-1.

Bibliography

Allen F. Repko (2013), '*Introduction to Interdisciplinary Studies,* Paperback Sage Publications, USA.

Anne Visholm, Lasse Grosen, Maria Theresa Norn and Rasmus Lund Jensen (2012), '*Interdisciplinary Research is Key to Solving Society's Problem*' publisher DEA Fiolstræde 44, 1171 København K, Denmark.

Arvind Kumar, '*Law and Dalits Social Inclusion in India'*, article accessed from - http://focusglobalreporter. com/article17.asp.

ASHE (2013), '*Annual Status of Higher Education of States and UTs in India*', MHRD, Government of India, New Delhi.

Bhatt, B.D. and Aggarwal, J.C. (1987), '*Educational Documents in India (1813-1986) Survey of Indian Education*', New Delhi: Arya Book Depot.

Biswal, A. and Agrawal, S. P. (1986), '*Development of Education in India: A Historical Survey of Educational Documents before and after Independence*', New Delhi: Concept Publishing Company.

C Butler Flora (2014), '*Social Justice: Preservation of Culture in Traditional Agriculture*', Encyclopedia of Agriculture and Food Systems, Vol. 5.

Chaube, S.P. and Chaube, A. (1999), 'Education in Ancient and Medieval India (A survey of the Main Features and a Critical Evaluation of Major Trends)', New Delhi: Vikas Publishing House Pvt. Ltd.

Chauhan, C. P. S. (2010), 'Higher Education in India: Issues and Challenges', in *Higher Education Quality and Management*, ed. Khurana, S. M., and Singhal, P.K., New Delhi: Gyan Publishing House.

Chettiparamb, A. (2007), '*Interdisciplinarity: a literature review*' The Interdisciplinary Teaching and Learning Group, Subject Centre for Languages, Linguistics and Area Studies, School of Humanities publication, University of Southampton.

Choudhary, Sujit Kumar (2008), '*Higher Education in India: a Socio-Historical Journey from Ancient Period to 2006-07*', Journal of Educational Enquiry, Vol. 8, No. 1.

Creso, M. Sa (2007), *'Interdisciplinary strategies' in U.S. research universities*', Paper Published online: 8 June 2007, High Educ (2008) 55:537–552 DOI 10.1007/s10734-007-9073-5.

Deepika Kumari (2014), '*Social Inclusion in Indian Higher education- Equity in Access'*, Centre for Civil Society, Researching Reality Summer Internship 2014, Working paper: 313.

Department of Economics and Social Affairs (2009), Report published on '*Creating an Inclusive Society: Practical Strategies to Promote Social Integration*'.

Dongerkery, S.R. (1997), '*University Education in India*', Mumbai: Manaktalas.

Elisabete, M. A. Pereira, Ana Maria Carneiro, Mirian Lucia Goncalves (2014), '*Innovation and Evaluation in the Brazilian Higher Education Culture: Interdisciplinary and General Education*', creative education, 2014, 5,1690-1701. http://www.scirp.org/journal/ce

Elisabeth, J. H. Spelt & Harm J. A. Biemans & Hilde Tobi & Pieternel A. Luning & Martin Mulder (2010), '*Teaching and Learning in Interdisciplinary Higher Education: A Systematic Review*'. This article is published with open access at Springerlink.com DOI 10.1007/s10648-009-9113-z

Garkovich, L. (1982), '*A proposal for Building Interdisciplinary* Bridges'. Teaching Sociology.

Ghosh, S.C. (2001) *The History of Education in Mediaeval India*, 1192 AD- 1757 A.D., Delhi: Originals.

GOI, (2016), '*Educational Statistics at a Glance*', MHRD, Department of School Education & Literacy, New Delhi.

Halder, Santoshi (2011), 'Bridging the Gap: Education for All', paper published in the edited book titled 'Reforms in Higher Education' edited by Bawa, S., K. and Padhan, Ananda, Chandigarh: Abhishek Publication.

Hommadi, A. H. (1985), 'Higher Education in Third World', Delhi: Indian Bibliographies Bureau, Balaji Enterprises.

http://data.worldbank.org/indicator/SE.TER.ENRR

http://ireport.cnn.com/docs/DOC-1108407

http://shodhganga.inflibnet.ac.in/bitstream/10603/68349/7/07_chapter%202.pdf http://www.life.illinois.edu/ib/102/Levetin/11.%20Origins%20of%20Agriculture.pdf

http://www.thehindu.com/features/education/Interdisciplinary-approach-in-higher-education/article16811839.ece

http://www.worldbank.org/en/topic/socialdevelopment/brief/social-inclusion https://www.ncbi.nlm.nih.gov/books/NBK44876/

Ingole, K. S., '*A Critical Study of Social Exclusion and its Implication*' http://www.ambedkar.org/research/SOCIAL_EXCLUSION_and_ITS_IMPLICATION.pdf

Jantsch, Erich (1980), '*Interdisciplinarity: Dreams and reality*' Prospects, Vol. X, No. 3.

Jules, Pretty (2002), '*Agri-culture Reconnecting People, Land and Nature*' London: Earth scan Publications Limited.

Kleinberg, Ethan (2008), '*Interdisciplinary Studies at a Crossroads*' Association of American College and Universities, Washington D.C. http://wesscholar.wesleyan.edu/div1facpubs/99/

Kockelmans, Joseph J. (1979), '*Interdisciplinarity and Higher Education (ed)*', The Pennsylvania State University Press, University Park and London.

Laurence, James, C. (2010), 'Higher Education and Development', New Delhi: Rajat Publication.

Lisowska, A., Wojciechowska, E. and Mitkowski, S. A. (2010), '*Interdisciplinarity in higher education- natural science electives for engineering students*' 1st World

Conference on Technology and Engineering Education, Krakow, Poland, 14-17 September 2010.

Lokhande, Dhananjay (2008), '*Youth in Education and Community Service*' Pune: Samajdarshan Prakashan.

Mandal, Bankim Chandra (2014), '*Globalisation and its Impact on Dalits*' Afro Asian Journal of Social Sciences Volume 5, No. 5.2, Quarter II 2014, ISSN: 2229 – 5313.

Mane, Vikas (2013), '*Globalisation and Indian Higher Education*', Pune: Scion Publication Pvt. Ltd

Martin Davies and Marcia Devtin (2007), '*Interdisciplinary Higher Education and the Melbourne Model*' Conference Presentation © 2007 Philosophy of Education Society of Australasia

Mary, Adler and Sheila Flihan (1997), '*The Interdisciplinary continuum: Reconciling theory, Research and Practice*' Report Series 2.36, National Research Center on English Learning & Achievement, University at Albany, State University of New York, Washington Avenue, Albany, New York.

Miller, Raymond (1982), '*Varieties of Interdisciplinary Approaches in the Social Sciences: A 1981 Overview*' Published in Issues in Integrative Studies: An Occasional Publication of the Association for Integrative Studies,

Mohapatra, Tanuja (2011), '*Tribes of Odisha: Issues of social inclusion, exclusion and cultural assimilation*' article published in Bodhy: An interdisciplinary Journal,5,ISSN:2091-0479.

Muravska,Tatjana & Zaneta Ozolina. (2011), '*Interdisciplinarity in Social Sciences: Does it Provide Answers to Current Challenges in Higher Education and Research?*' (ed.)Riga, University of Latvia Press.

Neelakandan Sanil and Patil Smita (2012), '*Complexities of inclusion and exclusion: Dalit students and higher education in India*' Journal of Social Inclusion 3(1) 2012.

Oommen T. K. (2015), '*Social Inclusion in Independent India*' http://uohherald.commuoh.in/social-inclusion-in-independent-india.

Pankajam, G. (2014), '*Issues in Education*', New Delhi: Gyan Publishing House.

Pongratz, Hans (1990), '*Cultural Tradition and Social Change in Agriculture*' Sociologia Ruralis. Vol. XXX-1.

Powar, K. B. (1995), Higher Education in India. In K.B. Power & S.K. Panda (eds), *Higher Education in India—in search of quality*, New Delhi: AIU,

Pramanik, Auditi (2014), '*Role of Interdisciplinary Studies in Higher Education in India*' Journal of Education and Human Development June 2014, Vol.3, No. 2

Rachel, Westfall (2010), '*Dimensions of Social Inclusion and Exclusion in Yukon*' Yukon Bureau of Statistics, December 2010.

Report on "*Interdisciplinarity*" (Problems of teaching and Research in Universities) Paris, Centre for Educational Research and Innovation (CERI), Organisation for Economic Cooperation and Development (OECD) 1972.

Ronald, F. and Inglehart (2016), '*Trump, Brexit and the Rise of Populism: Economic Have- Nots and Cutural Backlash*' Faculty Research Working Paper Series,

Harvard Kennedy School, https://research.hks.harvard.edu/publications/workingpapers/Index.aspx

Sandra Mathison, Melissa Freeman (1997), *'The Logic of Interdisciplinary Studies'*. the paper Presented at the Annual Meeting of the American Educational Research Association, Chicago.

Sharma, Shaloo (2002), 'History and Development of Higher Education in India' Vol. 5 perspectives on the History and Development of India Higher Education, New Delhi: Sarup and Sons.

Sharma, Sunita, Singh Machiavelli (2015), *'Interdisciplinary research: Transforming Higher Education in India'* International Journal of Interdisciplinary Research and Innovations Vol. 3, Issue 3, pp. 80-88, Month: July - September 2015.

Sonowal, C.J. (2008), *'Indian Tribes, and Issue of social inclusion and Exclusion'*, Article published in stud Tribes, Tribals, 6(2).

Sorokin (1956), *'Fads and Feables in Modern Sociology and related sciences'*, Chicago University Press.

Stirling, J. and McGloin, C. (2015), Critical pedagogy and social inclusion policy in Australian higher education: identifying the disjunctions. Radical pedagogy, 12.

Thiruvasagam, G. (2010), *'Interdisciplinary approach in higher education'* article published in the Hindu paper dated 2 Feb. 2010.

Thorat, Sukhadeo (2006), *'Higher Education in India Emerging Issues to Access, inclusiveness and Quality'* Nehru Memorial Lecture, University of Mumbai.

Twelfth Five Year Plan (2012-17), *'Faster, More Inclusive & Sustainable Growth'*, Volume I.

Veronica Boix Mansilla, (2010), *'Interdisciplinarity in United States Schools: Past, Present, and Future'* paper published in the journal Issues In Integrative Studies No. 28.

W. James Jacob, http://www.palgrave-journals.com/articles/palcomms20151

William H. Newell (2001), 'A Theory of Interdisciplinary Studies' Issues in Integrative Studies, No. 19.

Index

C

D

N

O

P

Q

R

S

T

U